Europe

Europe

RODNEY LEACH

A Concise Encyclopedia of
the European Union from
Aachen to Zollverein

PROFILE BOOKS

First and second editions published in Great Britain in 1998 by
Profile Books Ltd
52A Hatton Garden
London ECIN 8LX

Copyright © Rodney Leach 1998

The moral right of the author has been asserted.

Typeset in Bembo by MacGuru
macguru@pavilion.co.uk

Printed in Great Britain by Biddles Ltd

A CIP catalogue record for this book is available from the British Library.

ISBN 1 86197 133 8

To Jessica and Alice
who encouraged me.

Contents

Note to readers

Currency

The Community accounts are drawn up in ECUs. When the single currency is introduced they will be drawn up in euros, on the basis of a 1-for-1 exchange. As this book goes to press, the pound was worth approximately 1.5 ECUs. Many readers will be more at home with the dollar, which is presently worth about 10% less than the ECU.

The Treaties

The architecture of the EU is built on two core Treaties, Rome and Maastricht. The Treaty of Rome constitutes the European Community and its various institutions and has been significantly amended three times – by the 1986 Single European Act, the 1992 Maastricht Treaty and the 1997 Treaty of Amsterdam. The rules governing co-operation between member states outside the Community framework were created by some innovative sections of the Maastricht Treaty, and then amended by the Treaty of Amsterdam. This explains why it can be equally correct to refer to some clause as being contained in the Treaty of Rome or in the Maastricht (or Amsterdam) Treaty – it depends whether the emphasis is on the amendment itself or on the final consolidated result.

Common Market, EC and EU

The European Union grew out of the European Economic Community, or Common Market, which later became known simply as the European Community; it was at Maastricht that it became the European Union. Technically, the Community refers to the Union's supranational institutions and the Union refers to the wider whole, including co-operation among member states, although in common parlance the two terms are often used interchangeably. In this book the historically accurate terms are used when that is important for the understanding of an entry referring to the EU's earlier development.

Europe: the Union and beyond

Map ix

Acknowledgements

B y its nature an encyclopaedia draws on reference works and documentary sources too numerous to mention. That said, *Eurostat* is a prolific and co-operative supplier of statistics; *The Treaty of Amsterdam in Perspective*, compiled by British Management Data Foundation, is indispensable to an understanding of the main EU Treaties; *The Penguin Companion to European Union* is an informative guide, written largely from the European Parliamentarian's standpoint; the *European Journal* has published many thoughtful articles; and *The Economist Guide to the European Union* is a useful businessmen's survey of EU policies. This book is addressed to a less specialist audience and is less uncritical than most reference books on the EU.

The Commission has been prompt and courteous in answering questions. I have also learned much from the work of the more searching observers of the Community – among them Dr Hans Tietmeyer and Dr Otmar Issing at the Bundesbank; Professors Patrick Minford, David Currie, Tim Congdon, Pedro Schwarz and Martin Feldstein; several essayists published by the Institute of Economic Affairs; Christopher Booker; Martin Howe; John Laughland; Noel Malcolm; and Malcolm Pearson.

Oliver Segal and Rachel Willmot made valuable corrections to the entries on Community law. Keith Carson and *Eurofacts* answered several knotty questions. Gina Thomas on Germany, Niko Schmidt-Chiari on Austria, Gerald Flynn on Ireland, Sir Charles Powell on the Thatcher–Delors years, Mark Almond and Professor Colin Leach all made helpful suggestions. Andrew Cowgill, with his unrivalled grasp of the Union's Treaties, saved me from a number of errors. Daniel Hannan of the European Research Group generously read through the entire text in draft and improved it from his extensive knowledge. Susan Clifford went beyond the normal bounds of patience to type and retype the manuscript with unfailing good humour. James Barr worked closely with me in the closing stages, filling in a host of gaps and making it possible to turn a draft into a book.

Lastly, I would like to thank my colleagues at Jardines for their forbearance; my daughter Florence for her pointed questions; Penny Williams for her editing; and my publisher Andrew Franklin for his professionalism and the gentle relentlessness with which he pushed me to complete the work.

Rodney Leach

Introduction

The first edition of this book appears to have filled a gap. Students of the European Union had no ready place to turn for a succinct and reasonably comprehensive description of its many institutions, policies, laws and personalities. This gap was felt among voters preparing to face an eventual referendum on Britain's participation in the single currency; among politically conscious readers anxious to understand better what many sensed to be a period of constitutional upheaval; and among sixth form and university students (and teachers) of modern history, politics and economics, who recognised the growing influence of the Union but lacked a general reference book on its activities and felt themselves unduly reliant on Community sources for information about controversial European questions.

In this second edition I have where necessary brought the entries up to date, chiefly to reflect the further development of monetary union.

Preface

It is not only to the amateur that the EU is confusing. Even experts are baffled by the similarity of different institutions' names, the plethora of acronyms and initials, the changing titles and numbering of the Treaties. This book is addressed to anyone who has sought in vain clarification on some aspect of the Union or has encountered the sort of officialese which leaves the reader as perplexed after the explanation as before.

The choice of entries is based on one criterion only – whether or not a given subject is liable to crop up in an informed current discussion of the EU. Topics of interest only to historians have been omitted, as have expressions used exclusively by bureaucrats.

On certain subjects it is not possible to avoid an implicit political standpoint. The author's view is that both Continental federalism and British scepticism are grounded in the realities of history and self-interest. The federalist tide might recede, or Britons might be converted to European political union. These, however, seem less likely outcomes than a progressively imposed integration, increasing the UK's disenchantment or even in the extreme case leading to its withdrawal. The object of policy on both sides of the Channel should be to avoid that result. Given the EU's legal structure, a successful resolution of the impasse can probably be achieved only through incorporating into the Treaty of Rome the concept of permanently differing degrees of integration, sometimes known as flexibility or variable geometry. To see why this is so, a brief retracing of the Community's ideological development may be useful.

⌐

For 50 years since World War II, there have been two contrasting visions of Europe's destiny, one of which has come to predominate. The EU today is a would-be federation, half-way to its goal, steeped in bureaucracy but by no means static. Its ratchet structure makes it capable only of forward movement, an effect derived from the *acquis communautaire* – the doctrine that each new step towards integration is irreversible – and from the Treaty of Rome's paramount aim of 'ever-closer union'. This one-way system, commanding a budget of £60 billion and employing nearly 30,000 civil servants, is legitimised by the EU's claim to have created a new legal order outranking the constitutions and domestic laws of its member states. Its moral justification is the belief that the alternative to political union is antagonism and that Europe's contribution to civilisation entitles it to be more than a mere economic superpower.

The rival vision of Europe is of allies voluntarily co-operating and imposing only those common laws necessary to achieve common objectives. This concept bases its moral and legal position on the sanctity of the will of the people and the belief that democracies will never fight each other. Two above all have spoken in its name – General de Gaulle and Margaret Thatcher. Neither, however, framed their convictions in universal terms designed to appeal to other countries, de Gaulle being obsessed with French *gloire* and Thatcher concentrating her fire against what she saw as the prospect of the UK's submersion into Euro-socialism. Their redoubtable Commission opponents, Walter Hallstein and Jacques Delors, had little difficulty in characterising them as nationalists. Indeed, politicians who depend on popular votes, and who believe that the citizen's sense of belonging is largely attached to the nation state, are easy targets for federalists, who are apt to respond to the mildest proposal to block some integrationist policy by implying that such an action would be anti-European.

That federalism has won the upper hand is largely due to the forethought and subtlety of the Common Market's architects. Accepting that the people of Europe were not yet ready for political union, Jean Monnet taught his disciples in the 1950s and 1960s to steer towards their goal opportunistically, indirectly, retreating discreetly if rebuffed. Having successfully pooled France's and Germany's coal and steel resources in 1951, they next hoped to create a European army. When that ambition failed in 1954, they turned to the creation of an economic community, to which they tried to bolt on currency union in the early 1970s. When the currency project collapsed they bided their time, returning to it in the 1980s when the climate seemed more favourable.

This tactic of pursuing limited objectives, each of which could be portrayed as deserving in its own right, was successful. The ultimate goal of full political union was acknowledged in receptive circles but denied elsewhere, most famously in the 1975 British referendum. Each concrete advance was cast into Treaty law, institutionalised and administered by a supranational body. In this way the Commission was able to prevent relapses – and reform. It was a process which could be viewed from two perspectives: as the Machiavellian plotting of a secretive cabal, or as the enlightened planning of disinterested idealists who know what is best for the ordinary citizen and can get things done in a way denied to squabbling national governments. To Britons, reared on an unwritten constitution, an iconoclastic approach to the Establishment and the expectation that any policy can be reversed at the next election, the brick-by-brick construction of a European house based on unrepealable statute law was beyond their experience. Their heads in the sand, many opinion-formers chose not to understand it.

The Brussels bureaucracy could not have achieved its ends without political support. Such support was forthcoming from Europe's most powerful country, Germany. Racked by war guilt and not defining itself by nationhood (its borders have never been fixed and citizenship is a privilege of the *Volk*) Germany was more than willing to concede diminished sovereignty in exchange for reacceptance as a civilised society. From Adenauer to Kohl the submissive theme has gone unchallenged – a united Germany, safe from its own demons within a united Europe. To foreigners, bar a few transfixed by the past, the notion that modern democratic Germany needs protecting from itself in this way seems bizarre. Cynics, doubtless wrongly, take it for insincerity, concealing ambitions for hegemony.

Italians, too, supported political union. Embarrassed by the war, contemptuous of their domestic politics and with little sense of national identity (the country having existed for only 125 years and suffering from a sharp North-South divide), they considered that Brussels could hardly fail to be an improvement on Rome. Within the Common Market Italy prospered and left to others the more controversial aspects of building Europe.

The UK is often pilloried as the odd man out. Listening to a Europhile it would be easy to think that the UK's attitude stemmed from some flaw in the national character, perhaps a peculiar hostility to foreigners. The idea that one country alone has a fatal failing from which the other European countries are immune gives pause for questioning. Can it be that the Mother of Parliaments, the bastion of the rule of law and the only major European country to have consistently resisted both fascism and communism, is a moral defective? Or that the financial capital of Europe, a leading advocate of free trade, with unrivalled levels of inward and outward investment, is uniquely insular? The charges are not convincing.

Few realise how much the UK sacrificed to join the Community. The Treaty of Rome weakened the country's ties with the Commonwealth, with which there were sentimental links reinforced by shared suffering in two world wars. The CAP put an end to cheap food, at a cost of £1,000 per year for the average British family. Accession devastated the country's fishing industry and in numerous small ways (for example, the adoption of Continental weights and measures) disconnected people from their familiar world. By no means the richest of the European countries, the UK soon became the second highest contributor to the Community budget. Of no other member state could it be said that the tangible benefits of membership were so few and the tangible disadvantages so great. Added to that, the Anglo-Saxon model of economic management was so different from the Rhine model as to ensure that harmonisation along social market lines would be anything but harmonious.

If the UK, then, had good reasons for less than full commitment and Germany had good reasons for total immersion, France was torn. Under de Gaulle, the restoration of French pride was the priority. But that purpose did not survive his disappearance from the scene. His successors sought influence in playing Greece to Germany's Rome. As long as Germany remained politically passive, and as long as France dominated the Commission, Paris could regard itself as the true capital of Europe. On many an occasion Germany has been dismayed at French actions – over nuclear testing, over the near sabotaging of the 1994 GATT negotiations, over the original vetoing of the UK's entry. Yet each time it has gone quietly. While this situation persists, France will support European integration. If its perception ever changes, France will become less predictable: neo-Gaullist attitudes are rarely far below the surface.

Federalism's victories have come dear. Throughout Europe there is a sense of disillusion, often taking the form of disagreement with the priorities of the élites. A striking example is the German attitude to the single currency. Despite almost unanimous support for the euro among German politicians, backed by an expensive publicity campaign, a majority of the German population has reservations about losing the D-Mark. Their view of their government is that it ought to concern itself with unemployment, not monetary adventurism: their view of Europe is that it would be better occupied with issues such as the environment than with depriving Germans of their much prized currency.

There are other challenges, too, to integration, the most formidable of which arises from the recent collapse of the Soviet empire. If Europe's truest justification is the safeguarding of freedom and democracy from the Atlantic to the Urals, then the former communist countries of Central and Eastern Europe must be allowed to join. But the EU budget is shaped to serve a rich man's club with a few funds left over to ease the plight of distressed regions. The Community's finances would be stretched to breaking point if these regions were extended to include impoverished populations twice the size of Spain's.

To cater for British and Nordic independent-mindedness, 'variable geometry' has been allowed to grow since the 1992 Maastricht Treaty as a small tree in the shade of ever-closer union. The UK and Ireland have opt-outs from the abolition of frontier controls; the UK and Denmark have opt-outs from monetary union. When Poland, the Czech Republic and Hungary join the EU, they will have to be given exemptions on such a scale and of such duration as to be tantamount to opt-outs. To describe this process as a two-speed Europe, implying that integration is progressive and independence retrograde, is the language of federal determinism. What is needed is a new language. No one pretends that the Europe of nation states will be the victor in an ideological contest with federalism, for such an outcome would be unacceptable to

Germany, as well as to Italy, Spain and the Benelux countries. But nor must federalism be the outright victor. There is no iron law of history which makes European political union inevitable, ordaining success where so many other reluctant unions of nations have failed. The more sobering lesson of history is that populations deprived of their sense of identity, or feeling themselves to be remotely governed, will grow sullen and will eventually rebel.

It follows that if Europe is not to break apart, there must be room within it for different levels of unification on a permanent, not an interim, basis. Federation can remain the goal for those countries which freely elect to pursue it; but unless the principle that countries may set their own limits to integration is formalised within the Treaties of the EU, the running sore that has troubled Europe for 30 years will continue to trouble it indefinitely.

A–Z

I have always found the word 'Europe' on the lips of those who wanted something from other powers which they dared not demand in their own name.

Otto von Bismarck (1815–98), first chancellor of the German empire

---

A

Aachen

As the capital of Charlemagne's 9th century Christian empire, Aachen (Aix-la-Chapelle in French) could lay brief claim to being the first post-classical administrative and cultural centre of Europe. In all, 32 German emperors and kings have been crowned at Aix. The city also played host to the 1818 Congress to settle the peace of Europe after Napoleon's defeat – a conference which marked the high point of the unsuccessful attempt to govern Europe by international co-operation between the great powers.

Abatement

The temporary refund to the UK of part of its annual contribution to the EU budget. (See also **British rebate**, **Contributions** and **Fontainebleau Agreement**.)

Accession

The act of joining the European Union through a Treaty of Accession with the other member states. Applicants must be European states (among border-line cases Turkey qualifies but Morocco does not), respecters of the European Convention on Human Rights, willing to accept the *acquis communautaire*, democratic and not too poor. Neutrality, although at odds with EU policy, is no bar, as shown by the recent accession of Austria, Finland and Sweden.

The long-drawn-out application procedure involves obtaining a favourable Opinion from the Commission; gaining the majority assent of the European Parliament and the unanimous approval of the Council; negotiating a Treaty; and lastly getting this ratified by all the member states. New members are often given transitional periods in which to adjust. For example, the Accession Treaties of the UK and Spain led to a maze of interim arrangements and derogations over the Common Fisheries Policy. The anticipated accession of former communist countries from Eastern Europe will require exemptions on a range of EU policies, including EMU, the environment and the implementation of single market measures. (See also **Agenda 2000**.)

ACP countries

The 70 African, Caribbean and Pacific (ACP) countries, formerly colonies or dependent territories of EU member states, which enjoy Community aid and preferential access to Community markets under the Lomé Convention. (See Appendix 2.)

Action Committee for the United States of Europe (ACUSE)

Jean Monnet's integrationist lobby group, founded in 1955 and dissolved in 1975, by which time Monnet was 87 years old. ACUSE's greatest achievement was the preparation of the intellectual climate for the 1957 Treaty of Rome and the creation of the Common Market.

Acquis communautaire

The *acquis communautaire*, or Community heritage, is the irreversible body of laws, policies and practices which have at any given time evolved in the EU. The *acquis* is central to the way the European Commission ratchets up European integration. It prevents repatriation of powers to the member states by locking in previous federalising measures and it commits each signatory to the *finalités politiques*, or ultimate aims, of the Union. Thus the *acquis* not only inhibits reform but also paves the way to further unification.

The *acquis* particularly comes into play when new countries join the Union. These are required to accept all the Union's Treaties, legal obligations and policy positions and to 'take such measures as may be necessary to ensure their implementation'. A prime example was the reluctant acceptance by Denmark, Ireland and the UK of the Common Fisheries Policy, which had been rushed through at the last minute to enable the Six to lay claim to those countries' Atlantic and North Sea fish. Another example was the acceptance of the broad objective of EMU by Spain and Portugal 15 years before Economic and Monetary Union found legal expression in the Maastricht Treaty. Applicants are also required to acknowledge the judgments of the Court of Justice and the supremacy of Community law.

Although the concepts underlying the *acquis* have long been in existence, the term makes its first formal appearance in the Maastricht Treaty, under which an explicit objective of the Union is 'to maintain in full the *acquis communautaire* and build on it'.

Adenauer, Konrad (1876–1967)

In the chaos of post-war Germany Konrad Adenauer, in his 70s and with impeccable credentials as a non-Nazi, had the qualities of shrewdness, energy and unobtrusive determination that his country needed. As chairman of the Christian Democrats in the British zone, he helped to negotiate the constitution of the new Federal Republic of Germany and in 1949 he became the first federal chancellor, a position he held for 14 years.

During his span of office West Germany joined the Council of Europe in 1950 and NATO in 1955. Reconciliation with France was at the centre of his policy. In 1950 he proposed a complete union of France and Germany; in 1951 he signed the Treaty of Paris, under which French and German coal and steel production were placed under the common supranational authority of the European Coal and Steel Community (ECSC). In 1957 he signed the Community's founding Treaty of Rome; in 1959 he solved the vexed question of the Saarland, which lay in the French zone of occupied Germany, persuading France to allow it to be reincorporated into West Germany; and in 1963 he signed with Charles de Gaulle the Franco-German friendship treaty known as the Treaty of the Elysée.

All this time Germany's economy was recovering dramatically under the guidance of Adenauer's economics minister, Ludwig Erhard, while the Cold War helped erase the memory of German war crimes, as Stalin replaced Hitler as the symbol of evil. In 1955, two years after Stalin's death, Adenauer was able to negotiate the return of German prisoners of war from the Soviet Union. He cultivated good relations with the USA and the UK, adamant that the long-term purpose of German policy was to anchor the country in the West and find rehabilitation through suppressing German nationalism within an integrated Europe. Like his near contemporary Walter Hallstein and his later successor Helmut Kohl, he well understood the broader dimensions of economic actions, describing the foundation of the ECSC in 1951 as 'first and foremost political and not economic ... the beginning of a federal structure of Europe'.

Advocate-general

The role of the advocate-general in the European Court of Justice is to submit an Opinion on the case before the Court, analysing the facts, the precedents, the arguments and the relevant law, and to recommend a judgment. The Opinion is later published alongside the judgment, which generally (but not always) concurs with it. There are nine advocates-general, appointed by the Council of Ministers on renewable six-year contracts.

Agenda 2000

The Commission's perspective for the millennium, the centrepiece of which is its plan to incorporate into the EU the Czech Republic, Estonia, Hungary, Poland and Slovenia, as well as Cyprus. Notable for their omission are Bulgaria, Latvia, Lithuania and Romania, whose applications nevertheless command some support in the European Parliament and in certain member states. Economic liberalisation and political alignments are in flux in several of the candidate countries, which has prompted Romania to suggest an annual review of their progress. The admission of so many new members would require alterations in the EU's voting and institutional arrangements and would raise the cost of the Common Agricultural Policy and the structural funds, resulting in either a reallocation of subsidies among member states or an increase in the Community budget. Since Europe has little appetite for such developments, the prospect of reaching substantial agreement near the date of 2000 is, in reality, remote. Nevertheless, Agenda 2000 sketches out a draft EU financial perspective for the years 2000–06, the main feature of which is a provision of some 10% of the budget (approximately 10 billion ECUs per year) for the new members and other East European applicants.

Aid and development

The EU gives some 7.5 billion ECUs of external aid annually, of which 2.5 billion ECUs goes to 70 African, Caribbean and Pacific countries under the Lomé Convention and between 500 million and 1 billion ECUs to emergency humanitarian causes. Eastern Europe accounts for some 1.5 billion ECUs and the Mediterranean area 1 billion ECUs; the balance is divided between other developing countries. Most of these outlays pass through the EU budget, the exception being the Lomé funds, which are levied directly from member states but administered on their behalf by the Commission in the name of the European Development Fund.

The Community and its member states together provide nearly half the world's financial assistance to developing countries – more than twice as much as the USA or Japan. Such aid is increasingly called into question by donors as promoting a culture of corruption or dependency. It is also stigmatised by some recipients as selfish, a charge lent force by lucrative contracts won by European companies on assisted projects and by the EU's practice of counting as aid the dumping of unwanted food surpluses in competition with farmers in impoverished countries. The Community's Tacis and Phare programmes (for Russia and Eastern Europe respectively) have come in for stinging criticism from the Court of Auditors for wastefulness and lack of focus.

Airbus Industrie

A symbol (and a rare example) of successful European collaboration, the Airbus, assembled in Toulouse, is the sole major competitor to the US company Boeing in passenger aircraft manufacture. The principal partners are the French Aerospatiale, British Aerospace and Daimler-Benz Aerospace (Dasa) of Germany, with a smaller participation by Casa of Spain. The venture is a European Economic Interest Grouping, a non-profit-making consortium arrangement which hampers rationalisation, and which the partners are exchanging for a conventional structure. Their ambition of incorporating Airbus and making it the linchpin of the European aerospace and defence industry has won the approval of the administrations in France, Britain, Germany and Spain. Competition with the USA has been abrasive. The Americans accuse Airbus of receiving improper subsidies, while the Europeans accuse the US industry of being propped up by lucrative defence contracts. Both sides suspect the other of using every weapon of government, including diplomatic pressure and regulatory intervention, to further its cause.

Albania

After the death of Stalin in 1953 the Albanian Communist Party, led by Enver Hoxha, allied itself to China, considering Soviet policy too soft. Having been under Hoxha's grip for nearly 40 years, Albania is now a member of the Council of Europe, with a legitimate elected government, but it is the poorest country in Europe. In 1997 law and order broke down after a pyramid selling scandal, which ruined many citizens and gave a motley array of opponents, including members of the Mafia and ousted communists, the opportunity to create chaos, causing a refugee problem for the neighbouring EU states of Italy and Greece. The EU's muffled response was not untypical of the Common Foreign and Security Policy.

Andorra

See **Small countries**.

Anglo–American model

Sometimes contrasted with the Rhine model, the British and US economic systems are based on deregulation, free markets, labour flexibility, decentralised wage bargaining, low government involvement in the productive sector and widespread share ownership. The emphasis on shareholder values and open markets is also associated with takeover bids, which reallocate assets – in theory to their most efficient user – abruptly and without prior worker consultation.

The corporatist Rhine model is more closely controlled by the banks, themselves heavily regulated by a central bank. The stockmarket is of less importance and takeovers are rare. Wage bargaining is industry-wide, trade union representatives often sit on companies' supervisory boards, and government spending and the social costs of employment are high. Compared with the Anglo-American model the German system is said by its supporters to encourage long-term investment (as opposed to 'short-termism'), greater stability of employment and a more socially compassionate approach to the workforce.

Like the Swedish model before it, however, the Rhine model is not without its problems. Its labour market inflexibility has led to the export of jobs to more adaptable economies. Moreover, the combination of unemployment and some slimming of benefits has put the traditional employer–employee consensus under strain, whereas British labour relations have improved considerably. Continental industrialists are therefore beginning to look with increasing sympathy at aspects of the Anglo-American model and at the 'third way' practised in the Netherlands.

Approximation

Eurospeak for harmonisation, that is standardisation, whether of products, qualifications, laws or taxes.

Assent

Introduced by the Single European Act of 1986 and subsequently amended by the Maastricht Treaty, assent means right of veto, with particular reference to the European Parliament. The Parliament has to approve by absolute majority the accession to the EU of a new member state, and by simple majority the conclusion of an Association Agreement. This assent procedure applies to virtually all international agreements as well as to a limited range of legislative proposals.

Assizes

A conference of the European Parliament and the national parliaments of the EU's member states. There has only been one, in 1990, which (after a haggle about whether the seating plan should reflect nationality or political groups) led to a pair of Declarations about the desirability of involving national parliaments more in EU affairs.

Association Agreement

An agreement between the Community and a non-EU state or group of states. Such an agreement may be designed to pave the way to possible membership of the EU, in which case it is called a Europe Agreement, for example with Hungary, Poland and the Czech Republic. Or it may be an aid and technical co-operation agreement, as with certain North African and Middle Eastern countries; or a more comprehensive agreement with trade, aid, cultural and social dimensions, as with the African, Caribbean and Pacific signatories to the Lomé Convention. The EEA Treaty also counts as an Association Agreement.

Europe agreements provide for gradual integration into the Community, mutual free trade within ten years and progress towards compatibility with

Community law, within the framework of free elections, open markets and the rule of law. The process is carried forward by financial assistance and regular political meetings at head of state, ministerial, diplomatic and parliamentary levels.

Asylum

The abolition of internal border controls leaves the EU's external frontiers as the sole line of defence against unwanted asylum-seekers (asylum as between member states was barred in 1997). After the Dublin Convention of 1990, which shifted responsibility for assessing claims from the country where the refugee first enters the EU to the country where he or she first seeks asylum, there was no longer the same incentive for rigorous control at the external frontier. In some instances, all that was necessary for refugees to be waved through was to show that they were in transit to another member state, and in countries with long unpatrolled borders or coastlines the monitoring of illegal arrivals, a difficult task at the best of times, was seen by the destination countries as unacceptably slack.

With its central location and its possession of one of Europe's most generous social security systems, Germany receives more immigrants and more applications for asylum than any other EU country. A surge of Kurdish refugees early in 1998 led to criticism of Italy (and to a lesser extent Greece) for what Germany perceived as a negligent attitude to the transit problem. The UK, too, with its snail's-pace processing procedures and liberal attitudes, is an attractive destination. On arrival, applicants claim to have a well-founded fear of persecution at home; meanwhile, they can live off welfare or disappear into the big cities. By the end of 1997 the cases of over 50,000 asylum-seekers were still pending in the UK, and it was estimated that more than three times that number had become illegal immigrants. France and Sweden are also popular, receiving about the same number of applicants as the UK – some 250,000 between 1990 and 1997. The acceptance rate of asylum-seekers varies from country to country, ranging from over 40% in Scandinavia to under 20% in the UK and Germany.

The phenomenon of mass immigration into the EU is a function of poverty, repression and civil strife in neighbouring countries, from North Africa and the Middle East to the Balkans and the former Iron Curtain republics. It has exacerbated ethnic antagonisms and risks becoming a breeding ground for xenophobia and the ambitions of extremist politicians. (See also **Treaty of Amsterdam** and **Schengen Agreement**.)

Aubry, Martine (1951–)

The daughter of Jacques Delors, Martine Aubry is among the most influential socialist politicians in France. She provoked surprise and protest in 1998 as minister for employment and solidarity in Lionel Jospin's administration by her bill to tackle France's unemployment by cutting the working week from 39 to 35 hours without a reduction in the minimum wage.

Austria

Divided after World War II into four occupied zones, but with a single government, the Republic of Austria was not re-established as an independent state until 1955, when the Soviet troops withdrew after Austria had committed itself to neutrality. In 1960 the country became a founder member of EFTA. Germany, however, remained its main trading partner and the schilling has for over 20 years been closely linked to the D–Mark.

For most of the post-war period, Austria had grown at a higher rate than the European average, despite a stagnant political system in which much of the country's economic and civic life was controlled and shared out between the Social Democratic Party and the People's Party. In 1989, as the Cold War drew to a close and the single market gained momentum, Austria applied to join the EC, being formally admitted in 1995 to what had now become the European Union. Hopes that membership would provide an easy passport to sustained expansion soon gave way to the reality of austerity in order to meet the EMU criteria. Elections saw a sharp increase in the vote of the Freedom Party of Jorg Haider, who was much criticised as a xenophobe but was perhaps equally guilty of exposing political corruption in the traditional parties which formed the coalition government. As 1998 began, an intensive debate about the respective merits of neutrality and membership of NATO divided the coalition partners.

Accustomed to looking east, Austria has much to gain from the future accession to the EU of its neighbours, the Czech Republic, Hungary and Slovenia. The prospect of a prosperous *Mitteleuropa* and peaceful democracy on its borders has been unheard of since before World War I; but the spectre of low wage competition and a flood of economic immigrants is easily raised. Sharper competition within the existing EU, added to globalisation, has also brought doubts over Austria's consensus-based Rhine model style of industrial relations. Nevertheless, nationalism has no strong hold on the popular imagination and with its wealth and tranquillity it is hard to imagine the country lapsing into political extremism or turning its back on an acceptance of its future as an integral part of the EU.

Aznar, José-Maria (1953–)

Leader of the Partido Popular and Spanish prime minister since 1996, José-Maria Aznar started out as a state tax inspector, from where he rose through regional politics. His current position owes much to support from Basque and Catalan moderates, who have agreed to back him until Spain joins EMU. By 1998 Aznar was enjoying considerable prestige as a consequence of an economic upturn that enabled him both to increase spending without raising taxation and also to bring Spain into the first group of qualifiers for the single currency. Nevertheless, popularity continued to elude him, and with Spanish unemployment remaining the highest in the EU, he was expected to face a strong challenge from the Socialists in the election due in 2000.

B

The Balkans

The Balkans stand on a fault-line which has run though the south-eastern part of Europe since pre-history. There Helen's abduction led to the Trojan War and Greece fought off the Persian invasion. There lay the troubled border between civilisation and the so-called barbarians, from Alexander the Great to Julius Caesar and on until the fall of the Roman Empire. The Balkans marked the point where Eastern Christianity met Islam, Teuton met Slav, Europe met Asia. World War I started there, and the Bosnian massacres of the 1990s were but the latest in countless such ethnic or religious tragedies over the centuries.

The Balkans is an ill-defined term describing the region bounded by the Adriatic, the Aegean and the Black Sea. It is generally accepted to comprise Greece, Romania, Albania, Bulgaria, Yugoslavia (that is Serbia and Montenegro) and the former Yugoslav states of Macedonia, Bosnia-Hercegovina, Croatia and Slovenia. True to its history, the region remains full of tension and conflict, the latest trouble spot being Kosovo. Of its constantly shifting states, only Greece is a member of the EU, though several others have applied and Slovenia has been encouraged to expect membership early in the 21st century. (See also **Bosnian crisis**.)

Baltic states

Estonia, Latvia and Lithuania, formerly part of the Soviet Union, now all independent democracies, each of which is a member of the Council of Europe, has a Europe Agreement with the EU and has applied for full membership – though by the end of 1997 only Estonia, which had pulled far ahead of its neighbours, had been promised early admission. Under Soviet domination the Baltic states were integrated into the monolithic command economy of the USSR, making transition to market freedom a painful undertaking.

BECUs

Billion ECUs, sometimes written becus.

Beef crisis

In 1996 the British government announced a possible link between BSE, or mad cow disease, and a new strain of the fatal human brain illness, CJD. The scientific evidence was obscure and the number of reported human cases minuscule.

Nevertheless, outrage and panic ensued. The outrage came because BSE was more prevalent in England than elsewhere and the link with CJD had previously been denied. The panic was caused by predictions of a plague-like epidemic. In reality, BSE was on the wane, among its possible causes being pesticides and the overfeeding of British dairy cattle with sheep and cattle remains in the 1980s.

The EU inflamed the crisis by banning exports of British beef and beef products to non-EU countries. The British government then threatened to bring the workings of the Community to a halt unless the ban was lifted. This brought forth a half-promise to lift the ban progressively, provided the UK culled potentially affected cattle at a cost of several billion pounds. Despite the resultant slaughter the EU's ban remained, and British anger turned against the Community, which was perceived as favouring Continental farmers and breaching the principles of the single market. The affair, from which no party emerged well, soured relations within the EU and led to a welter of mutual accusations of insanitary practices, misreporting of BSE and evasion of import restrictions. By 1998 no solution had yet been found and the science remained debatable.

Belgium

Caught in both world wars in Germany's opening offensive against France, Belgium's instincts are defensive or neutralist. Its most prominent statesman during and after World War II, Paul-Henri Spaak, played a major role in many leading supranational institutions and in the negotiation of the Treaty of Paris and the Treaty of Rome, of which in each case Belgium was a founder signatory.

Even before the establishment of the European Coal and Steel Community in 1951, Belgium had been among the first members of NATO and had participated in Benelux, which prefigured many of the characteristics of the Common Market. The success of Benelux, allied to mistrust of its own domestic institutions, has made Belgium one of the EU's strongest supporters. Brussels is also the virtual capital of the Community, from which the country derives considerable revenue and an influence disproportionate to its size.

Since 1968 Belgium has gradually ceased to be a coherent state. Divided into the mutually antagonistic Flemish and Walloon (French-speaking) regions, together with some smaller minority regions, it has seven legislatures, with Brussels uneasily holding the reins. Its financial authorities have been accused of manipulating the level of national debt. Its judiciary is politicised, and Belgium must be unique among advanced Western economies in having witnessed popular demonstrations against the corruption of its politicians, judges and police. These domestic problems have reinforced the country's *communautaire* attitude, and although Belgium's indebtedness, at around 120% of GDP, far exceeds the ceiling set in the Maastricht Treaty's convergence criteria, its right to join the single currency was never seriously questioned.

Benelux

Originally a customs union conceived in 1944 by the exiled wartime governments of Belgium, the Netherlands and Luxembourg, Benelux came into being in 1948 and was reinforced by a Treaty of Union in 1960. With its headquarters in Brussels and its own supranational framework, Benelux is recognised as a regional union in the Treaty of Rome; and its ambitious – though as yet only partially fulfilled – plans for accelerated full economic and social union are regarded by integrationists as a model for the EU.

Within Benelux, Belgium and Luxembourg, despite the relatively greater strength of the tiny Luxembourg economy, share their gold and foreign exchange reserves and treat each other's currency as interchangeable.

Berlaymont

The star-shaped Brussels headquarters of the European Commission, rented from the Belgian government and found in 1991 to be riddled with asbestos and uninhabitable until cleansed. The Commission hopes to resume occupation in 2001.

Berlin

The youngest of Europe's great cities, Berlin was the historical capital of Germany, a position to which it will be reinstated a year ahead of schedule in 1999 when the government begins its move from West Germany's post-war capital, Bonn. The city, which lay in the Soviet zone of occupation when Germany was divided after World War II, was itself also divided, its eastern sector becoming the capital of the new Soviet satellite state, the German Democratic Republic. An oasis of freedom behind the Iron Curtain, Berlin was the focus of three dramatic episodes in modern European history. In 1948/49 it was blockaded on Stalin's orders but rescued from starvation by the Berlin Airlift, when the Western allies flew more than 275,000 relief flights. In 1961 the communist government built the Berlin Wall across the centre of the city to prevent the exodus of refugees from the East. And in 1989, the Wall's breach symbolised the disintegration of the Soviet Empire and the birth of German reunification.

The city's buildings, resonant of the country's militaristic past as well as the post-war occupation, are to be reused where they have survived. The Reichstag, home of the German parliament until 1933, when the Nazis set it ablaze in a plot to frame and discredit their opponents, is being rebuilt to resume its former function.

Black economy

Anecdotal evidence suggests that the unofficial 'shadow' or black economies of Europe have been growing, leading to an erosion of the tax base and the risk of mistaken (because based on misleading figures) policy decisions. Italy has even prided itself on the size of its black economy, relying on it in the 1980s to boast of *il sorpasso*, or the overtaking of the UK's GDP. Although no reliable economic analysis is possible, such estimates as have been made would put the black economies of Italy, Spain and Belgium at upwards of 20% of GDP, with the UK, France and Germany at approximately half that level and the Netherlands and Sweden mid-way between the two groups.

Black fish

Fish landed illegally, so as to avoid Common Fisheries Policy quotas.

Black Wednesday

See **White Wednesday**.

Blair, Tony (1953–)

Elected prime minister in 1997, Tony Blair had previously transformed the Labour Party by shedding its socialist past and embracing Margaret Thatcher's free-market reforms. Although sharing a leftist political label with the majority of his fellow EU premiers, Blair's substantive policies on European economic issues were little different from those of his Conservative predecessor, John Major.

Blair started his tenure with a strong predilection for playing a positive role in Europe, tempering a wait-and-see stance on EMU with statements that his government in principle favoured participation. He fulfilled a promise to sign up to the Social Chapter, which he now coupled with a pledge to block any legislation that would undermine British competitiveness – a pledge which would have to rely on persuasiveness, given the scope for passing measures by qualified majority voting. Blair had, however, attained power at a time of high unemployment in Germany and France and relative strength in the British economy. The political career of Chancellor Kohl was showing signs of mortality, and the EU was at sixes and sevens over a number of issues. Nor was Blair faced with a strong Commission president like Jacques Delors. Thus by 1998, his opportunity to exercise influence in Europe seemed as great as that of any prime minister since Churchill. The UK's presidency of the EU that year was, however, unfruitful, being overshadowed by a squabble over the leadership of the future Central Bank.

Bookerisms

Destructive and unnecessary rules, sometimes achieving the opposite of their professed aim, generally originating with Commission Regulations or Directives, the latter frequently 'gold-plated' by domestic officials as they pass in to national law. Named after Christopher Booker, a British writer who has compiled a graphic databank of bureaucratic wreckage. (See also **Cucumber Directive**.)

Bosnian crisis

The break-up of the former Yugoslavia in the early 1990s led to declarations of independence by Slovenia and Croatia and growing nationalist aggression by Serbia, which had inherited most of the Yugoslav army's weaponry. In 1991 Germany recognised Slovenia and Croatia, forcing the EU to follow suit in 1992. Bosnia's independence was recognised immediately afterwards, but that country (with a mainly Muslim and Croatian population) contained a large Serbian minority, and fighting broke out. Assisted by Serbia, which had also intervened militarily in Croatia, the Bosnian Serbs took advantage of a Western arms embargo to terrorise the country, besieging its capital Sarajevo.

While the EU attempted to broker a peace process, the Serbs embarked on the 'ethnic cleansing' of Bosnia's Muslims. This led to atrocities on both sides, but British and French reluctance to appear partial, allied to Germany's paralysis (doubtless the legacy of the Nazi occupation of Yugoslavia during World War II), left the Serbs free to commit genocide unhindered. A smattering of United Nations peacekeeping forces soon became more of a hostage than an effective military presence, and it was not until the USA lost patience and organised NATO bombing of Serbian positions in 1995 that a modicum of order was restored.

A partitioned Bosnia currently enjoys an uneasy peace. But the ineffectiveness of the EU has left a lasting impression of weakness and expediency, and gives the lie to the notion that Europe is yet capable of responding in a unified way to external crisis. (See also **Common Foreign and Security Policy**.)

Brandt, Willy (1913–92)

Willy Brandt's pedigree as a young socialist, who had escaped the Nazis and fled to Norway in 1933, spending the war partly in the Norwegian Resistance and partly as a journalist in neutral Sweden, fitted him well to lead a peacetime Germany which had reacted against the past with a strong orientation to social democracy. After serving in the Bundestag from 1949 to 1957, he was mayor of West Berlin during the Berlin crisis of 1961, when the Wall was built almost overnight. Elected chairman of the Social Democrats in 1964, within two years he had become foreign minister, a position he held until becoming chancellor in 1969. Having won the Nobel Peace Prize in 1971 for his contribution to East–West relations, he resigned in 1974 after a spy scandal involving a close aide.

Brandt had established his liberal credentials under Chancellor Konrad Adenauer, criticising the Hallstein doctrine of non-recognition of East Germany. An advocate of détente, he cultivated friendship with East Germany, allaying Soviet suspicions of West Germany's strategic role in NATO by his commitment to nuclear non-proliferation. Following the signature of treaties with the USSR and Poland, which settled the disputed East German border, Brandt was able in 1970 to ease the restrictions on contact between East and West Berlin. His *Ostpolitik* made him a welcome guest in the Warsaw Pact countries, a reception not accorded by his compatriots to his Stalinist East German counterpart, Communist Party secretary Erich Honecker.

After his resignation, Brandt served as an MEP from 1979 to 1983 and continued to play a role on the international political scene as president of the Socialist International and a champion of aid to developing countries.

Bretton Woods

The Bretton Woods Conference of July 1944 shaped the world's post-war monetary order at a time when German defeat looked inevitable. Its most important institutional creations were the World Bank and the International Monetary Fund. The Conference also designed a regime of fixed, but in the last resort flexible, exchange rates, which was to last for some 30 years. Under the Bretton Woods system each participating state tied its currency to the US dollar and maintained dollar reserves, but was able to adjust its parity if its economy fell fundamentally out of alignment. The weakening of the dollar in the early 1970s caused the system to collapse, to be replaced by floating currencies and by a series of European attempts to create an area of regional stability centred on the D-Mark.

Brezhnev Doctrine

Three months after the 'Prague Spring' was crushed by the Soviet military in 1968, Leonid Brezhnev declared the USSR's right, indeed 'socialist duty', to intervene in the internal affairs of its satellite states if communism was at risk. Effectively a restatement of the old Stalinist position, Brezhnev's doctrine was a negation of the widely accepted international principles of self-determination and freedom from outside interference. It was designed to frighten the East European countries, which already had Soviet troops stationed in their territory, into passive acquiescence in Moscow's hegemony, as well as warning NATO and the EC not to meddle in the Soviet sphere of influence. The Brezhnev doctrine was a contravention of the 1975 Helsinki Agreement, to which all the Warsaw Pact countries except Albania were later to become signatories, but it was formally abandoned only in 1988, by Mikhail Gorbachev.

British rebate

Known also as the British abatement, the UK's annual rebate from the EC was achieved by Margaret Thatcher after a long struggle in which she demonstrated that the UK was making a disproportionate contribution to the Community budget as a result of the workings of the Common Agricultural Policy. The rebate was finally agreed at Fontainebleau in 1984 and in its present form runs until 1999. Although it cannot formally be changed without British consent, the Commission has made it plain that it will propose a re-examination at the time of the EU's next enlargement. The rebate is calculated on a formula related to the VAT-based portion of the UK's contribution.

Brittan, Sir Leon (1939–)

A twist of fate brought Leon Brittan to his position as an influential vice-president of the Commission in Brussels. In 1986 he resigned from Margaret Thatcher's cabinet when a row about the rescue of the helicopter manufacturer Westland blew up into a political storm of which he became the victim. From 1988 to 1992 Brittan was the commissioner responsible for the Community's competition policy; he later took on external economic policy and played a key role in the successful conclusion of the difficult Uruguay Round of the GATT negotiations. His occasional forays back into domestic politics have been marked by hypersensitivity to criticism of the EU.

Brown, Gordon (1951–)

Chancellor of the Exchequer since Labour's 1997 election victory, Gordon Brown gave independent control of interest rates to the Bank of England and is a supporter of British entry into EMU, subject to a specially designed set of British convergence criteria.

Bruges Group/Bruges speech

Margaret Thatcher's 1988 speech at Bruges, praising a Europe of Nations and criticising the unaccountability of the EC's supranational institutions, shocked many at the time, although in retrospect it largely served to sharpen differences of vision which were already inherent in the European debate. The Bruges Group of anti-federalists took its name from that occasion.

Brussels (Treaty of)

Signed in 1948 by the UK, France and the Benelux countries, the Treaty of Brussels was the precursor to the WEU (Western European Union) and NATO. It envisaged economic and social collaboration as well as collective defence.

Budget

The Treaty of Rome decrees that the EU must run a balanced budget. On the revenue side, to give the Community financial independence, contributions from member states were replaced in 1970 by a system of own resources, which had to be revised in 1988 after the Single European Act had reduced the income from duties and levies. Currently, own resources consist of four classes of revenue:

⇒ tariffs on imports
⇒ agricultural levies and sugar duties
⇒ a percentage of each member state's VAT revenue (as determined by a special formula)
⇒ member state contributions related to their own GNP.

Of these revenue streams, the first two, known as the traditional resources, account for a declining share, currently under 20%. The VAT revenue is being reduced annually: at its height it accounted for over 60% of the budget, but by 1999 this will have fallen to around 30%. The GNP-related revenue, originally a mere balancing item, is rising rapidly and by 1999 will finance over half the budget. The overall effect of these changes has been an improvement in the fairness of member states' contributions, which in future should be a better reflection of national wealth.

EMU and growing federalisation are likely to lead in the long run to Commission demands for an expanded revenue base, with more direct access to national taxpayers, so as to support higher central spending and ease regional unemployment. The enlargement of the EU by the addition of poorer countries from Eastern Europe will also increase the cost of the Common Agricultural Policy and the need for structural funds. For the moment, such ambitious goals, which would require the unanimous approval of the Council of Ministers as well as the consent of national parliaments, are off the agenda. Indeed, the emphasis until 2000 is on restraint. Nevertheless, integrationists recall with nostalgia the 1977 MacDougall Report, which reckoned a small Community spending target at up to 7% of the total GNP of the member states and a large target at up to 25%, that is, from five to 20 times the present budget level.

The budget is driven by the expenditure plans, which are drafted by the Commission, approved by the Council of Ministers and then read by the European Parliament, which proposes amendments and returns the budget to the Council. An artificial, but not clearcut, distinction between compulsory and non-compulsory spending determines the next phase of negotiation (the Council has the final say on compulsory spending, which includes agricultural price support, and the Parliament has the final say on non-compulsory spending). Lastly, the Parliament either adopts or rejects the budget. If a budget is in limbo, awaiting further amendments or the resolution of differences, expenditure is eked out month by month at the rate of one-twelfth of the previous year's spending.

I consider it an assumption of heroic proportions to believe that the Monetary Union can function in the long run ... if the European Central Bank were isolated from financial and wages policy.

Dr Hans Tietmeyer, president of the Bundesbank, Freiburg, January 13th 1997

Inside the total expenditure ceiling (some 91 billion ECUs for 1998) agricultural price support accounts for around 45% of the budget; the structural funds for over 33%; internal policies (mainly research) for 6%; external action, or development assistance, for 6%; and administration for 5%. No other items approach 2%. The overall budgetary proportions are set by heads of government, meeting as the European Council, the last such financial perspective being agreed at the 1992 Edinburgh summit, covering the years from 1993 to 1999 and stipulating a 1% per year decrease in the percentage taken by agricultural guarantees.

Despite current efforts at budgetary discipline and a boost since 1993 from rising world agricultural prices, the wider picture is that Community spending has risen from 0.03% of the member states' aggregate GNP in 1960 to 0.53% in 1973 and a projected 1.27% in 1999 – an increase in real terms of some 40 times. The Commission argues that some of this represents costs transferred from national governments to the EU; if so, national governments (other than the main financial beneficiaries, Ireland, Greece, Portugal and Spain) evince little gratitude for the diminution of their burdens. (See also **Contributions**, **Fraud**, **British rebate** and **Court of Auditors**.)

Bulgaria

Impoverished, ridden by hyperinflation and unreconstructed, Bulgaria was ruined after World War II by the communist dictator Todor Zhivkov and failed to take advantage of his dismissal in 1989. A succession of weak governments was followed by a reformist administration in 1997, but positive results are yet to show and the country's application for early membership of the EU has failed to win the recommendation of the Commission.

C

Cabinet

The private office of a European VIP.

CAP

See **Common Agricultural Policy**.

Capital of the European Union

There is no capital of Europe, the nearest approximation being Brussels, which houses the Commission, the Council of Ministers and parts of the European Parliament. Three-quarters of the Commission's staff work in Brussels – a rich source of rent and restaurant trade. It has been estimated that Brussels earns around $1.5 billion a year from European officials and their multifarious visitors.

Luxembourg serves as the second city of the EU, playing host to the European Court of Justice, the European Investment Bank and the Court of Auditors. The third city is Strasbourg, home of the European Council and principal home of the European Parliament.

Cassis de Dijon case

The 1979 Cassis de Dijon ruling of the European Court of Justice was a landmark judgment. It established that a product sold lawfully in one member state may not be prohibited in another member state except on public health grounds – the so-called mutual recognition of products principle.

Cecchini Report

The 1988 Cecchini Report, named after the chairman of a Commission-appointed committee of experts, is chiefly famous as a cautionary tale. Basing their results on econometric models and a survey of 11,000 businessmen, the authors of the report forecast that the single market would add around 5% to the GDP of the Community's member states, reduce prices by 6%, raise growth by 7%, create several million extra jobs and 'put Europe on an upward trajectory into the next century'. In the event, the achievement of the single market in the 1990s coincided with stagnation and a massive increase in structural unemployment – evidence, if evidence were needed, of the shallowness of economic predictions, especially by businessmen.

Censure

Under the Treaty of Rome, the European Parliament has the right, rarely threatened and never in practice employed, to force the Commission to resign *en bloc* on a motion of censure carried by a two-thirds voting majority, representing an absolute majority of all MEPs. The Parliament has no right of censure against the Council or against individual commissioners.

CERN (Centre Européen pour la Recherche Nucléaire)

CERN is the French acronym for Europe's Geneva-based advanced non-military high energy physics research centre. It is financed by European governments, including certain non-EU countries, and strictly speaking is not a Community organisation. The CERN particle accelerator has produced interesting pure science results but the Centre's main practical benefits have been by-products, notably the invention of the worldwide web.

CFP

See **Common Fisheries Policy**.

CFSP

See **Common Foreign and Security Policy**.

Channel Islands

See **Small countries**.

Channel Tunnel

See **Eurotunnel**.

Charlemagne (742–814)

Europeans who like to trace the history of unification to the past have a number of candidates to choose from. The Romans gave Europe law, roads, the Latin language and the spreading of Christianity, Napoleon gave it conquest and a modernised legal code, but it is the name of Charlemagne that is most frequently invoked. Scarcely less bloodthirsty than Napoleon, he conquered France, Belgium, North Italy, Saxony, Bavaria and North Spain, turned the clergy into a tame bureaucracy and centralised taxes, administration and theology. His empire, with its capital at Aachen, comprised a remarkably similar geographical area to that of the six original EEC members. It did not long survive his death.

Charter of Paris

See **OSCE**.

Chirac, Jacques (1932–)

A Gaullist who had twice served as French premier, Jacques Chirac was elected president of the republic in 1995, reluctantly inheriting the commitment to EMU of his Socialist predecessor François Mitterrand at a time when economic stagnation seemed to be threatening France's ability to meet the Maastricht convergence criteria. A national election, called by Chirac in 1997 to gain endorsement for his policy of austerity, backfired when, despite his personal popularity, the Socialists won a majority in the Assembly, with Lionel Jospin replacing Chirac's Gaullist ally, Alain Juppé, as premier. Jospin's old-fashioned make-work manifesto was incompatible with Chirac's centre-right economic views, and although both co-habitants of France's highest offices now proclaimed loyalty to the single currency, concern arose in Germany that France would be a weak link, possibly to the extent of undermining the ability of the Euro to match the strength of the D–Mark.

Chirac's loss of political authority coincided with a weakening in the domestic standing of Chancellor Helmut Kohl of Germany. There was little love lost between the two men, and for a time the erstwhile solid Franco-German partnership came under strain. Disagreement arose over matters ranging from foreign policy to Italy's suitability for the single currency and the independence of the future European Central Bank. The Amsterdam conference of 1997, intended to reform the EU's institutional structure and pave the way for the admission of former communist countries, ended inconclusively. Some, mindful of Chirac's inconsistency and the historical French desire to dilute Germany's influence in Europe, questioned the durability of France's commitment to a politically unified supranational Europe.

By 1998 economic recovery had enabled France to achieve compliance with the financial qualifications for EMU; and despite a last-minute attempt to politicise the European Central Bank by putting a Frenchman at its head, a breach with Germany was avoided. But an irresolute Chirac, at odds with his Socialist premier and dismayed by the strength of the extreme right National Front party, presided over a rudderless France, whose *joie de vivre* was strained by unemployment and whose vision of the EU veered between the influences of federalism and traditional aspirations for independence.

Christian democracy

The nearest approximation to a transnational centre-right political creed in Europe. (See also **Religion** and **Political groups**.)

Churchill, Winston (1874–1965)

Winston Churchill's incomparably distinguished political career ended with his retirement from the premiership in 1955, nearly ten years before his death and 17 years before the accession of the UK to the EEC. It is thus an anachronism to enlist him on either the Eurosceptic or the Europhile side; it is, however, relevant to recall that his mother was American and that he held a fervent faith in the Commonwealth and the Anglo-American alliance. Perhaps his ultimate loyalty was to the English-speaking world.

In the summer of 1940, with France near collapse, it was a typically bold gesture on Churchill's part to agree with Jean Monnet and Charles de Gaulle a proposal for a complete union between the UK and France; France fell and the idea came to nothing. For his considered thoughts on Europe after the war, the primary source is his speech made in September 1946 in Zurich, in which he called for the building of a 'kind of United States of Europe', of which the UK would be a 'friend and sponsor' – natural words in the context of the times, with much of the Continent lying in ruins. This is not very different from his earlier published observations in 1930 ('We are with Europe but not of it. We are linked but not comprised'); and when he said in 1948 that if Europe united was to be a living force, the UK would have to play its full part as a member of the European family, the words are sufficiently vague to admit of more than one meaning.

It is easier to state that Churchill was in favour of European unity than that he would have favoured UK entry into the EEC, still less that he would have acceded to Walter Hallstein's and Jacques Delors' vision of a supranational Europe; it is inconceivable that he would have been willing to compromise British sovereignty or forget the UK's obligations to the Commonwealth. The fact that he was president-of-honour of the 1948 Congress of Europe owed more to his prestige, and to the content of his Zurich speech, than to any coherent pan-European strategy. Churchill alone had played a leading role in the century's two world wars, both of which had started in Europe; nobody could speak with more authority about the necessity of radical new thinking to prevent a third one.

Citizenship

It is no accident that European citizenship conjures up the image of a country called Europe. The idea first found expression in 1984 with proposals for a People's Europe designed to improve the flagging popularity of the Community and strengthen the sense of European identity by creating a raft of miscellaneous citizens' rights. Many of these were enacted into Community law over the ensuing years. But it was not until the Treaty of Maastricht in 1992 that citizenship itself (at Spain's urging) was formally recognised as part of the *acquis communautaire*. The Treaty ordained that all nationals of member states must also be citizens of the Union. Initially, the privileges conferred by European citizenship are modest: the right to complain to the European Parliament, to vote or stand in local or European elections, to obtain diplomatic protection in countries where the citizen's member state is unrepresented and to reside anywhere in the Union. But the Treaty envisages these rights being strengthened or expanded; thus the intent of multiplying the trappings of a single state appears evident.

The requirements for EU citizenship are left to member states. For example, British subjects with the right of abode qualify, whereas those with Dependent Territories status, with the exception of Gibraltarians, do not. Germany faces a particular dilemma. It houses many more recent immigrants than other European states. Yet under an Imperial Decree of 1913 it bases the right to citizenship on blood descent, which rules out children of foreigners even if born in Germany. Anxious to win a reputation for enlightenment, many German parliamentarians wish to change the law. Chancellor Helmut Kohl, however, has blocked reform, fearing an influx which would add to the country's 7 million immigrants (of whom 2 million are Turks) and facing down accusations of fanning xenophobia through discrimination.

The City of London

The suggestion is sometimes made (pessimistically by British Europhiles, optimistically by Parisians and Frankfurters) that London might lose its position as Europe's leading financial centre if the UK does not join EMU. In reality, the City is a centre for world, rather than European, finance; it relies on market freedom, as likely to be stifled as enhanced by the tight regulations likely to accompany the single currency; and the English language and law are the *lingua franca* of international markets. It would be difficult to replicate the City's range of activities elsewhere in the European time-zone. (See also **Convergence criteria (2)**.)

Clarke, Kenneth (1940–)

As Chancellor of the Exchequer from 1993 to 1997, Kenneth Clarke inherited an economic recovery which coincided with the pound's ejection from the ERM. His attitude to EMU puzzled his many admirers. Disdaining to read the Maastricht Treaty, he scorned the opponents of the single currency as a dissentient minority 'capable of being fitted into a taxi' and did not acknowledge a connection between monetary and political union. On being succeeded by Gordon Brown in Tony Blair's administration, he broke Conservative Party ranks by declaring his personal support for British adoption of the euro.

Closer co-operation

Closer co-operation, or flexibility, is a significant principle introduced by the 1997 Treaty of Amsterdam. It provides that as a last resort a majority of member states may use the Community's institutions to develop closer links with each other, without involving the remaining member states. The Treaty makes it plain that this Article is not intended as a loophole for preventing the advance of the *acquis communautaire*, still less for reversing it. The intention rather is to allow certain countries to move ahead with integration faster than others. (See also **Two-speed Europe**.)

Club Med countries

Italy, Spain, Portugal and Greece, so named because of their supposedly relaxed financial policies and southern temperament, in contrast to the stern discipline of the northern hard core. Paradoxically, the impending introduction of EMU in 1999 saw the Club Med countries making equally determined efforts as Germany and France to prove their fiscal rectitude. In the event, Italy, Spain and Portugal were admitted as immediate entrants to the euro. Greece, too, seemed likely to be accepted within five years.

Cockfield White Paper

In the early 1980s the Common Market had substantially ground to a halt. Progress in freeing trade was blocked by indecision in the Council of Ministers, resulting in a heavy backlog of draft Directives and Regulations which seemed unlikely ever to see the light of day. At the 1985 summit meeting of heads of state, the Commission was instructed to draw up a remedial programme with a timetable. The task was entrusted to the British Commissioner for the Internal Market, Lord Cockfield, whose White Paper identified some 300 necessary measures and set the end of 1992 as the target date for completing the single market. The White Paper divided the obstacles into three categories: physical (for example, frontier controls); technical (for example, product standards, public procurement policies and restrictions on free trade in services); and fiscal (for example, differing rates of VAT and excise duty). The Cockfield proposals were an important formative influence in the Single European Act of 1986.

Co-decision

Co-decision means joint decision by the Council of Ministers and the European Parliament. Established by the 1992 Maastricht Treaty, the procedure allows the Parliament to veto (by absolute majority) any legislation on which it has not reached agreement with the Council; co-decision also reduces the role of the Commission as an intermediary, replacing this by direct negotiations between the Council and the Parliament in a conciliation committee. In both these respects, co-decision gives more authority to the Parliament than the co-operation procedure brought in by the 1986 Single European Act. Co-decision applies currently to a limited range of policies (such as the single market, education, the environment, consumer protection and health) but the 1997 Treaty of Amsterdam will extend its scope to new areas, including employment, social policy and transport.

Co-habitation

The power-sharing which arises, especially in France, when there is a leftist president and a rightist prime minister, or vice versa.

Cohesion Fund

See **Structural funds**.

College of Europe

Founded in Bruges in 1949, the College of Europe, which is part-funded by the EU, offers postgraduate courses in European integrationist studies to some 200 students. It was here that Margaret Thatcher made her celebrated anti-federalist speech in 1988.

Comecon

Established in Moscow in 1949 and dissolved in 1991, Comecon was the Soviet-dominated organisation for co-ordinating communist economic policy in Eastern Europe and later Mongolia, Cuba and Vietnam. Co-ordination amounted in reality to abject subservience to the Soviet Union. The former Yugoslavia was never a member. Albania, which considered the USSR soft after Stalin's death, left Comecon in 1961.

Comitologie

The science of committees, a necessary skill in Brussels, where advisory, management, regulatory and other committees jostle for influence – cynics would say for the privilege of power without responsibility. The general rule is that the Commission is obliged to take account of committee Opinions, but not to follow them unless ordered to do so by the Council. The European Parliament, resentful of secret committee proceedings and Commission dominance, favours requiring the Commission's committees to supply more information to the Parliament's committees.

Commission

See **European Commission**.

Committee of the Regions

Established on a German–Spanish initiative by the 1992 Maastricht Treaty, the Brussels-based Committee of the Regions consists of 222 representatives (most of them holding regional or local elective office in their home countries) who advise on the impact of EU legislation. The Committee's remit covers five sectors – education and vocational training, culture, public health, transport systems, and economic and social cohesion – although the Treaty allows the Commission and the Council of Ministers to consult it on other issues. Under the Treaty, the Committee may also volunteer Opinions on regional matters. No EU institution is, however, obliged to follow its advice, whether solicited or unsolicited. The Committee shares certain services and a reputation for imaginative expense accounts with the Economic and Social Committee. It was censured in 1997 by the Court of First Instance for nepotistic recruitment (including the hiring of political cronies) within its own 80-strong bureaucracy. (See also **Regionalism**.)

Common Agricultural Policy (CAP)

The CAP is a protectionist system for supporting agriculture in the EU. Established by the Treaty of Rome in 1958, it was for many years the only significant Community policy, accounting for over two-thirds of the budget, providing vast subsidies and substantially raising the cost of food to consumers. The CAP has enriched some farmers, saved others from poverty and ensured plentiful home-grown production; but at the same time it serves as an unwilling accomplice to fraud and disrupts international markets through import levies, subsidised exports and the creation of unwanted surpluses disposed of by intermittent bouts of dumping.

In more recent times some reforms have been progressively brought about by financial constraints and pressure from the GATT. The effect has been to reduce the cost of the CAP to about half the EU budget and to make some inroads on surplus production. But many member states have a vested interest in resisting change and the reforms have fallen far short of a genuine liberalisation of agricultural trade. With the approaching accession of new countries, some, like Poland, poor and with large rural areas, others with Arctic or mountainous conditions, further modifications to the CAP are inevitable if the Union is not to run out of funds. As long, however, as the CAP is seen as a talisman of European integration and a battlefield of free traders versus protectionists and interventionists, it will continue to attract passionate controversy.

Origins (1958–73)

The five aims of the CAP as set out in the Treaty of Rome were couched in elevated terms: increased productivity, a fair standard of living for the agricultural population, stabilised markets, regular supplies of food and reasonable prices for consumers. The underlying political reality was that France wanted to guarantee high prices to farmers in return for enlarging the markets for German industry. Fear of social instability and vivid memories of food shortages increased the determination of the member states to create a prosperous farming community and to make Europe self-sufficient in staple items.

Launched in 1962, the CAP was to be based on three principles:

⇒ a single market in farm products, with common prices and free movement within the Community
⇒ Community preference, that is, a tariff system of import levies and export refunds on trade with non-members
⇒ shared responsibility for costs.

In the context of these policies, the UK's application to join the Six was both a threat and an opportunity. The opportunity lay in the fact that the UK was one of the world's largest food importers; if it could be persuaded to switch suppliers, the EC would gain an additional paymaster and a new market. The threat lay in the UK's predilection for free trade and cheap Commonwealth food. Charles de Gaulle's vetoes of British entry in the 1960s had much to do with the UK's initial unwillingness to abandon its Commonwealth trade links by agreeing to Community preference. The withdrawal of de Gaulle from the political scene and the concession by Prime Minister Edward Heath of most of the UK's negotiating points (with the exception of some special arrangements for New Zealand and the Caribbean) brought this phase to a close, clearing the way for British entry, at a cost to the consumer estimated in recent years at around £1,000 per year per family of four.

Mounting problems (early 1970s–late 1980s)

The need to restructure inefficient Continental agriculture had led to the 1968 Mansholt Plan, featuring import protection and compensation for job losses. A watered-down version of this plan was adopted by the EC in 1972 and funded by the European Agricultural Guidance and Guarantee Fund (known by its more pronounceable French initials, FEOGA). The resultant combination of improved productivity and generous guaranteed prices proved little short of disastrous to everyone except farmers left on the land. Agricultural incomes were in the main sustained not by direct subsidies to subsistence farmers but by unlimited intervention buying of any produce which could not be sold at a higher price on the open market. As a result, market discipline was virtually non-existent. By the early 1980s wine lakes, butter mountains and large surpluses of dairy produce, cereals and sugar were accumulating.

To the cost to consumers of overpriced food was now added the cost to taxpayers of storing or disposing of stockpiles. The easy answer was dumping, through export refunds, gifts in aid or cut-price deals. Such action caused extensive international ill-will, as competing exporters were undercut and low-cost agricultural economies were hit by a flood of produce at prices which even they could not match.

The scale and complexity of FEOGA's operations gave rise to growing scope for exploitation and fraud, which an expanding bureaucracy was unable to control and which there was little incentive for offending countries to expose. Public bewilderment was compounded by the artificial system of green currencies and monetary compensation amounts, designed to make up for currency fluctuations and create the illusion that farmers were operating in a single European currency zone.

The accession to the EC of Greece in 1981 and Spain and Portugal in 1986; the impending round of GATT negotiations, at which trade agreements appeared sure to be conditional on some degree of agricultural liberalisation; and the spectre of the Community budget being stretched to breaking point – together these factors demanded reform. From 1983 onwards the Commission and the member states wrestled with proposals to tackle over-production and limit subsidies, hampered for a while by the weakness of the dollar, which increased the gap between world prices and European prices. In 1988 a package of measures was agreed by the Council of Ministers, of which the principal elements were that the overall growth of CAP expenditure would be not more than 74% of the growth of the budget; that farmers would be paid not to farm (the notorious set-aside); that output quotas and levies on excess production would be extended (leading to an unseemly rush to swell the volumes on which the ceilings would be based); and that the Community's structural funds would be retargeted to include among their objectives the easing of agricultural reform and aid to rural areas.

Recent developments
The 1988 measures failed to address the radical changes which the British wished to see and which the USA and the Cairns Group of agricultural countries, led by Argentina, Australia, Canada and New Zealand, considered essential to a healthy international market. The biggest stumbling blocks to progress were the

antipathy of the French and German governments to any action which might jeopardise countryside prosperity and their fear of adding to unemployment, anxieties which were exacerbated by the disproportionate power of farm lobbies and rural voters in France and Bavaria. Moreover, the complexity of the CAP had given it a bureaucratic life of its own. It was the centrepiece of the EC. It favoured Denmark, Ireland and the Netherlands, among others, and it had provided such scope for abuse that negotiations over reform were invariably painful and protracted.

Nevertheless, some change continued to be eked out in response to budgetary pressures and the worldwide trend towards freer markets. In the early 1990s Commissioner MacSharry's labyrinthine proposals to cut prices and surpluses by moving away from price guarantees towards direct income support narrowly averted the failure of the GATT Uruguay Round. In theory, the MacSharry proposals should in the long run reduce the cost of the CAP. But no provision has been made for the approaching accession of poor countries with large rural areas, including Poland, Hungary, the Czech Republic and Estonia. These former communist states will, like East Germany, pose additional budget strains, which as the CAP is presently structured will cumulatively exceed the EU's financing capacity.

Amid this catalogue of shortcomings, it is fair to say that most of the original Treaty objectives have been achieved. Productivity has increased, with agricultural employment falling between 1958 and 1995 from 20% of total Community-wide employment to an estimated 5%. Farmers' incomes have risen, Europe is self-sufficient in temperate foodstuffs and prices have been reasonably stable. It is the cost that has been inordinate, not only to taxpayers and consumers but also to the moral standing of an EU which ought to be more sceptical of bureaucratic interference and less tolerant of corruption and waste.

Common commercial policy

A term used to denote the Community's external trade policy, which under the Treaty of Rome is required to be uniform for all the member states. By and large the Treaty objective has been met. The Commission negotiates on behalf of the member states with the GATT and the WTO, and the Lomé Convention ensures equal treatment for 70 former dependent territories of EU countries; various Association Agreements have a similar standardising effect on trade relations with other states. There remain, however, certain non-tariff barriers which are not uniformly applied. These include the German, French and Italian voluntary quotas for Japanese car imports, which expire in 1999 and have been approved by the competition commissioner as a transitional measure. Although not quite liberal enough for convinced free traders, the Community's common commercial policy has played a significant part in the global reduction in trade barriers since World War II.

Common currency

A common currency differs from a single currency by operating alongside national currencies, not in substitution for them. In 1990 John Major proposed abandoning EMU in favour of the creation of a strong European common currency, the hard écu. If enough people used it, the plan was that it might come to replace domestic currencies by a process of natural evolution, much as the dollar has replaced various local currencies throughout the world. The hard écu was rejected by the other EU member states as insufficiently integrationist. Ironically, when the euro is introduced it will have considerable opportunity to compete with the pound as long as the UK stays outside EMU. The euro will thus be not unlike a common currency within the UK, although it will serve as a single currency elsewhere in Europe.

Common External Tariff

As a customs union, the Community has no internal tariffs but a uniform external tariff, which is one of the main sources of revenue for the EU budget. Following the 1994 Uruguay Round of GATT negotiations, the weighted average Community external tariff has fallen to some 3% and is expected to decline further.

Common Fisheries Policy (CFP)

The saga of the CFP is an unhappy episode in the UK's relations with Europe. In 1970 the UK, Norway, Ireland and Denmark were negotiating entry into the EU's predecessor, the Common Market. The four countries were rich in fish, which the existing members of the Community coveted. Having no legal justification for their ambitions (the Treaty of Rome covered only fish products) the Six hastily created the CFP, under which all member states would have equal access to Community fishing grounds, which would become a common resource. Anxious to secure the prize of membership of the Community, the British prime minister, Edward Heath, gave way. Despite public assurances that the CFP was unacceptable, the British government contented itself with a ten-year derogation, which temporarily protected coastal fishing. The UK signed its Treaty of Accession in 1972. The same year, Norway rejected the CFP and voted against joining the Community.

The UK's derogation allowed it to extend its fishing limits from six to 12 miles. In 1976 the British government passed an Act of Parliament raising its limits to 200 miles. The Act accorded with international law, but when tested in the courts it proved subordinate to Community law, which did not recognise exclusivity as between Community fleets beyond 12 miles. Meanwhile, Canada, Iceland and Norway had also extended their limits to 200 miles, barring Community vessels from many of their habitual fishing grounds and driving them into other waters.

At the end of 1982 the UK's derogation expired. Revised arrangements, for two further ten-year periods, granted the UK rights to just over one-third of the Community's fish, compared with its contribution of some two-thirds of the Community's total resources. In January 1983 a Danish fisherman was fined for fishing inside the UK's 12-mile limit. The European Court overruled his conviction on the grounds that he had been fishing while no derogation was in force and was therefore entitled to equal access. This judgment exposed the weakness of the UK's negotiating position: the alternative to losing half of its fishing rights was to lose them all.

In 1986 Spain and Portugal joined the Community, bringing with them limited resources but adding two-thirds to the Community's combined fleets. To reduce disruption and over-fishing, the Community entered into fishing agreements with some 30 maritime countries and put in place interim arrangements for quotas and fleet reduction; meanwhile, Spain's full integration into the CFP would be delayed for 16 years. Spanish owners responded by quota-hopping, a practice banned by a 1988 Act of Parliament but reinstated when the European Court again overruled the English courts to allow Spanish fishermen flying under the British flag to catch against the British quota.

In 1994 Spain and Portugal gained accelerated integration into the CFP by threatening otherwise to veto the enlargement of the EU. Ironically, a referendum in Norway, one of the successful new applicants, rejected membership of the Community for the second time, after a campaign which featured the need to protect the Norwegian fishing industry. The CFP now forced Community fishermen to scrap their surplus capacity. As their village communities declined, the British were so dismayed that they even failed to take advantage of the EU funds available for decommissioning and modernisation.

The CFP's quota system limits the catch on a species-by-species basis and specifies mesh sizes to allow young fish to escape. Amid a welter of mutual accusations it was hard to establish the truth, but Spanish compliance was said to have been lax, resulting in indiscriminate fishing and heavy dumping of unwanted by-catches. The resultant environmental damage and depletion of stocks prompted the setting up of a reform movement, Save Britain's Fish, in 1995. Its objectives were conservation and the restoration of the UK's fishing limits.

When the UK's derogation expires in 2002, the Mediterranean states command enough votes to block any renegotiation which goes against their interests. Moreover, the next stage of the CFP, embodied in the 1995 Accession Treaties of Austria, Finland and Sweden, envisages the Commission controlling all aspects of Community fishing via permits. A campaign to place the UK in the same position as Norway by withdrawing from the CFP has attracted considerable popular sympathy but is a lost cause, since it would mean breaching Community law and reneging on Treaty obligations.

The verdict on the CFP, therefore, is that it has evolved into a complex and incoherent system which deters Norway and Iceland from joining the EU and is particularly disadvantageous to the UK, but for which, given the multitude of conflicting national interests, no equitable solution is likely to be found. (See also **Factortame**.)

Common Foreign and Security Policy (CFSP)

One of the two intergovernmental pillars of the EU formalised by the Maastricht Treaty, the Common Foreign and Security Policy is the successor to the previous system known as 'European Political Co-operation'. For 25 years before Maastricht, Community circles had discussed the idea of co-ordinating foreign policy, a subject not mentioned in the Treaty of Rome. Following two reports in the early 1970s by a Belgian diplomat, Etienne Davignon (later a prominent commissioner), regular meetings and exchanges of information were set up, but nothing of value resulted. The obstacles were forbidding. Not all the member states were signatories to NATO, whereas three European countries (Norway, Iceland and Turkey) were in NATO but not in the Community. The 1982 Falklands Campaign, the 1991 Gulf War and the prolonged Bosnian crisis each revealed major rifts in European national positions. The neutrality of several countries was another problem, as was West Germany's *Ostpolitik* in the 1970s and 1980s. Among European countries only France and the UK possessed the nuclear deterrent and independent seats on the UN Security Council. Denmark refused to recognise the Community's competence in matters outside the scope of the Treaty of Rome, and Greece had its own agenda. In reality, therefore, repeated Declarations and expressions of the Community's determination to 'assert itself on the international stage' amounted over the years to little but words, the only common actions being the occasional joint imposition of economic sanctions against errant third countries.

Maastricht changed the rhetoric, emphasising ambitions for a European military dimension. The Treaty states that the CFSP covers 'all questions related to the security of the Union, including the eventual framing of a common defence policy, which might in time lead to a common defence'. The Treaty goes on to identify the WEU as the future defence arm of the EU, despite the fact that Ireland, Denmark, Austria, Finland and Sweden are only observer members of the WEU, a more passive role than the associate member status of Iceland, Norway and Turkey. The Amsterdam Treaty reiterates the Maastricht proposals in more specific terms and strengthens the position of the Commission in policy formation, without, however, clarifying how the inherent contradictions are to be addressed.

How much the substance of the CFSP has been changed by the two Treaties is debatable. The old obstacles remain and Europe is as reliant as ever on the USA and NATO for strategic defence, despite the formation of the 50,000-strong Eurocorps in the mid-1990s. The proposal that forces assigned to the WEU should also be assignable to NATO ('double-hatting') is a grudging recognition of military realities, though it is doubtless fortunate that the collapse of the Warsaw Pact makes it unlikely that the EU's new security arrangements will be put to the test. Under Maastricht, joint action in the CFSP area is subject to national veto, whereas detailed arrangements for implementation are subject to qualified majority voting. Such complications, and such concepts as constructive abstention, could hardly survive a genuine emergency.

The logical conclusion of the CSFP would be that both France's and the UK's nuclear deterrent should be placed in the hands of the WEU and that their permanent seats on the Security Council should be merged into a single European seat. This, however, would require a *communautaire* single-mindedness which neither country has shown. Despite withdrawing from the integrated military command of NATO in 1966, in protest against American domination, and despite its leading role in advocating a Europe-centred defence strategy, France appears determined to maintain an independent nuclear capability. As for the UK, it remains wedded to NATO and the Anglo-American alliance, as was illustrated when a renewed crisis in Iraq during the 1998 British presidency found Prime Minister Tony Blair shoulder to shoulder with US President Bill Clinton but at a loss to develop a coherent EU response.

Once we have a single currency we will immediately have
a single foreign policy.
Michel Rocard, former French premier, September 1996

The CFSP also raises questions of sovereignty, which have been of particular significance to the UK and Denmark, although they have also troubled France and the neutral countries. It is of the nature of foreign and security policy that for most of the time it appears to the electorate unimportant compared with domestic issues; but on the rare occasions when it matters to ordinary citizens it engenders powerful emotions, the more so when lives are put at risk. The

European Parliament is not capable of serving as a safety valve for feelings of the sort occasioned by war or by a threat to the vital interests of a nation. The fact that the EU failed to construct a satisfactory CFSP during the Cold War, when the Soviet Union provided a common enemy, poses a fundamental question mark over the rationale of a collective defence policy in the more complex world which faces the next generation. (See also **WEU**.)

The Common Market

For many years the generally used term for the European Economic Community, later re-named the European Community. The term is sometimes still used to refer to the single market, now that the wider political, social and economic set of policies and institutions has become known as the European Union.

Common position (1)

The position agreed by the Council of Ministers after the first reading stage of legislation, that is, after taking account of any amendments proposed by the European Parliament.

Common position (2)

An agreed common stance of member states in foreign affairs or home affairs. Once such a position is reached, which can only be by unanimity, any resultant action would generally be governed by qualified majority voting.

Common transport policy

The Treaty of Rome envisages a common transport policy, but not in language specific enough to presuppose any particular course of action. In 1982 the European Parliament brought proceedings against the Council of Ministers for failure to carry out its Treaty obligations in the transport area. The Court of Justice delivered a split ruling: it supported the Parliament in limited respects, based on the general principle of freedom to provide services, but it held that the common transport policy itself was too vague to be relied on in a court of law.

There followed a variety of Commission initiatives – on road safety, on frontier documents, on commercial lorries, on rail links, on infrastructure (trans-European networks), on safety at sea, on liberalisation of air fares, on state airline monopolies, and so forth. Each of these, however, could be dealt with as single market legislation or under EU competition policy, and although many aspects of transport are well suited to supranational governance (air traffic control in Europe, for example, is notoriously chaotic), it remains the case that a comprehensive common transport policy is unlikely to take shape unless the EU becomes a fully federal entity.

Communautaire

In the spirit of the Community, that is, integrationist. In the corridors of Brussels, *communautaire* denotes the ultimate in politically desirable attitudes.

The Community

See **European Community**.

Community law

The starting point for Community law was the 1951 Treaty of Paris, which established the European Coal and Steel Community. The 1957 Treaty of Rome extended its scope and in the *Van Gend en Loos* case in 1963 the European Court of Justice (ECJ) ruled '... the Community constitutes a new legal order ... for the benefit of which the States have limited their sovereign rights ...'. Unlike international law, community law goes beyond agreement between states and has a direct impact on citizens and businesses throughout the EU. Where it conflicts with national laws it claims superiority, based on the Treaties of Accession, in which each signatory state acknowledges the subordination of its own law.

Community law advances in three ways: by new Treaties, which add to or amend the Treaty of Rome, notably the Single European Act, the Maastricht Treaty and the Treaty of Amsterdam; by the issuance of Regulations, Decisions and Directives, at the instigation of the Commission or the Council of Ministers; and by case law created by the ECJ, building on the preambles or principles enunciated in Treaties or at summit meetings. As Community law expands, its clashes with national law grow more frequent; and since the ECJ is Treaty-bound to support an integrated Europe, the Court's decisions generally go against individual countries.

No longer is European law an incoming tide flowing up the estuaries of England. It is now like a tidal wave bringing down our sea walls and flowing inland over our fields and houses.
Lord Denning, former Master of the Rolls, 1991

A Regulation counts as domestic law without need for further action, being, in the words of the Treaty of Rome, 'binding in its entirety and directly applicable in all Member States'. In theory based on specific Treaty Articles but in practice often reliant on general principles, Regulations are the main instruments of the Common Agricultural and Common Fisheries Policies. Decisions are similar but more narrowly focused, being binding only on 'those to whom they are addressed'. Directives are binding in terms of the result, leaving the form to the individual country. Normally, national legislation has to be passed for a Directive to become effective, but in the *Francovich v. Italy* case the ECJ gave a citizen the right to damages where a member state had failed to transpose a Directive into domestic law.

In addition to these formal instruments, there is a grey area of Opinions, Resolutions and Declarations, which, like the Treaty preambles, are often mistakenly dismissed as mere rhetoric. Although not enforceable, these create a framework, paving the way for future legislation and guiding the courts on the underlying purpose of Community law. As such, they are a reminder of the difference between English law, which is based on the literal meaning of the text, and Community law, which serves a grand design.

The secrecy of the European law-making process is protected in several ways. The ECJ does not publish dissenting judgments. The Council of Ministers meets privately, rarely issuing minutes of its deliberations. The Commission's unaccountability, to be expected in a bureaucracy, sits less happily with that body's executive and legislative powers (including the unique right of initiative to propose new legislation). Lacking the checks and balances of the US constitution, the Commission and the ECJ in tandem draft, interpret and enforce the law with a remarkable lack of transparency considering the democratic nature of the EU's membership.

The Treaties obtain their legal effect through enabling legislation; for example, in the UK's case, the European Communities Act of 1972 enacted British accession to the EEC and validated the operation of Community law in the UK. The 1972 Act was obliquely worded with regard to the treatment of conflicts. It was clear that Community law would be superior to pre-existing English law and to subordinate regulations, such as Orders in Council. It was less clear whether a subsequent Act of Parliament would be overridden by the 1972 Act, since it is a fundamental constitutional doctrine that no Parliament can bind its successors. This doctrine would be in jeopardy if Parliament was to be bound permanently by the 1972 Act, unable either to revoke it or to enact any law which conflicted with it.

The best view is that Parliament does still retain its ultimate supremacy, in that it could repeal or supersede the 1972 Act if it did so with that intent; but in the absence of an express provision, Community law will continue to prevail over any Act of Parliament. Nevertheless, given the UK's unwritten constitution and the traditional reliance of its courts on precedent, the anxiety has been expressed that, if ECJ rulings continue to expand unchallenged, the doctrine might gain ground with the passage of time that the sovereign power of Parliament had been surrendered.

In countries with written constitutions the original draftsmen rarely envisaged a progressive ceding of sovereignty. Thus the situation of Continental countries is little clearer than that of the UK. Each country has its own way of resolving conflicts between Community law and the national constitution. In France, for example, there is a constitutional committee, while Germany has a constitutional court. Scandinavian countries more often resort to referendums. The 1997 Treaty of Amsterdam marked the first specific assertion of the supremacy of Community law over the constitutions of member states, but the effectiveness of this assertion, which has received little attention, remains to be tested.

Community method

The principle that the EU should instigate common action in areas where the initiative was formerly left to the member states, such as foreign policy and judicial co-operation.

Community preference

Community preference denotes the CAP regime of import tariffs and export refunds designed to advantage Community agricultural produce as compared with produce from elsewhere. The system is a negation of the principles of trade liberalisation in the Treaty of Rome and is a cause of dismay in Eastern Europe and in other impoverished countries which rely on farming but are faced with dumping and import levies on their trade with the EU. For the UK, the switch from Commonwealth preference to Community preference on joining the Common Market was a painful and costly experience.

Community trade marks

Since 1994 trade marks throughout the European Economic Area can be protected by registration with the Office for Harmonisation in Alicante, Spain.

Competence

The right to decide or legislate in a given field of activity. A competence is described as either exclusive or shared, depending on whether the Community has the sole authority to act or whether member states also have some jurisdiction. Under the Treaty of Rome, the European Court of Justice ultimately determines where a competence lies; the Court is entitled to rule in its own favour when the supremacy of Community law over national law is in dispute. External negotiations fall within the competence of the Community, rather than that of individual member states, if the Court decides that the issue in question would have been a matter for the Community had it been internal to the EU. This is called the doctrine of implied competence.

Competition and merger policy

Any anti-trust policy has inherent contradictions, and that of the EU is no exception. The Treaty of Rome prohibits price-fixing, market-sharing, discriminatory agreements and abuse of dominant position, with the aim of promoting free trade; but it is a sufficient defence to prove public benefit. Thus state aid, theoretically forbidden as a distortion of markets, is justified in many Continental countries by elastic interpretation of clauses in the Treaty permitting aid for restructuring, regional problems and development. The clearest example of systematic anti-competitive activities is the Common Agricultural Policy, which is exempted by the Treaty from the general ban on restrictive practices, on the grounds that it aims to ensure rural prosperity and stability of food supply.

The Commission, subject to the ultimate jurisdiction of the Court of Justice, is responsible for the execution of competition policy. It has draconian powers, deriving from a Regulation of the Council of Ministers, which supersedes national law. It can enter premises without warning, seize documents, terminate agreements and fine an offender up to 10% of its annual turnover. In practice, many cases of suspected restraint of trade are settled by negotiation under threat of sanction; others are pre-cleared or exempted.

The progressive integration of the EU, allied to the advent of the single market and the determination of successive commissioners, Leon Brittan and Karel Van Miert, has led to an increasingly activist prosecution of competition policy. Since 1990 the Commission has also had specific authority to block or approve substantial mergers, provided that at least 250 million ECUs of the turnover of the companies concerned is generated in more than one member state. The assumption of this power was a sensitive matter, although some companies have found that the Commission's remit – to judge amalgamations on competition grounds – has provided more predictability than the politicised decisions often made by national monopoly-policing authorities.

The Commission growingly asserts extra-territorial jurisdiction. Restrictive practices within the EU on the part of subsidiaries of non-EU companies fall incontestably within the Commission's ambit, but alliances between European companies and, for example, US companies (such as between British Airways and American Airlines) would once have been considered the province of the relevant national regulators. A particularly controversial Commission action was its ruling in 1997 that the amalgamation of two US companies, Boeing and McDonnell Douglas, could not go through unless they rescinded 20-year exclusive supply contracts with three US airlines to which Airbus had ambitions to sell aircraft. Doubtless an element in the Commission's decision to intervene was resentment at the extra-territorial activity of US regulators. The

Commission's policy adds complexity to the regulatory hurdles which any sizeable merger now faces.

The Commission's attempts to curb state aid have often been frustrated by chauvinism, notably its failure in 1998 to block France's £2 billion cash injection into Air France. Nevertheless, it has had its share of successes, backed by the Court of Justice. Among its best-known cases have been those of Renault and Crédit Lyonnais; and it has also taken on German state aid to Volkswagen and the Bremer Vulkan shipyards and an attempted Belgian government bail-out of a steelworks. In 1997 it embarked on a campaign to dismantle European telephone monopolies. These activities have incurred the displeasure of governments, which take an elevated view of their own motivation and are sensitive to any move which might affect employment. On the other hand, the Commission is criticised by liberal economists for allowing too many subsidies, nor has it yet made significant inroads into opening financial services to free competition. Continuing tension is inevitable so long as authority for competition policy is divided between national governments and Brussels.

A new avenue for intervention currently proposed by the Commission concerns fairness of treatment of shareholders in takeover bids. Avowedly basing itself on the success of the British Takeover Code, the Commission would like to introduce a Directive to enforce similar provisions by law. This proposal would offer the shareholder less protection than is afforded by the British Code; but by substituting the law for the voluntary nature of the UK system, it would open the way to expensive delaying tactics, thereby helping to entrench management and frustrate bids. The outcome of the proposal, which is being opposed by the UK, remains uncertain.

Compliance

As a result of the European Parliament's requests, the Commission publishes an annual statistical table of individual states' application of EU Directives. In its 1997 report, covering the period to the end of 1996, the Commission noted that it was increasingly difficult to monitor compliance and commended the value of individual citizens' vigilance in reporting cases of failure to implement Community legislation. (See also **Directives**.)

Compulsory expenditure

Compulsory expenditure is the term for that part of the EU budget (about two-thirds of it, mainly CAP expenditure) which arises directly from the fulfilment of Treaty obligations. The European Parliament has little say in this category of spending, which is decided by the Council of Ministers. The Parliament can, however, amend the non-compulsory section of the budget within strict financial limits, subject, in case of disagreement, to conciliation with the Council. In an annually renewed three-way budget battle, the Commission drafts expenditure proposals, the Council routinely cuts them and the Parliament unsuccessfully tries to expand non-agricultural spending. From time to time Parliament and the Council also argue over the classification of items as compulsory.

Concentric circles

The metaphor of concentric circles is designed both to explain and to persuade. The idea is of a galaxy. The central core consists of model EU states, surrounded by less *communautaire* members such as the UK and Denmark; Norway and Switzerland are more distant planets in a third circle; and aspiring candidates with association agreements are in a still more remote fourth circle. In the farthest outer ring are temporarily rejected applicants such as Turkey and Bulgaria, while the fringes of space are occupied by countries in the Russian orbit, which have European connections but no prospect of membership of the Union. The implied message is of an irresistible centripetal pull towards the core.

There is considerable disagreement about whether it is proper for the EU's institutions to be fully involved in activities undertaken by the inner core alone, or whether the Community's machinery should be reserved for policies common to the entire membership of the Union. This seemingly arcane debate has much importance for the future of the EU. (See also **Two-speed Europe**.)

Conciliation procedure

Since 1975 budget disagreements between the European Parliament and the Council of Ministers have been resolved (in cases where the Council cannot decide unilaterally) in a conciliation committee consisting of representatives of each body. As the powers of the Parliament grow, the scope of this procedure is gradually expanding to embrace the resolution also of legislative disputes.

Congress of Europe

Modelled on the 1815 Congress of Vienna after the Napoleonic wars, the Congress of Europe was held in The Hague in May 1948 and attended by 800 eminent political, professional and academic figures under the presidency of Winston Churchill. The Congress led to the foundation of the European Movement and the Council of Europe and indirectly to the European Convention on Human Rights, but despite its 'Message to Europeans', calling for a united Europe with its own Assembly and freedom of movement, ideas and goods, the Congress lacked concrete ideas for reconstruction or integration and is remembered as a romantic event rather than as the foundation of the EU.

Conservatism

Conservative as a political party name is confined in the EU to the UK and Denmark. The centrist wing of the British Conservative Party is close in ideas to the Christian Democrats of Germany. The free-market wing of the party, once symbolised by Margaret Thatcher, has only one counterpart in the EU (the Partido Popular in Portugal), partly because of its reservations about federalism – a supposed mark in most European countries of political extremism – and partly because of the pervasive Continental faith in the social market economy. In the negative sense of not being socialist, the Partido Popular of José-Maria Aznar in Spain and the neo-Gaullist party in France are natural allies of the Conservatives. (See also **Political groups**.)

Constitution of the European Union

The EU has no formal constitution, but as it has come increasingly to resemble a federal state, its Treaties, which perform an equivalent function, have grown in size and complexity. Its essential structure revolves round two documents:

⇒ the 1957 Treaty of Rome, as modified by the 1986 Single European
  Act, the 1992 Maastricht Treaty and the 1997 Treaty of Amsterdam
⇒ the intergovernmental segment of the Maastricht Treaty, as modified
  by the Treaty of Amsterdam.

The member states bind themselves into the EU and accept the supremacy of Community law through their individual Treaties of Accession. Principally of historical interest are the 1951 Treaty of Paris and the 1957 Euratom Treaty. (See also **Treaty on European Union**.)

Contributions

By far the biggest contributor to the EU budget is Germany, a feature long seen as a just reflection of that country's wealth and its war-time debt to society. The second largest net contributor has generally been the UK, although from the start of its membership it was by no means the second richest state. This led to Margaret Thatcher's notorious five-year confrontation with the Community, culminating in 1984 with the British rebate.

The Commission, which alone is in full possession of all the detailed figures, is reticent about member countries' receipts and contributions, arguing that the figures are unrepresentative and that the unquantifiable economic benefits of membership of the EU are so great that it is unhealthy to focus on actual numbers. In its defence, the Commission makes some strong points. Such estimates as are available take no account of multiplier effects, are far from homogeneous (for example, outright subsidies are not comparable with loans or purchased goods and services) and are flawed by unallocated expenditure and other distortions (thus levies or rebates on imports or exports at Rotterdam are treated as if they formed part of the Dutch balance). It is, nevertheless, clear that over the years the main beneficiaries have been Ireland, Denmark, Greece, Portugal and Spain, with France paying less than its prosperity would suggest and the Netherlands and Sweden joining Germany and the UK as the main paymasters.

The impending enlargement of the EU, with the accession of impoverished countries from the former Soviet bloc, will add to the demands on the budget. Germany already makes vast internal transfers to the eastern *Lander* it acquired on reunification, and in 1997 it signalled for the first time that it considered it was paying too much to Brussels. This move, which caused consternation among its partners, was promptly echoed by the Netherlands and presages battles ahead. (See also **Agenda 2000**.)

Convergence criteria (1)

Before joining the single currency, member states, according to the Maastricht Treaty, are supposed to achieve a 'high degree of sustainable economic convergence'. This entails meeting four (some would say five) tests – the so-called convergence criteria. These are:

⇒ inflation close to that of the three best performing member states
⇒ elimination of excessive public sector debt, that is,
  – annual budget deficit under 3% of national output
  – outstanding government debt under 60% of national output
⇒ low exchange-rate variability against the other European currencies in the ERM
⇒ long-term interest rates within 2 percentage points of the three best performing member states.

The convergence criteria are open to interpretation, especially those relating to excessive public debt and to sustainability. Temporary aberrations may be overlooked, and continuous progress towards an acceptable level may be taken as equivalent to actual convergence. Throughout 1997 the debate swung back and forth as different countries altered their budget forecasts, struggling to qualify. Germany initially took the position that the criteria (especially the 3% deficit ceiling) should be construed strictly and made permanent. Some, notably Italy and Belgium, could not come near to meeting the test relating to the level of debt, yet were determined to join the single currency; in 1998, after a year's hard lobbying, both countries were admitted, the final decision being taken by heads of government under qualified majority voting.

In evaluating the suitability of the applicants, the European Council relied on data supplied by Eurostat and on evidence from numerous sources, including Ecofin, the Commission and central banks. The non-political witnesses for the most part expressed a jaundiced view of the measures taken by governments to manipulate budgets in order to claim compliance with the criteria. Italy was alleged to have fallen short in several respects, chiefly by deferring liabilities and taking credit for a one-off tax. Belgium was accused of shuffling assets on and off balance sheet over the year-end, and France of assuming France Telecom's pension liabilities in return for an immediate cash payment. Even Germany had massaged its figures and attempted in 1997 to accrue a special dividend from a revaluation of gold reserves, before the Bundesbank's frown induced a hasty retreat. The exposure of these exercises in creative accounting, however, weighed little against political considerations, and once the Commission had accepted nearly all the applicant states' numbers at face value it became clear that the only country that would be rejected was Greece.

Although regarded as sensible goals so far as they go, the convergence criteria have been criticised for failing to take account of more important real economy yardsticks, such as unemployment, productivity trends, taxation and unfunded pension liabilities. The effort to conform with the criteria by a set date also sometimes gave the impression that temporary convergence would be acceptable, which is contrary to the underlying concept of sustainability. Public opinion in Europe about the single currency remains far from uniform. Many French voters associate convergence with austerity and unemployment. In Germany, by contrast, the fear is that a relapse to loose budgets may undermine the euro. Support is strongest in Italy and Spain, with their history of high interest rates and weak currencies.

The UK's opt-out from EMU has enabled the government to declare that it will not participate in the first wave of participants in the single currency in 1999, although it favours later entry in principle. The UK is therefore freed from any pressing obligation to adhere to the criteria. However, owing to the sound management of its economy, by 1998 the UK (like Sweden, which has chosen not to apply, and the other opt-out country, Denmark) met the most demanding Maastricht tests; ironically, it failed one criterion, that of exchange rate stability, not because of weakness but because the pound had become a strong safe haven from the anticipated problems of the euro. (See also **EMU.**)

Convergence criteria (2)

The British government has set out its own five convergence tests to be met before the UK enters EMU:

⇒ Compatibility of business cycles and economic structures
⇒ Sufficient flexibility to meet any problems
⇒ Better conditions for capital investment in the UK
⇒ Positive impact on the City
⇒ Promotion of growth, stability and jobs.

A sixth test is political: that the electorate should have approved abolishing the pound in a referendum.

A Treasury assessment in 1997 concluded that without sustainable convergence with Continental economies EMU (even if otherwise successful) would do the UK more harm than good, but that EMU has the potential to enhance growth and employment. In the Treasury's view, convergence did not at present exist. A curious omission both in the criteria and in the Treasury paper was that no mention was made of the risk of exchanging the pound for the euro at an uncompetitive rate – a flaw that had helped to undermine the UK's brief participation in the ERM in 1992. Discerning commentators have also noted that of the five criteria few are capable of objective measurement.

Co-operation Agreement

An aid-and-trade agreement between the EU and a less developed country, often nowadays containing human rights conditions, to the irritation of the recipient government.

Co-operation procedure

Introduced in 1987 by the Single European Act, the co-operation procedure allows the European Parliament to be consulted twice before legislation is enacted – first at the draft stage, and second after the Council of Ministers has considered both the Commission draft and the Parliament's Opinion, in final form. If the Parliament rejects the proposal, the Council needs to be unanimous to proceed. If the Parliament adopts an amendment, the Commission becomes involved again and the need for unanimity in the Council lapses if (but only if) it accepts the resultant revised Commission draft. The co-operation procedure was intended to load the decision-making scales more in favour of the Parliament, with the idea of redressing the democratic deficit. It is, however, cumbersome and limited in scope, covering only a few policy areas, including the European Social Fund. The co-decision procedure brought in by the Maastricht Treaty differs chiefly in cutting down the role of the Commission and allowing Parliament the ultimate weapon of veto.

COREPER

See **Permanent representatives**.

Corpus Juris

Consciously echoing the title of a section of the great sixth century compilation of Roman law under the Emperor Justinian (*Corpus Juris Civilis*, or The Collected Works of Civil Law), *Corpus Juris* is a project designed by the 20th Directorate-General of the Commission to create an *éspace judiciaire européen* in the field of criminal justice, with a European public prosecutor, or investigating judge, having powers of arrest, committal to trial and the overruling of national prosecuting authorities. Trial by jury (established in England by Magna Carta in 1215) could be threatened and *habeas corpus* (passed in 1679) weakened. Although *Corpus Juris* has not been formally proposed to the Council of Ministers – and is initially intended principally to combat EU fraud – the Treaty of Amsterdam paves its way by introducing the concept of legal harmonisation and invoking the detection and prevention of organised crime as a reason for strengthening Europol. Although doubtless unlikely to survive in its first draft form, *Corpus Juris* illustrates the extreme centralism which actuates certain Commission officials.

Council

See **Council of Ministers**.

Council of Europe

Despite its name and its seat (like the European Parliament) in Strasbourg, the Council of Europe has no connection with the EU. It should not be confused with the European Council (the summit meetings of the member states of the EU) or the Council of Ministers (the EU's regular ministerial-level decision-making body).

The Council of Europe contains not only the 15 members of the EU but also the members of EFTA, various European islands and mini-states, including Malta and Cyprus, and the majority of the former communist countries of Eastern Europe – in all, 44 countries including special guests from the former Eastern bloc. Apart from Turkey, every member is European (albeit many are Slavonic); indeed, it is Turkey's membership that qualifies it to apply to join the EU.

Founded four years after the end of World War II, the Council of Europe has stood for much that the British have wanted in Europe but that the Continental powers have rejected. It consults, rather than dictates. When it reaches agreement, it issues conventions or charters rather than laws or directives – it is up to member governments whether to convert these into legislation. Its lack of a supranational dimension has, however, deprived it of the ability to get things done, and only two years after its formation France and Germany began to go their separate way with the Treaty of Paris.

Having long since lost the authority that once made it the natural forum for the expression of Winston Churchill's vision of the future of Europe, the Council now concentrates on such areas as culture, the environment, ethics and law, its best known products being the European Convention on Human Rights, the European Social Charter and the Convention on Data Protection. Its Court of Human Rights has made the occasional splash, notably on the treatment of IRA terrorists; and since the fall of the Berlin Wall the Council has staged something of a comeback, serving as a constitutional adviser to emerging democracies and a seal of approval to countries trying to shed a reputation for authoritarian rule. None, however, but the specialist needs to be familiar with its structure of Committee of Ministers, Parliamentary Assembly and Congress of Local and Regional Authorities; and with the constant expansion of the *acquis communautaire* it is, perhaps, only a matter of time before the EU assumes what little remains of the Council's prerogatives.

Council of Ministers
(Council or Council of the European Union)

The Council of Ministers (easily confused with the European Council of heads of government) is in theory the most powerful institution of the EU, being on the one hand the interface between member states and the Community's supranational entities and on the other hand the Union's highest regular decision-making body. In reality the Commission is at least as influential, having the advantage of greater continuity as well as executive and legislative powers far exceeding those of a conventional bureaucracy.

The presidency of the Council rotates between the EU's member states, changing every six months. It is composed of ministers (one from each state) appropriate to the subject under discussion, the most important gatherings being Ecofin (for economic issues), the Council of Foreign Ministers and the Council of Agriculture Ministers, each of which meets monthly. The arrangements are flexible enough to allow less frequent meetings of other ministers and occasional cross-departmental Councils. The Council of Foreign Ministers used always to be regarded as the senior body, but this status has now been largely assumed by Ecofin as integration proceeds and EMU takes centre stage.

The Council's representatives are required by the Treaty of Rome to be 'authorised to commit the government' of their member state. The significance of that provision is that it diminishes the power of national parliaments to scrutinise and approve decisions which affect their interests. Since the Council meets in secret and normally votes by qualified majority, it is in practice substantially unaccountable (although Denmark, for example, keeps a tight grip on its representatives).

In respect of the intergovernmental pillars of Foreign and Security Policy and Home Affairs, the Council takes joint actions or adopts common positions as permitted by the Maastricht and Amsterdam Treaties (though many would say that it more often papers over disarray, as in the cases of Bosnia and Iraq). Its Resolutions, Conclusions, Recommendations, Opinions and so forth are not legally binding, although it is unwise to disregard them, since they are apt to lead to subsequent legislation and constitute evidence of intent, which shapes the interpretations of the European Court of Justice. As a legislature, it issues Regulations, Decisions and Directives, sharing with the Commission responsibility for the several thousand new legal instruments which each year affect European citizens. The European Parliament is consulted about the Council's legislative proposals and can in the last resort veto them, but only in limited areas of activity. More often, the Parliament secures amendments.

Despite the theoretical primacy of the Council, however, the key to real power in Brussels is the bureaucracy. The Council is served by three different types of bureaucrats: the permanent representatives, or national delegations, who meet as a committee under the name COREPER to prepare the agenda for Council meetings; the Council's own permanent secretariat (over 2,000 officials in six departments); and the ubiquitous Commission, which rarely misses a meeting at any level. Even if a national delegation has a strong domestic mandate, the pressures of 'Community spirit' and the universal tendency to strike compromise deals generally combine to produce results which are acceptable to the Commission.

Over the years, the Council's powers have evolved along the lines of the Community's own development. In the 1960s, reflecting Charles de Gaulle's battles with Walter Hallstein, decisions in practice were generally taken unanimously to avoid confrontational vetoes (see **Luxembourg Compromise**). After de Gaulle's retirement, the veto continued for a decade to exert its influence without actually being invoked, but by common consent it could now be used only where a vital national interest is at stake.

The democratic deficit arising from the unaccountability of Community institutions and the absence of a powerful body directly answerable to voters has prompted numerous constitutional suggestions. Some integrationists favour a system whereby the Council would become an upper chamber, leaving the Commission and the Parliament to divide effective authority between them. Some in France, and many in the UK, would like national governments to increase their control of the Council. The probability is that its position will be left broadly unchanged but that it will have to share more power with the Parliament under the co-decision procedure.

Court of Auditors

Among the most admirable, and certainly among the most neglected, of Community institutions, the Court of Auditors, based in Luxembourg, is not a court in the accepted sense, having no powers other than to draw attention to financial incompetence and irregularity. Set up in 1977, it replaced the former Audit Board, with the remit of auditing all the EC institutions as well as the official bodies in the member states which receive Community funds. With its staff of some 400, the Court is under-resourced even for its limited statutory function of reconciling accounts and monitoring the legality of underlying transactions, let alone for any wider role of investigating value for money. It works largely by sampling and extrapolation, its members (one from each state) serving six-year terms of office.

The Court's reports present a devastating year-by-year indictment of neglect and incompetence. The Commission generally downplays these findings, except to the extent that they support the concepts of legal harmonisation and greater powers of intervention by Brussels. (See also **Fraud**.)

Court of First Instance

The Court of First Instance was created under the Single European Act as an attachment to the European Court of Justice (ECJ). It shares the burden of the ECJ by taking on lesser cases, such as staff disputes, certain actions against the Community and actions relating to competition policy. Appeals against the Court's decisions on points of law may be made to the ECJ.

Court of Human Rights

See **European Court of Human Rights**.

Court of Justice

See **European Court of Justice**.

Crédit Lyonnais

A state-owned French bank, encouraged under President François Mitterrand's regime to conquer the financial world. Eventually, after a lending and spending binge, it was rescued in the second half of the 1990s at a cost to French taxpayers estimated at over FFr150 billion – arguably the largest banking disaster in European history. The Crédit Lyonnais scandal revealed numerous irregularities, epitomised the shortcomings of politically motivated management by *énarques* and brought France into conflict with the European Commission, which considered the bail-out terms to be anti-competitive.

Crocodile Club

For some years eclipsed by Jean Monnet, Altiero Spinelli assumed the role of spiritual and intellectual leader of the European federalist movement after his rival's death in 1979. In 1980 he founded the Crocodile Club, named after the Strasbourg restaurant where he used to meet with a small group of MEPs. There they plotted to turn the European Parliament into a proper legislature, with the Commission serving as the executive arm of a refashioned European Union and the nation states reduced to provinces. These ideas, vehemently opposed by Margaret Thatcher, survived in much watered down form in the Single European Act of 1986 and the Maastricht Treaty of 1992.

CSCE (Conference on Security and Co-operation in Europe)

See OSCE.

Cucumber Directive

A paradigm of Eurocracy, the 2,000 word Cucumber Directive specifies the permitted length, circumference, arc, curvature and crookedness of cucumbers. Embarrassed Europhiles claim that it was drafted on a Danish government initiative. (See also **Bookerism**.)

Customs union

An area with free internal trade but a common external wall of tariffs or quotas. In the context of the World Trade Organisation (formerly the GATT), a customs union is a permitted exception, as a regional trading arrangement, to the rules forbidding discrimination. In post-war Europe, Benelux was the first example, followed in 1957 by the European Economic Community, set up to establish a customs union in traded goods between its six member states.

The UK's initial caution about joining the Common Market was largely based on its Commonwealth links, including preferential tariffs and cheap food, and its belief in free trade. These features were incompatible with the protectionist Common Agricultural Policy and the European customs union. In the event, the UK sacrificed Commonwealth preference to join the Community; but the feared general increase in trade barriers did not materialise, for over the years industrial tariffs were sharply reduced throughout the developed world, reaching negligible levels by 1998.

The persistence of non-tariff distortions, such as subsidies, state monopolies and purchasing discrimination, means that the underlying purpose of the European customs union − to create a perfect internal market − remains uncompleted. Nevertheless, it has formidable achievements to its credit and was largely responsible for the remarkable growth of the Community in the 1960s. (See also **Zollverein**.)

Cyprus

See **Small countries**.

Czech Republic

Created with artificial boundaries after World War I, Czechoslovakia surrendered its German-speaking territory to the Nazis after the notorious Munich Agreement of 1938 and was later invaded and occupied by Germany until its liberation in 1945. In 1948 a communist coup brought the country under the domination of the Soviet Union. Alexander Dubcek's 'Prague Spring' of 1968 was quickly crushed, ending an attempt to introduce 'Socialism with a human face', but the 1989 'Velvet Revolution', in which the Communist Party Central Committee was forced to resign after a massive popular protest, was in the Czech tradition of intellectual independence going back to a 15th century martyr, Jan Hus. It was thus natural that it should fall to a dissident writer, Vaclav Havel, to lead a mixed government through a programme of political and economic reform, until the elections of 1990 brought the defeat of the remaining communists. Nationalist feelings, long suppressed under the grip of the Soviet Union, came to the fore with freedom, soon leading to the separation of the Czech and Slovak states. In 1993 Havel was elected president of the new Czech Republic (a post to which he was re-elected in 1998).

There followed a period of triumph and setback. At first, under Prime Minister Vaclav Klaus, the Republic appeared a model of Thatcherite success. Regulation and investment incentives were eschewed and industry was privatised on an unprecedented scale through the issue of vouchers to the population. Foreign investment was attracted and economic growth was rapid. The Republic was accepted as a future member of NATO and the EU (despite the European Commission's bizarre challenge to the Czech policy of banning former secret police and communist activists from holding public office). But the unfettered operation of free markets proved a mixed blessing. Bank-dominated investment funds bought up the privatisation vouchers and the stock exchange became a crooked paradise. Industrial restructuring was held back by corruption, bankruptcies and the conflicting lending and ownership roles of the financial sector. Growth stalled and the foreign trade deficit grew. Pollution inherited from the communist years was a menace to public health.

Late in 1997 Klaus was forced to resign, brought down as much by the realisation that his economic miracle was evaporating as by allegations that his party had accepted bribes in return for ensuring the success of a privatisation deal. Nevertheless, with the highest standard of living, the lowest inflation and the strongest democratic traditions of the major East European countries, the Czech Republic's future as a member state of the EU seems assured.

D

Data Protection, Convention on

The Council of Europe's 1981 Convention on Data Protection aimed to limit the ability of organisations to hold or circulate data on individuals without their agreement. The convention was generally welcomed as a contribution towards curbing the irresponsible use of a mushrooming mass of personal information and was reflected in various pieces of national legislation (in the UK's case, the 1984 Data Protection Act). Differences between the practices in EU member states led, however, to a wish for greater conformity and in 1985 a Directive was introduced which should result in new Community-wide legislation by the autumn of 1998. Some concern has been expressed in the UK that the revised Data Protection Act will be costly to charities and small businesses without materially advancing the protection of affected individuals.

Decision

A narrowly focused instrument of Community law which directly affects those to whom it is addressed, that is, without the need for national enabling legislation. (See also **Directive** and **Legal instruments**.)

Declaration

A detailed recital of points agreed by the European Council. Like Resolutions and Conclusions, Declarations have no status in law, but create a framework for Community legislation.

Deepening

Increasing the degree of integration between the EU's member states. Often contrasted with widening, or enlarging the number of members, on the theory that the two aims may be incompatible. The basis for this presumption is that new members, especially from Eastern Europe, are unlikely to be able to meet the criteria for joining in certain common policies, such as EMU: thus their accession would undermine the integration process and contribute to a two-speed Europe.

Defence policy

See **Common Foreign and Security Policy** and **WEU**.

De Gaulle, Charles (1890–1970)

The illustrious career of Charles de Gaulle, president of the Republic of France from 1958 to 1969, who ended the civil war in Algeria and was the architect of his country's recovery of self-confidence after its retreat from Indo-China, needs no repetition here. During his long wartime period in the UK as leader of the Free French he had unrivalled scope to assess the nature of his hosts, with whom – including Churchill – his relations were often far from easy. His acute sense of nationality enabled him to recognise the same spirit in others. Seeing France as temporarily weak, he wanted no rival for leadership in Europe. Hence it was mainly *Realpolitik* which motivated him to veto (in 1963 and again in 1967) the UK's application to join the EEC. Additional factors were the UK's ties with the Commonwealth, its special relationship with the USA and its predilection for free trade, which threatened the Common Agricultural Policy and ran counter to French mercantilism. In retrospect, de Gaulle's judgement that the UK and the Community would not be ideally suited to each other is hard to fault.

De Gaulle's independence made him a difficult colleague in European counsels, especially since his reign coincided with the Commission presidency of Walter Hallstein, that keen advocate of full European integration. The two men first clashed in the early 1960s over the Fouchet Plan, in which de Gaulle tried to amend the Treaty of Rome, reduce the Commission's powers and put authority in the hands of national parliamentarians. Rebuffed, he sharpened his proposals, aiming to weaken the Council of Ministers and end the supremacy of Community law. At the same time he suggested revising Europe's defence arrangements to sideline the UK and the USA.

What's the point of Europe? It must serve to prevent domination either by the Americans or the Russians.

General de Gaulle to Alain Peyrefitte, 1962

The collapse of de Gaulle's initiative led to paralysis in the Community and fierce infighting. France threatened to leave the EEC, boycotted meetings and blocked the extension of qualified majority voting. The crisis was only resolved by the 1966 Luxembourg Compromise, which preserved the veto if national interests were at stake. The same year, de Gaulle pulled France out of NATO's integrated command. Not until after his retirement in 1969 did the Community start to recover its poise and invite the UK to resume its quest for membership.

That even de Gaulle (despite his close alliance with Konrad Adenauer, marked by the 1963 Treaty of the Elysée), like Margaret Thatcher, signally failed to shift the Community from its path towards becoming a European superstate showed that it is easier to promise than to achieve a halt to the advance of federalism. (See also **Soames affair** and **Empty chair crisis**.)

Delors, Jacques (1925–)

After periods as a socialist in the European Parliament (1979–81) and a left of centre finance minister in French national politics (1981–85), Jacques Delors became president of the European Commission in 1985 and, having had his office twice renewed, served until 1995. During his presidency the European Union was enlarged and significantly deepened. He oversaw the Single European Act (1986), German reunification (1990) and the Maastricht Treaty (1992), and the Delors Report of 1989 made important recommendations on EMU (Economic and Monetary Union).

The only child of a working-class family, Delors did not have a university education, though he was intelligent and metaphysically inclined. From his early years he was much influenced by his 'personalist' Catholic faith – a doctrine which stresses communal (as opposed to collectivist or individualistic) values. No instinctive friend of parliamentary democracy, he was sensitive to criticism and instilled fear, as well as loyalty, in subordinates. His fanatical work ethic, his determination and his consistent integrationist vision ensured him an ascendancy in the Commission unrivalled since the heyday of Walter Hallstein.

> *The proverbial level playing field that was part of M. Delors' flat earth economics.*
>
> Dr Pedro Schwartz, Spanish economist, October 1996

Delors' unpopularity in the UK owed something to Margaret Thatcher's antagonism, echoed by the tabloid press, but probably more to his patent distaste for liberal Anglo-Saxon ways, allied to the dawning British realisation that his model of the EU comprehended political as well as economic fusion, objectives at odds with the UK's traditional concept of parliamentary sovereignty. His quintessentially French perspective also led to suspicions, belied by his integrity, that he used his presidential position to further French interests. In reality, he perhaps showed more partiality towards Germany, owing to his 'blood brotherhood' with Chancellor Helmut Kohl and his sense that while he personally held the key to German reunification, Kohl held the key to the realisation of Delors' own European dreams.

Democratic deficit

The democratic deficit refers to the loss of legitimacy arising from the transfer of powers from sovereign nations to the supranational institutions of the EU, sometimes with the implication, especially among German commentators, that this could be rectified by increasing the powers of the European Parliament.

The problem cuts deep. Few of the Founding Fathers of Europe much admired democracy. Jean Monnet and Walter Hallstein were technocrats who saw nations as anarchic obstacles to the process of building Europe. Jacques Delors was in the same mould, his convictions reinforced by his religious beliefs. The European Court of Justice owes its allegiance to the Treaty of Rome's objective of ever closer union and does not publish dissenting judgments. The Commission can in theory be dismissed *en bloc* by the Parliament, but this right is a façade. The Council of Ministers meets and votes in secret, its accountability further compromised by qualified majority voting. When the independent European Central Bank comes into being, the EU will have a full panoply of undemocratic quasi-sovereign powers.

I have never understood why public opinion about European ideas should be taken into account.

Raymond Barre, former French premier and European commissioner

---

This unhealthy situation owes its origins to the post-war Continental mistrust of nationalism combined with Monnet's conviction that European co-operation could only proceed by concrete steps agreed behind closed doors. As the role of the nation state was devalued, so supranational commercial policies, such as the Common Agricultural Policy and the European Coal and Steel Community, were elevated into political substitutes. The ultimate aim of the technocrats, for which they considered public opinion unready, was to turn nations into regions of a superstate. How the evolving 'country called Europe' would achieve democratic legitimacy was a question often asked but as often postponed and never convincingly answered.

Nobody brought up on robust Anglo-Saxon parliamentary traditions supposes that the European Parliament is capable of curing the democratic deficit, for in its present form the Parliament is ineffective and remote from ordinary people, a problem that can only deteriorate with the EU's enlargement. Nor is the Gaullist and Thatcherite vision of a Europe of Nations currently on offer or capable of winning over the majority of member states. It is perhaps this very intractability that might generate the political will for fresh answers, in that the Union may be reaching the limits of integration that some of its electorates will tolerate.

Denmark

A founder member of the Council of Europe, NATO, the Nordic Council and EFTA, Denmark applied to join the EC with the UK in 1961 and was admitted, again with the UK, in 1973, having in the interim been effectively blocked by de Gaulle's veto on British accession (trade between the UK and Denmark was too great to risk disruption from the Community's tariff wall).

Denmark's courageous behaviour during World War II, together with its democratic traditions, gives it a moral authority disproportionate to its small size. This is reinforced by the country's socially responsible attitudes and its success in bringing its budget close to balance while reducing unemployment to levels below the Community average. Denmark also ranks among the EU's richest states, largely because of its efficient agriculture.

From the standpoint of the Commission and a number of the member states, however, Denmark is an awkward ally, since its attitude to federation has been as reserved as the UK's. The Danish representative in the Council of Ministers is obliged to check back with the Danish parliament before agreeing to any significant integrationist steps. The parliament voted against the Single European Act in 1986, although a subsequent referendum ratified it; in 1992 the roles were reversed when the parliament voted for the Maastricht Treaty but a referendum rejected it. A second referendum in 1993 was influenced by a united media front stressing the risks of isolation; in addition, the government had won certain concessions, including an opt-out from the final stage of EMU and the right not to participate in defence measures. As a result, the Yes side prevailed, with some 57% of the votes. Nevertheless, grass roots resistance to Maastricht – and subsequently to the Treaty of Amsterdam – continues in Denmark, on the grounds that the Danish constitution bars the transfer of sovereignty except in specified areas, whereas these Treaties grant wide-ranging sovereign-type powers to the EU.

Derogation

Temporary exception to, or exemption from, a Regulation, Directive or Treaty provision, for example as part of a transitional arrangement when a new state joins the EU. A member state which fails to meet the convergence criteria for EMU is given an automatic derogation from the single currency.

De Silguy, Yves-Thibault (1948–)

As the commissioner in charge of monetary and economic affairs, Yves-Thibault de Silguy was a key figure in the negotiations leading up to the 1998 agreement on EMU. A right-wing aristocrat, an *enarque* and an ardent fan of European integration, de Silguy shocked many of his colleagues when he announced, with the backing of President Jacques Chirac, his wish to run for political office in France without giving up his position in Brussels. The mini-scandal was averted when President Jacques Santer ruled that de Silguy's ambition was incompatible with the Maastricht Treaty's provisions. Credited with helping to dissuade Chirac from incipient Euroscepticism, de Silguy has turned his attention to promoting broad economic harmonisation throughout the EU.

Détente

A policy of reducing tension between countries. The term was especially used of East-West European relations in the Cold War between the late 1960s and the collapse of Soviet communism around 1990. Among détente's leading exponents was Chancellor Willy Brandt of Germany, with his *Ostpolitik*, or policy of conciliation with the Soviet bloc, during the early 1970s. Détente was essentially a one-way strategy: in the West it meant making concessions, such as recognising borders or regimes imposed by force; whereas behind the Iron Curtain it was principally a propaganda manoeuvre to undermine Europe's NATO-based security.

DG

See **Directorate-General**.

D'Hondt system

Invented by a Belgian in the 19th century, the d'Hondt formula is still used in Europe, including by the European Parliament, to distribute impartially any given number of posts in a coalition. Suppose, for example, that three allied parties have respectively 120, 90 and 36 seats in an elected assembly and that they have the right to appoint six cabinet ministers between them. The number of seats is divided first by two, then by three, then by four, and so on, and the resulting figures are ranked in descending numerical order, with the positions going to the top six numbers. Thus:

	Party		
	A	**B**	**C**
Number of members	*120(1)*	*90(2)*	*36(6)*
Divided by 2	*60(3)*	*45(4)*	18
Divided by 3	*40(5)*	*30(7=)*	12
Divided by 4	*30(7=)*	22.5	9

The italicised figures rank as the top six. In the above example, therefore, Party C would not qualify to nominate a cabinet minister if only five positions were available; if eight positions were available, Parties A and B would each have the right to one extra nomination.

Direct effect

The principle that certain rights under Community law may apply directly to EU citizens, regardless of whether they have been enacted into national law.

Directive

Directives have come to symbolise the new constitutional order of Europe even more than their legal brethren, Regulations and Decisions. At the summit of this order stands Community law, enshrined in the Treaty of Rome, as amended by subsequent Treaties. Directives are subordinate instruments, in that they must reflect Treaty provisions, but they are endowed with the same supremacy over national law.

Unlike Regulations and Decisions, which once issued pass directly into effect throughout the EU, Directives have first to be enacted nationally before obtaining legal force (although the Francovich case showed that failure to implement a Directive promptly can lead to remedy by the European Court of Justice). Thus member states have flexibility over the form of the legislation, a privilege which some countries use to minimise the impact of Directives, whereas others, most notoriously the UK, seize the opportunity of 'goldplating' by the addition of unnecessary complications.

While the Common Agricultural Policy is mainly implemented by Regulations, the single market operates through 'horizontal' Directives, which set out industry-wide standards, and 'vertical' Directives, which specify the minutiae of business processes in excruciating detail. These Directives are drafted by the Commission, ratified (generally unread) by the Council of Ministers, occasionally discussed by the European Parliament and finally passed into national law with the barest of scrutiny. The Parliament of Westminster makes some attempt to vet them, but it is overwhelmed by the volume of documents, including the Statutory Instruments which the civil service deploys to transpose Directives into law.

It is difficult to obtain an accurate picture of the size of the problem, since the official statistics are deficient, partly through under-recording and partly through double counting. One British estimate suggested that in 1995 the Commission issued 2,801 Regulations, 3,025 Decisions and 35 Directives, as well as 600 draft proposals, and in 1996 1,832 British Statutory Instruments were registered, of which an unknown number related to Directives and other forms of EU legislation. Many of these were lengthy, complex and brought up either at short notice or when the Houses of Parliament were in recess. A Danish MEP stated in 1997 that by 1996 over 23,000 EU legal acts were officially in force (nearly 9,000 relating to agriculture), although this figure evidently included some superseded Directives. An *Economist* calculation put the *acquis communautaire* at

80,000 pages, more than twice the length of the *Encyclopaedia Britannica*.

This system, whereby 370 million Europeans receive (or so it is estimated) one-third of their law and over two-thirds of their business law from distant middle-ranking bureaucrats, has started to concern more than just sceptics. There is, however, no solution in sight, and the increasing use of Regulations foreseen by the Commission will deprive national governments of even the vestiges of control. (See also **Legal instruments**.)

Directorates-General (DG)

There are 24 Directorates-General within the European Commission, each responsible for one or more specific areas of policy-making. In addition, the Commission provides legal, translation, statistical and other support services. The responsibilities of commissioners do not correspond exactly with the DGs; for example, DG I is split between three commissioners. (For a table of DG portfolios, see Appendix 6.)

Discrimination

Discrimination among EU citizens is generally barred under Community law, although non-EU migrant workers enjoy considerably less protection. The 1997 Treaty of Amsterdam laid particular emphasis on the elimination of sexual discrimination, but simultaneously undermined the principle of equal treatment by authorising member states to pursue positive discrimination to ease the career path for the 'under-represented sex' (Eurospeak for women).

Discrimination on nationality grounds
An exception to the general prohibition is that public service employment may be reserved for nationals: this includes civil servants, the armed forces and the police.

Sexual discrimination
Since the mid-1970s the Commission has been producing Directives aimed at giving women equal rights in the workplace – of occupation, conditions, promotion and social security. More recently the focus has been on extending the interpretation of equal pay for equal work, first to include equality of pension entitlement and then to define equal work as work of equivalent value – an echo of the ancient concept of the just wage.

In addition, the Commission regularly proposes action programmes for voluntary implementation by the member states. These programmes range from practical proposals to improve training and career guidance, to politically correct objectives such as the promotion of gender awareness and the removal of stereotypes from educational books. Between these extremes lie suggestions of a social market nature, such as guaranteed maternity leave and the protection of pregnant women from loss of promotion. Ironically, the Commission itself, which claims credit for the rising status of women within the EU, appointed no female commissioners until 1989. Four of Jacques Santer's 20 commissioners, however, are women.

Dublin Convention

The Dublin Convention of 1990 was designed to prevent would-be immigrants from making serial applications for asylum to one EU member state after another, in order to extend their stay. In practice, it had the effect of encouraging lax external border control, since the Convention transferred the responsibility for processing asylum applications from the country of first arrival to the country of first application. This led to an increase in bogus refugees, who gained easy access to the EU by promising to transit from the frontier states to another EU country, relying on the Community's internal freedom of movement.

Duisenberg, Wim (1935–)

In 1997, after 15 years as president of the Dutch Central Bank, Wim Duisenberg, an economist of impeccably anti-inflationary credentials, was appointed president of the European Monetary Institute, which is due to become the European Central Bank (ECB) in 1999. Initially considered a certainty to be the first head of the ECB, he was shocked when France unsuccessfully counter-proposed Jean-Claude Trichet as a candidate – a proposal which underlined the French wish to politicise the ECB and led eventually to an uneasy compromise whereby Duisenberg agreed informally not to serve out his full term.

E

EBRD

See **European Bank for Reconstruction and Development.**

EC

See **European Community.**

ECB

See **European Central Bank.**

Ecofin

When the Council of Ministers meets on economic affairs it comprises all the finance ministers of the EU and is known as Ecofin. Ecofin's authority as the supreme arbiter of the Union's financial policy may, however, be challenged after 1999 when a smaller committee, Euro-X, is due to be created, drawn exclusively from member states participating in EMU.

Economic and Monetary Union

See **EMU.**

Economic and Social Committee (ESC)

The EU's Economic and Social Committee, or EcoSoc, has 222 members and 222 substitutes, all unpaid and divided into three groups – employers, trade unionists and other interests. On issues such as workers' rights, the first two groups usually vote against each other, leaving the third group (consumers, academics, farmers, the self-employed and so forth) to decide the outcome. EcoSoc is a perfect work of corporatist bureaucracy, with its rotating presidency, its tripartite managing bureau, its working groups, its draft reports and its specialist sections. In 1997 it was on the receiving end of a stinging rebuke from the Court of Auditors for abuse of expense accounts.

EcoSoc must, under the Treaty of Rome, be consulted on various issues, though there is no obligation on the Commission or the Council to take its advice. It may also offer opinions (and minority 'contrary opinions') on any other subject on which its members wish to pronounce. The idea of abolishing EcoSoc was often canvassed until the Maastricht Treaty surprisingly bolstered it by attempting to graft onto it the newly created Committee of the Regions, with which it shares certain services in Brussels.

ECSC

See **European Coal and Steel Community**.

ECU (European Currency Unit)

The ECU's predecessor, the European Unit of Account (EUA), was not a currency but a book-keeping convenience to avoid expressing EC statistics (including the budget) in dollars or in D-Marks. After the introduction of the European Monetary System the ECU replaced the EUA in 1981 and assumed some embryonic characteristics of a real currency. It is, for example, occasionally used as a denominator for bank deposits, travellers cheques and international money and bond market transactions. It is not, however, legal tender, nor is it available in the form of paper or coin. The value of the ECU is derived from adding the values of a basket of all the national EU currencies, each currency representing a percentage of the whole, weighted according to the individual member state's GDP, with an adjustment based on its share of intra-Community trade. The composition of the ECU was fixed in 1993 to reduce uncertainty in the run-up to EMU (see Appendix 5).

The currencies of all the EU member states form part of the ECU basket, regardless of whether they also participate in the ERM. Consequently, the central banks are all obliged to make available 20% of their gold and dollar reserves to the European Monetary Institute to enable it to conduct stabilisation operations. The system of internal maintenance of the values of the basket currencies against each other is, however, confined to the ERM participants. Although the Maastricht Treaty provided that the ECU would become the new European single currency, the European Council agreed in 1995 to abandon the name in favour of the euro. This change was in deference to German concern that the ECU would not be a credible replacement for the D-Mark, given its track record of repeated devaluation occasioned by the weakness of several of its component currencies, notably the lira, the peseta, the escudo and the drachma.

Education

The Maastricht Treaty encourages the Community to 'develop the European dimension in education'. Apart from Directives aimed at mutual recognition of professional qualifications (essentially a freedom of movement right), EU policy has taken the form of voluntary programmes, of which the best known is ERASMUS, the scheme for exchanges of university students. Other well-known projects include Lingua (foreign language learning), the European University Institute, the College of Europe, the European Institute of Public

Administration and the nine European Schools for children of employees of Community institutions.

EEC

See **European Economic Community**.

EEA

See **European Economic Area**.

EFTA (European Free Trade Association)

After World War II the UK favoured an expansion of free trade in Europe rather than the customs union with federalist ambitions which was created by the Treaty of Rome in 1957. In 1960 the UK took the lead in forming EFTA, the other signatories being Austria, Denmark, Norway, Portugal, Sweden and Switzerland (collectively known as the Seven, as opposed to the Six member states of the EEC); these were subsequently joined by Finland, Iceland and Liechtenstein. The objective was to establish a free trade area in industrial goods, first between the EFTA members and then throughout western Europe, without, however, imposing uniform external tariffs or submitting the signatories to the authority of supranational institutions.

Some 18 months after EFTA's formation, Harold Macmillan's government applied to join the EEC. Charles de Gaulle twice vetoed the UK's entry, but by 1973 the UK and Denmark had deserted EFTA for the Community, later followed by Portugal (1986) and Austria, Finland and Sweden (1995). Norway has twice been accepted into the Community but has rejected membership by referendum. By 1998, therefore, EFTA consisted only of Iceland, Liechtenstein, Norway and Switzerland, of which all but Switzerland were closely linked to the EU by the Treaty constituting the European Economic Area.

EIB

See **European Investment Bank**.

EMI

See **European Monetary Institute**.

Employment

To the Commission's disappointment, the EU's policy on employment goes no further than monitoring it, regulating some of its aspects and expressing concern that it is not in more plentiful supply. There are policies on vocational training, regional aid (through the structural funds) and hours of employment (through the Working Time Directive). In addition, the Social Chapter of the Maastricht Treaty committed the signatories to measures on workplace conditions, while the Treaty of Rome proclaims the objective of a 'high level of employment'. The Commission produces White Papers on employment and the Council of Ministers calls summit meetings on the subject, where it agonises over the contrast between the success of the USA in creating 25 million new jobs since 1980 and the EU's chronic unemployment, running at 18 million, or 12% of the working population, at the start of 1998. The culmination of much fruitless discussion was the formulation of an Employment Chapter in the 1997 Treaty of Amsterdam. This, however, amounted to little more than phrase-making, since there is within the EU no consensus on the appropriate policy response to the problem.

France and the Commission have advocated public-sector job-creation schemes and harmonisation of tax and social policy, so as to deny competitive advantage to less costly countries. At the other extreme, since Margaret Thatcher's time the UK has advocated privatisation, deregulation and flexible labour markets. Germany mistrusts the spending of taxpayers' money on artificial employment but has long regarded statutory job protection and consensual employer–union relations as central to its social market economy. A 'third way', pursued by the Netherlands, has been successful in reducing nominal unemployment through voluntarily negotiated wage restraint, reduced hours and early retirement, albeit at the cost of falling real wages and disguised joblessness in the form of widespread disability and sickness leave.

The ultimate European verdict on these alternative strategies is less clear than it would have been in the 1980s and early 1990s. Then the Rhine model appeared over the years to have outperformed the Anglo-American model, at least as practised by the UK. But when Tony Blair announced in 1997 that the UK would renounce its opt-out from the Social Chapter, he spoke from strength in putting jobs at the top of the European agenda and emphasising the validity of the British approach, for the economy that he had inherited from the Conservatives was among the most effective in Europe, with unemployment running at half the EU average (doubtless helped by cyclical factors) and the public finances in a healthy condition.

Beneath the surface, business has been more flexible than governments, and there is less rigidity in Continental employment practices than is often assumed. France regulates lay-offs, enforcing consultation with works councils, but although severance is expensive and slow the courts rarely block redundancies. To avoid anti-dismissal laws in Spain and Germany – and high social security costs in several countries – there has been a marked increase in part-time and short-term employment throughout the EU. By 1998 over one-third of all jobs in Spain were filled by temporary workers, and nearly two-fifths of employment in the Netherlands was part-time.

Empty chair crisis

In July 1965 President Charles de Gaulle ordered a French boycott of the Council of Ministers, withdrew France's permanent representative to the Community and instructed the Gaullists to absent themselves from the European Parliament. This empty chair policy was occasioned by the ending of a transition period in the Common Market, after which a range of decisions, previously requiring unanimity, would be taken by qualified majority voting. De Gaulle, who in 1963 had unilaterally vetoed the UK's application to join the EEC, had already been fighting with the Commission president, Walter Hallstein, over the growing power of the bureaucracy in Brussels. The last straw was Hallstein's supranational zeal – in particular, his proposals to make the Community financially self-sufficient, to extend the budgetary powers of the Parliament and to revise the financing of the CAP. The prospect of being outvoted on such matters was anathema to de Gaulle; moreover, he had a French presidential election to fight in December. The dispute paralysed the Community for six months and was not resolved until January 1966, through the Luxembourg Compromise, which essentially condoned the French position and restored the unanimity principle, albeit recognising that this constituted a breach of the Treaty of Rome.

EMS

See **European Monetary System**.

EMU (Economic and Monetary Union)

Early experiments

The goal of Economic and Monetary Union was first proclaimed by the French president, Georges Pompidou, and the German chancellor, Willy Brandt, in 1969, immediately after President Charles de Gaulle's departure from the scene. The blueprint set out in the resultant Werner Report did not, however, succeed. France was unwilling to surrender more than a modicum of financial autonomy. Moreover, the collapse of the dollar-based Bretton Woods international monetary system in 1971, followed by an unprecedented rise in oil prices and global inflation, led to unstable foreign exchange markets in which no artificial attempt to link European currencies could have expected to survive without the sturdiest of political and institutional underpinnings.

In 1977, four years after the demise of the Snake, EMU was relaunched by the Commission president, Roy Jenkins, supported by the next generation of

French and German political leaders, Valéry Giscard d'Estaing and Helmut Schmidt. The revised scheme, known as the European Monetary System, was designed to bring about a zone of currency stability in Europe through the Exchange Rate Mechanism (ERM) and a new quasi-currency (not legal tender but usable in wholesale transactions) called the ECU, or European Currency Unit. The ERM came into effect in 1979. More sophisticated and more firmly backed by central banks than the earlier arrangements, it lasted more or less unscathed for some 12 years, although the ECU, whose value was based on a basket of currencies, did not match the strength of the D-Mark.

The Maastricht era
The ERM had initially been a flexible framework, with room for rate adjustments. But in 1989 a committee of central bankers and economists headed by Jacques Delors made recommendations for a concrete three-stage process of harmonising national economic policies, fixing exchange rates and finally adopting a single currency. From the Delors Report would spring the Maastricht Treaty, which made EMU its centrepiece. Alone among European leaders, and despite being undermined by dissent in her own cabinet, Margaret Thatcher attempted to stand out against these developments.

The Maastricht Treaty, signed in 1992, closely followed the Delors proposals. Stage One of EMU would involve the abolition of exchange controls, the entry of all currencies into the narrow band of the ERM and steps towards economic convergence. Stage Two, starting in 1994, would see the creation of a European Monetary Institute and the granting of independence to national central banks, paving the way for a European Central Bank (ECB) free of government interference. In Stage Three, from which the UK and Denmark negotiated opt-outs, countries meeting the convergence criteria would fix their rates irrevocably and move towards the transformation of the ECU into a genuine currency, with a target date of 1997 but some allowance for slippage.

The UK had reluctantly participated in the ERM for the first time in October 1990, a period which coincided with a domestic recession, German reunification and the inauguration of an increasingly rigid policy of European currency management, which in practice meant locking every country's exchange rate to the D-Mark. A series of disasters ensued. It suited Germany, which had over-inflated its money supply in the process of exchanging D-Marks one-for-one for East German Ostmarks, to keep interest rates high. Other countries, especially the UK, needed low interest rates to stimulate their economies. The Maastricht Treaty proved extremely controversial. Denmark rejected it in a referendum. It barely passed through the British Parliament and doubts arose over its ratification in France. In September 1992 these strains culminated in violent currency speculation, resulting in the departure of the pound and the lira from the ERM and the devaluation of the peseta. A year later, renewed currency turmoil destabilised the franc and virtually destroyed the European Monetary System.

The chaos of 1992 and 1993 appeared for a while to have wrought such havoc that the whole EMU project might fail or be postponed. Nevertheless, a five-year period of budgetary stringency and relative monetary calm, albeit accompanied by heavy unemployment on the Continent, gradually enabled most of the would-be participant countries to fulfil, or at least lay claim to fulfilling, the majority of the convergence criteria. Moreover, the momentum in the corridors of power was well-nigh unstoppable. European governments had from the beginning recognised EMU as an essentially political concept. Unable to force the pace of constitutional integration, because of the reluctance (the Commission would say unpreparedness) of voters, François Mitterrand, Helmut Kohl and Jacques Delors had pressed forward with monetary integration instead. Economic integration would follow, then full federation. The lesson of history, that political unification should have preceded a single currency, as it had done in the USA, Germany, the UK and Italy, was understood, but consciously rejected in favour of an inversion of the natural order of events. Only in the UK, where Thatcher had been ousted late in 1990, did politicians delude themselves, and seek to persuade the public, that EMU was primarily economic in intent.

Throughout Europe, big business generally supported the project. Little caring for national political independence, the multinational corporations saw in EMU the prospect of regional currency stability, enabling them to plan capital expenditure and to budget costs and revenue with more assurance. Their opponents they decried as nationalistic or devaluationist. In Germany and France, prominent businessmen were under considerable pressure to conform to official thinking. In the UK, business opinion was divided. The country's financial structure, its trading patterns and the timing of its economic cycle were so different from those of the Continent that the arguments for staying out of the single currency were stronger than elsewhere. In many countries, small and medium-sized businesses, more entrepreneurial and less susceptible to political influence than the big corporations, were opposed, seeing in the euro (the ECU's name having been quietly dropped) unavoidable costs and unconvincing benefits.

Among central banks, the Bundesbank was the most outspoken, articulating the dangers of EMU in a series of articles and speeches. The scope of its arguments was comprehensive: monetary union could not work well without unified tax and spending policies; this implied political union. In the absence of interest and exchange rate flexibility the cost of adjusting to economic change must be felt in jobs, wages, inflation and migration; Europe's labour rigidity and the immobility of its populations (caused by language and cultural differences) were obstacles to the success of the single currency. The euro was not indispensable to the single market and would be weak unless financial discipline were maintained indefinitely; the convergence criteria were ill-chosen and the French desire to politicise the European Central Bank could be the excuse for previously inflationary countries to revert to bad habits. The Bank of England echoed many of these sentiments. Both central banks couched their warnings in cautious words, careful not to trespass too far into political territory.

Throughout the 1990s EMU dominated the political scene in Europe. Thatcher's fall from power had been partly due to her hostility towards it; John Major's defeat in 1997 owed much to the pound's ignominious expulsion from the ERM in 1992; Mitterrand's authority was never the same after his wafer-thin majority in the French referendum on the Maastricht Treaty. By 1998 German unemployment had climbed over 4.5 million, the highest since 1933. President Roman Herzog spoke of a national malaise, but Kohl seemed obsessed with monetary union to the exclusion of other concerns. Denmark (ordered by its partners to hold a second referendum in 1993 after the first had gone wrong) was cowed into a reluctant Yes, but the electorates of Switzerland (in 1992) and Norway (in 1994) voted down their governments' applications to join the EU. Le Pen's extremist nationalist party exploited antipathy to EMU to gain ground in France; communist parties won the balance of power in France and Italy, where they reluctantly came to terms with belt-tightening measures which offended leftist orthodoxies but were necessary to meet the convergence criteria. In 1997 Jacques Chirac lost his conservative Assembly majority when a snap election to endorse the French austerity drive backfired with a victory for the Socialists. Less than a year away from the 1999 starting date for the single currency, unemployment in the member states stood at close to 20 million and, although the Continental economies were at last recovering, there were few politicians in the EU who had not been scarred by the preparations for the new monetary order.

Nevertheless, in the contest against economic Cassandras and supporters of the nation state, victory had gone to the integrationists. Their assertions that European unity, even peace, depended on EMU had not convinced ordinary people, who remained largely resistant to losing their currencies in Germany, France, the UK, Sweden and Denmark (in Italy and Spain, as in the de facto D-Mark zone of Belgium and the Netherlands, the population was more favourable). But the citizens of France and Germany would have no say in the matter, for no further referendums were planned and the major parties in both countries were committed to the single currency. Accordingly, by January 1999, the last date permitted under the Maastricht Treaty, the currencies of qualifying member states will become irrevocably fixed to each other, and in 2002, when the mints and printing presses have done their work, the euro will replace the D-Mark, the French franc and the other participating national currencies.

The choice of participants

Which countries would be included was decided by the European Council in the spring of 1998. All but the UK, Denmark and Sweden had declared their wish to join as soon as possible, although Greece's financial condition prevented its immediate admission. Germany, with vivid folk memories of wheelbarrow money in its Great Inflation of the 1920s, would have preferred to confine the single currency to a small group of countries with a northern sense of discipline, reinforced by an independent ECB modelled after the stern Bundesbank. France, afraid equally of deflation and of German dominance, favoured a higher degree of political control and the inclusion of the southern states of Italy, Spain and Portugal. Both France and Germany would have liked the UK to be included – France to dilute German influence, Germany because of the UK's strong finances – but the British government, concerned about the mismatch of economic cycles and the hesitance of the British electorate, indicated that, although in principle positive, it was in no hurry to join. Ironically, whereas the UK readily met the main qualifying tests laid down in the Maastricht Treaty, neither France nor Germany, the two prime movers of EMU, found it easy to do so.

The resolution of these differences of opinion proved less difficult than had been expected. The Latin countries based their claim on the sincerity of their conversion to fiscal rectitude. Accused of creative accounting, Italy retorted that even Germany was not above the devices it criticised in others. If Italy and Spain were rejected, their interest rates would soar and the cohesion of the EU would be severely tested. Accordingly, despite German qualms, when the Commission recommended that the Mediterranean nations be included in the single currency, the heads of government agreed without demur. At the Cardiff summit, eleven nations adopted the euro. The UK, Denmark, Sweden and Greece alone would retain their own currencies.

Difficulties and opportunities

With less than a year to run before the introduction of the new currency, the technical obstacles came into sharper focus. There was anxiety about the possibility of speculation during the period of several months after the participants were selected in the spring of 1998 but before the existing national currencies became mere subdivisions of the euro in 1999. Another problem was the adaptation of systems. As the range of complications proliferated, so the estimates of expenditure escalated. The anticipated software costs were compounded by the revelation that few computers were programmed to cope with the transition from the 20th to the 21st century. There might not be enough technicians to handle both the euro and the millennium simultaneously. The cost of switching systems to prepare for the new currency was widely estimated at $150 billion – but the US computer company IBM, which was well placed to evaluate the question, let it be known that it considered this a vast understatement.

The plans for directing future monetary policy grew more rather than less confusing as the deadline approached. It was originally intended that the ECB alone would be responsible for interest rates and the money supply, with price stability its main objective. But France pushed for employment to figure as an equal priority. The proposed ministerial Stability Council, or Euro-X club, seen by Germany as an earnest of permanent fiscal prudence on the part of member states, was seen by France as a political counterweight to the ECB. Moreover, exchange rate policy, allocated under the Maastricht Treaty to the ECB, was agreed during the 1997 Amsterdam summit to be a joint responsibility with the Stability Council. Since exchange and interest rates are inextricably linked, this development appeared to threaten the independent anti-inflationary thrust of monetary policy on which Germany's consent to EMU had been predicated. The European Parliament also pressed its case for an oversight role and France suddenly turned the choice of the ECB's first head into a political controversy, unsuccessfully demanding the position for Jean-Claude Trichet, president of the Banque de France.

Further difficulties kept emerging. The management of the maturity profile of the EU's debt would be outside the control of both the ECB and the Stability Council. There would be no lender of last resort in the event of systemic risk. State pensions, especially in Germany, Italy and France, proved to be gravely underfunded, jeopardising the validity of the convergence criteria. There would be legal problems, too. The redenomination of contractual assets and liabilities into euros would change the rights and long-term expectations of investors, pensioners and life assurance policy-holders. The Bundesbank protested that it would be the principal loser of seigniorage, or the benefit of interest-free liabilities such as bank notes and free deposits, having belatedly realised that the volume of such liabilities in D-Marks far exceeded that in other European currencies.

While the politicians were concentrating on bringing EMU to fruition, it paid them to paper over all such difficulties. Sooner or later, however, the underlying issues would have to be faced. As long as the EU's economies were enjoying an upswing, as they were in 1998, doubtless any disagreements would appear inconsequential. But time would bring the strains to the surface. Some observers concluded that the single currency must eventually lead to a material increase in centrally disbursed EU subsidies to alleviate the burden of regional economic adjustment. This would entail paying more taxes to Brussels, an outcome for which the voters had not been prepared. Pessimists foresaw a disaffected public, rising unemployment, a Fortress Europe mentality and even the disintegration of the EU. Informing and overshadowing every aspect of EMU was the realisation that the direction of the economies of Europe would in future be disconnected from the will of the people, a phenomenon known as the democratic deficit.

> *There is no example in history of a lasting monetary union*
> *that was not linked to one state.*
> Dr Otmar Issing, chief economist, Bundesbank

Against these anxieties other more positive expectations should be recorded. The single market might receive fresh impetus from the elimination of currency fluctuations. Increased pricing transparency should raise business efficiency, enabling Europe-wide giants of industry to spring up, capable of challenging the strongest US and Japanese competitors. The pressures of more intense competition might be the most effective way of forcing governments to undertake much needed tax and labour market reforms. Although the euro would not be immune from exchange rate volatility against the dollar and the yen, intra-European stability would improve the ability of industry to plan for the long term, while broader capital markets might assure the new currency the liquidity enjoyed by the dollar. It was argued that the inevitable compromise of national sovereignty was an outdated concern in a world where markets are all-powerful and security is collective.

Thus was the intellectual ground staked out in opposing camps as the EU confronted the consequences of a decision which was certain to define much of the Union's fate for decades to come.

Enarque

Enarque is the colloquial name for a graduate of the *Ecole Nationale d'Administration*, the elite French institute of higher education dedicated to preparing young people for careers in public administration. *Enarques* of all ages call each other *tu* and expect to run the great departments of state; many go on to high positions in public-sector industry.

Energy

Panic after the 1973 oil shock led to a fruitless search for a Community energy policy, which despite the earlier Euratom and European Coal and Steel Community Treaties had not previously been formulated. The Community imports about half its energy requirements, only the UK and the Netherlands being net exporters, but there are profound strategic differences between the member states. France and Belgium rely – controversially, many would say – on nuclear power; Germany, France, the UK and Spain produce uncompetitive high-cost coal; and many countries are dependent on oil or gas from politically vulnerable sources. The resulting patchwork of energy supply, some in the private sector, some nationalised, does not lend itself to supranational official policy-making. Nevertheless, successive position papers, updating a strategic review undertaken by the Commission in 1974, have provided a framework within which to consider energy issues. The main thrust of these papers has been the promotion of energy efficiency, renewable resources, cross-border links, security of supply and advanced research, in some cases assisted by EU grants or loans from the European Investment Bank. In 1994 a European Energy Charter Treaty was signed by the Community, 12 former Soviet republics and 37 European and other states, the aim being to guarantee oil and gas supplies from the East in exchange for transfers of Western technology and capital. Initial experience of the Russian approach, however, has not been promising, since foreign capital has been regarded there with suspicion.

Enlargement

The usual term for the widening of the European Union by the addition of new member states. The collapse of the Soviet empire around 1990 resulted in a new wave of recently liberated applicants, among which the Czech Republic, Hungary, Poland, Slovenia and Estonia were singled out in 1997 for recommendation by the Commission, with Bulgaria, Romania and the other Baltic republics not far behind. Cyprus was also recommended, but Turkey's long-standing candidature was again unsuccessful. In the long run it cannot be ruled out that such former USSR republics as Ukraine might be admitted.

This massive prospective enlargement gives rise to problems and opportunities of a magnitude that has been temporarily obscured by the more immediate issue of the introduction of EMU. The poverty of the East European states will impose heavy strains on the Community budget, which could only be relieved if other member countries (notably Spain, Portugal, Ireland and Greece) were to agree to surrender part of their privileged access to subsidies; and the voting and representational arrangements of the Union, originally designed for six nations, will have to be reformed radically to accommodate new members, whose ultimate number is unknown.

These difficulties have led some in the Community to doubt the practicability of enlargement or to view it as a Trojan Horse carrying within it the seeds of the EU's self-destruction. Others regard it as the Union's ultimate moral justification, the means of creating a secure, prosperous and democratic area from the

Atlantic to the Ural Mountains. The resolution of the institutional aspects of enlargement raises questions of great importance to the future of the EU, which will renew old differences between integrationists and their opponents. In particular, enlargement may strengthen the hand of those who believe that Europe is too populous and diverse to be managed by a central bureaucracy under the sole banner of ever closer union and that henceforth variable geometry may have to play a permanent, rather than a transitional, role in the Community's constitution. (See also **Agenda 2000**.)

Environment

Although controversy dogs the Commission's involvement in other spheres, public support for EU involvement in environmental protection is strong. Governments, too, have been content to devolve some of their responsibilities in this area to the Community, which is well placed to organise European co-operation over such issues as emission controls and climate change. Anything approaching a coherent EU policy on the environment is, however, of recent origin. The original Treaty of Rome was silent on the subject. The 1986 Single European Act set out three priorities: improving the quality of the environment; health protection; and the conservation of natural resources. Since then, the Commission has issued Directives on matters ranging from atmospheric pollution to water quality and has set up the European Environment Agency in Copenhagen to liaise with national governments and collect scientific research. The 1997 Treaty of Amsterdam required the Community to incorporate the protection of the environment into all relevant legislation.

Despite its popular appeal, environmentalism is full of pitfalls. At the Kyoto Summit of 1997 the EU delegation pointed out that unilateral reductions in power station or vehicle emissions would put Europe at a competitive disadvantage unless matched by US, Japanese and developing country reductions. Moreover, much of the scientific evidence is bogus or debatable. Doubts have, for example, been raised in serious quarters over the explanation of global warming, the phenomenon widely believed to threaten the existence of the planet and therefore to justify massive preventive expenditure. Another battleground is the cost-effectiveness of legislation. The struggle between polluting businesses and health police – the latter armed with draconian powers to penalise infringements of sometimes inappropriate regulations – appears set to be a recurrent EU theme as the 21st century approaches, with the warring parties citing uncertain scientific hypotheses and the rival claims of health and employment. Yet another major theme will be the clean-up of the pollution caused by industry in the former communist countries of Eastern Europe. A rectification programme is a precondition for accession to the EU, but few outsiders understand the scale of the devastation which has been perpetrated in these countries over the last 50 years. (See also **Green parties**.)

ERASMUS

Perhaps the most high profile of the Community's educational initiatives, ERASMUS (an acronym for European Community Action Scheme for the Mobility of University Students) has offered nearly 50,000 students and teachers annually the opportunity to spend a year in another university within the EU. In 1995 ERASMUS became part of the wider SOCRATES programme for co-operation in the educational field.

Erhard, Ludwig (1897–1977)

The acknowledged father of West Germany's post-war economic miracle, Ludwig Erhard was Chancellor Konrad Adenauer's economics minister from 1949 to 1963. A convinced free-marketeer, he dismantled Hitler's state-directed system and devoted himself to export-led revival, based on free enterprise but with a concern also for social welfare. The social market economy is associated with Erhard's name, although he came to regret the phrase's connotation of featherbedding, labour rigidity and high employment costs.

He had grave doubts about federalism, accepting the ECSC and the Treaty of Rome only after much agonising. He was also suspicious of the idea of a customs union, fearing it would encourage protectionism. During his tenure of office, West Germany's exports grew eightfold and the economy outpaced every other European country. Low inflation, high savings and a persistent balance of trade surplus were the hallmarks of this period, which launched Germany on its path to becoming Europe's leading industrial power.

ERM

See **Exchange Rate Mechanism**.

ESA

See **European Space Agency**.

ESCB

See **European System of Central Banks**.

Estonia

Sandwiched between Russia and the Baltic Sea, Estonia has historically been dominated by its eastern neighbour. Its declaration of independence in August 1991 was its second this century, the previous attempt at the end of World War

I having been the culmination of years of fighting, first with the Germans, then with the Soviet Union. The USSR seized Estonia in 1940 under the infamous Molotov-Ribbentrop pact, lost it to the Nazis in 1941, recaptured it in 1944 and held it as a subject state until November 1989, when the Estonian Supreme Soviet declared the annexation illegal. Multi-party elections were held in March 1990. The constitution of 1992 followed, securing freedom for the press and committing the state to privatisation and market liberalisation.

The radical right-wing party elected in 1992 governed for two years, before being replaced in 1994 by a series of centre-left coalitions, based around the Rural People's Union (KMU). The popularity of the KMU reflects the character of the Estonian economy, based on light industry and agriculture. Since independence, the country has benefited from an influx of foreign investment and a switch of trading partners: by 1997 two-thirds of its trade was with the EU. Estonia has secured an Association Agreement with the EU and applied for full membership in 1995, obtaining a favourable recommendation from the Commission.

EU

See **European Union**.

Euratom (European Atomic Energy Community)

The Euratom Treaty was signed in 1957 on the same day as the Treaty of Rome, which established the European Economic Community, and six years after the signing of the Treaty of Paris, which had established the European Coal and Steel Community. Together the three institutions were called the European Communities; they were substantially merged in 1967 and eventually became known simply as the European Community. In its early days Euratom was considered of immense potential importance, on military as well as non-military grounds. France, however, went its own way in nuclear weaponry, as did the UK before and after it joined the Common Market. In 1970 Euratom's research budget became part of the overall Community budget, whereupon the organisation ceased to have a meaningful independent existence.

Euro

The unlovely name for the proposed European single currency. The originally planned name was the écu. This was rejected because Germany disliked the implied reference to the weak European Currency Unit (ECU). Names with honoured traditions in European history, such as florin, shilling or ducat, failed to survive committee decision-making, and euro was settled upon as a compromise.

Eurobond

So called because the market originated in Europe, a eurobond is an internationally owned debt instrument, issued by governments or companies, whose interest is paid without withholding tax. The (mainly dollar-based) market is centred in London.

Eurocommunism

A term used to denote communism modified by democracy. The Franco-Italian Eurocommunist Manifesto of 1975 abandoned the idea of one-party rule and the dictatorship of the proletariat in favour of free elections. Thereafter, however, the French Communist Party stayed close to the Moscow line and it was the Italians who became identified with Eurocommunism, earning the opprobrium of the Soviet Union and evolving ideas little different from those of ordinary socialism. Before the advent of Eurocommunism, which was supportive of European integration, old-fashioned Marxist-Leninists in Western Europe had opposed the Common Market (the maverick federaliser Altiero Spinelli being a rare exception to this rule) on the grounds that Soviet interests were best served by a divided free world. The collapse of the Soviet Empire around 1990 spelled the end of Eurocommunism as a distinctive force.

Eurocontrol

Eurocontrol, founded in 1960 with its headquarters in Brussels, is inoperative and in regular danger of being closed down. If properly activated, it would be one of the EU's most useful bodies. Its object is co-ordinated air traffic control – an urgent need in Europe, where control of airspace is jealously guarded by national governments and co-operation is inadequate, causing unnecessary risk and delays to passengers.

Eurocorps

A joint initiative of President François Mitterrand and Chancellor Helmut Kohl, the Eurocorps was inaugurated in 1993, based on a proposed 35,000-strong Franco-German force. It became operational in 1995 with over 50,000 French, German, Belgian, Luxembourg and Spanish troops, Belgium having committed nearly half of its 45,000-strong army to the corps. Membership is open to all the WEU signatories, some of which, including the Netherlands, Italy and Poland (a WEU associate), have signalled their interest. Forces allocated to the Eurocorps are also assigned to NATO, on which the corps would be reliant for support services in a sustained emergency. The role envisaged for the Eurocorps is that of peacekeeping and crisis management, with the WEU providing the political framework and NATO the military umbrella – a format not perhaps ideally suited to fast-moving operational conditions. (See also **Common Foreign and Security Policy**.)

Eurocrats

European bureaucrats, recruited from all the member states, some working their way up as career officials, others at senior level parachuted in from outside (*parachutage*). These officials, over two-thirds of whom work for the Commission, owe their loyalty and pay their taxes to the EU. Europhiles make play of how few Eurocrats there are (around 29,000), but equally to the point is their influence on the tens of thousands of national civil servants who are seconded to them. This process, known as *engrenage*, or meshing, is designed to indoctrinate the officials of member states in European attitudes by seating them on joint committees with Eurocrats, where they collaborate in detailed technical work, for example on product safety, fish quotas or agricultural issues.

Eurodollar

A dollar deposited outside the USA, especially in a European bank or branch.

Eurofanatic

A person who uncritically and enthusiastically accepts all proposals and defends all policies of the European Union.

Eurofighter

A joint British, German, Italian and Spanish project, the Eurofighter is an advanced fly-by-wire military aircraft, whose commercial viability depends principally on orders from the partner countries. As a short-range interceptor which has attracted doubts about its capabilities and its suitability for modern warfare requirements, the Eurofighter is often defended more on political than on strategic grounds.

Euroland

Those EU member states which adopt the euro as their currency. Or, the EU as a state – a term coined (perhaps initially in jest, by analogy with Disneyland) as a pithier alternative to Federal Europe or United States of Europe.

Euromyth

A term used by the European Commission to denote false stories of intrusive and unnecessary Directives or Regulations emanating from Brussels, such as those specifying the shape of strawberries. Unfortunately, rather too many of these stories prove on investigation to be substantially true, as chronicled by

Christopher Booker in *The Mad Officials*. A feature on which Eurosceptics and Europhiles agree is that many of the most oppressive rules stem from over-zealous drafting or enforcement by national (especially British) officialdom of relatively innocuous proposals originated in Brussels. From the victim's stand-point, however, the result is the same, so long as redress is blocked by the ability of officials to shelter behind the Community as their legitimising authority.

The term is used in the opposite sense by sceptics, to denote misleading or exaggerated Commission claims; for example, that the Community has been responsible for preventing war, or that EMU will create millions of jobs, or that subsidiarity brings decision-making closer to the people.

Europe (1)

With their unique gift for imagery, the ancient Greeks symbolised Europe in the myth of Europa, the lovely daughter of the King of Tyre, who was abducted by Zeus after he had taken the form of a bull. She later married the King of Crete and bore a son, King Minos, who built the notorious labyrinth. Thus within a single story Greek mythology perfectly captured Europe's abiding beauty, its propensity for political rape, its descent into labyrinthine bureaucracy and the ambiguity of its eastern borders.

Europe (2)

After the Roman conquests, Europe's western border was established as the Atlantic north of Gibraltar. But to the east the situation has never been clear. The Romans fought incessantly with barbarians along the Rhine and the Danube. Some considered that Asia began at the River Don. Today it is fashionable to talk of Europe stretching from the Atlantic to the Urals, which accommodates the Baltic states, Ukraine and Slovenia, but still makes Turkey a surprising candidate for the EU.

Europe (3)

Europe as referred to by EU statesmen or officials is a mystical idea, sometimes called 'our European house', to suggest a pan-European vision while glossing over the awkward absence of such states as Norway and Switzerland.

Europe *à la carte*

An alternative term for variable geometry, that is, the concept that member states may pick and choose whether to take part in any given EU policy or institutional arrangement. Disliked by integrationists, Europe *à la carte* is nevertheless already a reality in certain fields, owing *inter alia* to the Danish and British opt-outs in the Maastricht Treaty, certain British opt-outs in the Treaty of Amsterdam and the neutrality of four member states. It is likely to gain further support when the former Eastern bloc countries join the EU, since these will find it difficult to meet the convergence criteria for EMU or to adopt the whole of the *acquis communautaire*. (See also **Two-speed Europe** and **Closer co-operation.**)

Europe Agreement

An Association Agreement with a non-EU country, providing a framework for the associated country's gradual integration into the Community via free elections, the rule of law and open markets.

Europe of Nations

The idea that nation states should be the main determinants of the future of Europe. Charles de Gaulle used the term *Europe des états* to denote his vision of a Community built on co-operation, as opposed to an integrated Union in which power lay predominantly with the Commission and other supranational bodies. Margaret Thatcher later adopted the same theme. (See also **Federalism.**)

European Agricultural Guidance and Guarantee Fund (EAGGF or FEOGA)

See **Common Agricultural Policy** and **Structural funds.**

European anthem

Generally assumed to be the anthem of the European Union, the theme (Schiller's 'Ode to Joy' set to the last movement of Beethoven's Ninth Symphony) is in fact the anthem for the members of the Council of Europe, currently 44 countries, many of which are outside the EU. (See also **European identity.**)

European Bank for Reconstruction and Development (EBRD)

The EBRD was set up in 1991 with a callable capital of 10 billion ECUs, mandated to assist the transition to free markets of the former communist countries of Central and Eastern Europe. The aim was to prove the EU's financial muscle and expertise, but doubt soon turned to embarrassment as President François Mitterrand's friend and adviser Jacques Attali, the bank's first president, spent over £200 million on marble, furnishings and French chefs at his London headquarters. The EBRD's meagre profits have been consumed by loan loss provisions, and although the next president, Jacques de Larosière, brought discipline to expenses and lending, it is hard to see what the bank has to offer that could not be as well done by private enterprise, the World Bank or the European Investment Bank.

European Central Bank (ECB)

Like its predecessor, the European Monetary Institute (EMI), the ECB will be located in Frankfurt. It was ordained by the Maastricht Treaty to come into being as an integral part of the final stage of EMU. The Treaty technically makes the new institution part of a European System of Central Banks, but in practice the role of the participating national central banks is transitional. Once the ECB is operational, they will give it advice, supply members to its Governing Council (due to meet ten times a year) and implement its decisions. Their independence of action, however, will cease.

The primary objective of the ECB, probably to be pursued through targeting the money supply, is price stability in the euro zone. The Treaty stipulates that the bank will be free of political influence and that it will define monetary policy, conduct foreign exchange operations and manage the reserves of the participating countries. Under French pressure, however, employment has been elevated as a priority. It had originally been planned – at least by Germany – that a Stability Council of finance ministers would ensure that the ECB's monetary prudence would be reinforced by fiscal discipline in the single-currency countries. But the Stability Council soon became known as Euro-X, with an informal remit to co-ordinate monetary and economic policy and a vague mandate to intervene more in exchange rate management than the Maastricht Treaty had envisaged. A failed attempt by the French government to appoint a French banker, Jean-Claude Trichet, as the ECB's first president further fuelled concern that its independence would be compromised (the natural candidate was the Dutchman, Wim Duisenberg, president of the EMI). Uncertainty reigned as to how future policy differences would be reconciled, given the clouding of the clear line of authority granted to the ECB in the Maastricht Treaty.

Other issues, too, became embroiled in the dispute. The smaller countries were not happy to see the choice of president of the ECB (the prerogative of all the participant states on consultation with the European Parliament) settled behind closed doors by France and Germany, with an unofficial deal that Duisenberg would not serve out the full term of his presidency. The UK sought in vain to join Euro-X, and was offered instead an assured seat on the ECB's six-strong Executive Board if, or when, the country decided to adopt the single currency. The non-participants expressed anxiety lest Euro-X usurp the Treaty-based primacy of Ecofin in economic decision-making. Although the choice of initial participants in the euro passed off in spring 1998 without undue incident, it seemed that the six years since Maastricht had not been entirely well spent if so many critical questions remained unanswered so late in the day. (For a fuller description of the political and monetary background, see **EMU**. See also **Convergence criteria** and **Single currency**.)

European Centre for Nuclear Research

See **CERN**.

European Championships (Football)

Started in 1958, the European Championships are played every four years, ranking second in importance only to the World Cup, with which they alternate at two-year intervals. They are open to 51 national teams from Europe as far east as the Caspian Sea and the Ural Mountains, including Russia, Georgia, Ukraine, Belarus, Turkey, Armenia and Azerbaijan. Northern Ireland, Wales, Scotland and England are permitted to enter separate teams, an arrangement mirrored by no other European country, not even by those with the strongest regional allegiances (there is a similar dispensation for rugby internationals, except that Northern Ireland and Eire play in these as a united Irish side, a triumph of island loyalty over constitutional niceties). The impact of the passionate national rivalries of football followers is not inconsiderable – perhaps even enough to have played some part in the desire for political devolution in the UK's Celtic fringe.

European Coal and Steel Community (ECSC)

The ECSC was the acorn from which grew the EU. The brainchild of Jean Monnet, it was created by the 50-year Treaty of Paris in 1951 following a proposal of the French foreign minister to pool the French and German coal and steel industries (the Schuman Plan). The object was to make war between those countries impossible by putting essential production under the control of a supranational body. Germany immediately agreed, and when Italy and the Benelux countries decided to join as founder signatories, the Six came into being. In 1957 the same countries formed the EEC through the Treaty of Rome.

The ECSC was the institutional model for the EEC, with a Council of Ministers representing the member states, a High Authority (equivalent to the Commission, with Monnet as its first president), an Assembly of national parliamentarians and a Court of Justice, all based in Luxembourg. The guiding philosophy of the project was political; economically, its policies were a compromise between free-market ideas and interventionism, the reduction of internal trade barriers being offset by price harmonisation and the right to curtail production and imports.

Reluctant to compromise its sovereignty, the UK did not participate. Even among the members there was disagreement about the appropriate sharing of powers between the High Authority and national governments. The advent of the more comprehensive EEC, however, soon began to render the ECSC redundant; in 1967 the two Communities were substantially merged, many of their functions being consolidated in Brussels. Although the Treaty of Paris is still occasionally invoked for purposes of industrial restructuring, when it expires in 2002 it will doubtless be finally replaced by the Treaty of Rome.

European Commission
(Commission or Commission of the European Communities)

The engine-room of the European Union, the European Commission in Brussels is at once its civil service and its government, sharing the latter role with the Council of Ministers. Its powers are immense. Under the Treaty of Rome it has 'its own power of decision' and may 'participate in the shaping of measures taken by the Council and by the European Parliament'. It has the right of initiative in legislating. It has the power to enforce the Common Agricultural Policy and Competition Policy. It negotiates treaties on behalf of the Union and draws up the Community's budget. It manages and dispenses the Community's external aid and internal structural funds. It is the guardian of the Treaties. Whether in its executive or its bureaucratic function, it dominates the EU's affairs.

In intergovernmental matters the Commission is less authoritative. But it has the right to be fully associated with all developments in regard to the Common Foreign and Security Policy and Justice and Home Affairs Policy (no casual matter – each policy has its own department, headed by a commissioner). The president of the Commission attends international summit meetings on a par with heads of government. The smaller states attach great importance to this role, which they see as a safeguard against the weight of the larger countries.

The European Parliament has made repeated efforts to encroach upon the power of the Commission and has made some progress in that direction. In particular, it has the right to be consulted about the choice of president, to dismiss (or refuse to appoint) the commissioners *en bloc* and to decide certain matters jointly with the Council. The Commission, however, has retained *de facto* power virtually unchallenged, through its mastery of its briefs, its unique access to information and its proximity to decisions.

The Treaty of Rome enjoins strict independence on Commissioners, who owe their duty only to the Commission. The president is chosen by member governments, which in practice has meant by France and Germany (see **Treaty of the Elysée**), although this could change if, for example, the UK, Italy, Spain and the Scandinavian countries were to adopt a common candidate. The 20 commissioners are also nominated by member states, and their portfolios are allocated by mutual agreement, the president effectively deciding in case of dispute. Currently, the five largest states (Germany, France, the UK, Italy and Spain) supply two commissioners each, but the approaching enlargement of the EU, combined with the provision that each country has the right to appoint one of its own nationals, is bound to lead to modifications.

The Commission's portfolios are divided into departments, known as directorates (more accurately, directorates-general or DGs). Each commissioner is responsible for all or part of the work of each DG, assisted by the departmental head, or director-general, and a private office, or *cabinet*. Commissioners also take on miscellaneous other individual responsibilities, for example, for translation or statistics. The overall administrative head of the Commission's nearly 20,000 employees has the title secretary-general (see **Eurocrat**).

The most influential of the Commission's nine presidents were indubitably its first, Walter Hallstein, who had led the West German negotiations over the Treaty of Paris in 1951 and the Treaty of Rome in 1957; and its last but one, the Frenchman Jacques Delors, who ushered in the Single European Act in 1986 and forced through the Maastricht Treaty in 1992. Both men were dedicated federalisers, with strong characters and the backing of their own national governments (Delors also enjoyed the support of Germany's Chancellor Helmut Kohl). Both gained stature from being reappointed and were prepared to take on powerful political opponents – respectively Charles de Gaulle and Margaret Thatcher. And both were at heart technocrats more than democrats. Next to them, the president who made the greatest impact was perhaps Roy Jenkins (1977–81), who relaunched EMU in 1979 with the Exchange Rate Mechanism.

Commission presidents

1958–67	Walter Hallstein	Germany
1967–70	Jean Rey	Belgium
1970–72	Franco-Maria Malfatti	Italy
1972–73	Sicco Mansholt	Netherlands
1973–77	François-Xavier Ortoli	France
1977–81	Roy Jenkins	UK
1981–85	Gaston Thorn	Luxembourg
1985–95	Jacques Delors	France
1995–	Jacques Santer	Luxembourg

European Communities

The European Coal and Steel Community, the European Economic Community and the European Atomic Energy Community. In 1967 the three Communities were effectively merged by being given a common Council of Ministers, a common Commission and soon afterwards a common budget. Technically still distinct, they became collectively known as the European Community.

European Communities Act

The 1972 Act of Parliament which brought the UK into the European Community, thereby accepting the *acquis communautaire*, including the supremacy of Community law. (For a synopsis of British relations with the Community, see **The UK and Europe**.)

European Community (EC)

In ordinary parlance, the former Common Market, the European Economic Community (EEC), the European Community and the European Union (EU) are often treated as interchangeable terms. Over the years the names have been changed as the Community's economic character has given ground to its political character. The EEC officially became the EC in the Maastricht Treaty, although EC had been in use from the early 1980s. The distinction between the terms lies in the fact that the Community refers to the EU's institutions, whereas the European Union includes also co-operative agreements between the member states – the so-called intergovernmental pillars. (See also **Treaty on European Union**.)

European company

There is no such thing as a European company, there being no uniformity of company law within the EU. This defect detracts from the single market, for example, by impeding cross-border mergers. The Commission's first attempt to create a European Company Statute was made in 1975 but foundered on its proposal for a German-style two-tier board, with compulsory worker representation on the supervisory board. The Commission's emphasis on building the protection of workers' rights into a Europe-wide statute has been seen by some states as inimical to competitiveness and has ensured continuing opposition to the idea.

European Convention on Human Rights

After World War II the United Nations adopted the Universal Declaration of Human Rights. Two years later, in 1950, the Council of Europe drew up its Convention for the Protection of Human Rights and Fundamental Freedoms (commonly known as the European Convention on Human Rights), and set up the Court of Human Rights. Signatories were obliged to recognise the Convention's principles but not necessarily to enact them into domestic law (the UK agreed to do so only in 1997).

The freedoms contained in the Convention are added to from time to time and are in the main uncontroversial. Nevertheless, the encroachment of the EU into the field of social rights gives rise to concern that the concept of rights may be expanded to include a growing number of contentious, or politically correct, entitlements. Another consequence is that the European Court of Justice may parallel the Court of Human Rights as the tribunal of last resort. The degree of overlap between the two courts' spheres is illustrated by the fact that the Amsterdam and Maastricht Treaties (including the Social Chapter) not only recite the Convention as establishing principles of Community law but also recognise, or pave the way for, such entitlements as the right to employee–employer dialogue, equality between the sexes and freedom from exclusion. Whether these are properly classed as fundamental human rights, and how they should be interpreted and applied, is far from clear.

In external relations, pragmatism or cynicism towards human rights issues on the part of the larger member states has generally been the order of the day. A blind eye is turned to abuses committed by powerful countries or those with export potential. The EU itself, however, and particularly the European Parliament, has sought to raise the profile of these issues, refusing membership and blocking Association Agreements where applicant states fail to abide by the Convention. In the late 1960s Spain, Portugal and Greece were affected by this stipulation, as in the late 1990s have been Turkey and Slovakia.

European Council

The European Council (not to be confused with the Council of Ministers) refers to the biannual, or occasionally more frequent, summit meetings of EU heads of government (plus the directly elected presidents of France and Finland) and the president of the Commission. The meetings, which are also attended by foreign ministers and one Commission vice-president, are intended to be small, grand and informal, in settings which encourage the formulation of European strategy and the solution of problems considered intractable at lower levels, such as the selection of countries for the single currency. The decisions of the Council are normally expressed as Conclusions, Resolutions or Declarations, having no status in law but creating a framework for Community legislation. Virtually all major Community policies are launched or approved in the Council, which offers its participants, with the media in close attendance, irresistible opportunities for eye-catching initiatives.

European (Single) Court of Human Rights

The Court (from November 1998 the Single Court) of Human Rights in Strasbourg is an adjunct of the Council of Europe and is unrelated to the

European Court of Justice (ECJ) in Luxembourg, although both are colloquially known as the European Court. The Court, which accepts a case only when national remedies have been exhausted and has no independent powers of enforcement, decides about 25 cases a year, the whole process, including the determination of admissibility, taking five years or more.

The UK, which regards itself as a leading defender of freedom, has fallen victim to some controversial judgments by the Court, including the condemnation of its treatment of IRA terrorists. So long as the UK (although a signatory) had not incorporated the European Convention on Human Rights into domestic law, such decisions had no legal impact. In 1997, however, Tony Blair's government announced its intention to enact the Convention into law, thereby making human rights a matter for the judiciary, perhaps in conflict with Parliament. Moreover, the Treaty of Amsterdam not only recognised the Convention as establishing principles of Community law but also added a raft of other social entitlements, with the probable consequence that the ECJ will increasingly come to parallel the Court of Human Rights as the ultimate arbiter in this highly subjective field.

European Court of Justice (ECJ)

The ECJ in Luxembourg is the highest court of the EU. Where Community law conflicts with national law it outranks the domestic supreme court, superseding Parliament and the House of Lords as the ultimate legal authority in England and Scotland. There is no appeal from its rulings. It effectively makes law, through its constructive interpretation of the European Treaties, and as a result it increasingly challenges or strikes down national law. The ECJ is, therefore, central to any discussion of sovereignty.

The ECJ was one of the first Community institutions, being set up by the Treaty of Paris in 1951 and enjoined by the Treaty of Rome in 1957 to ensure the legal observation of all the European Treaties. Its judges, one from each member state, sit in panels, delivering only collegiate judgments (dissenting judgments, if any, are not published). Cases are summarised by an advocate-general in a reasoned submission, which the judges consider together with the written arguments of the parties to the action. The ECJ deals principally with failures of omission, for example failure by member states or Community institutions to meet their Treaty obligations. It also has powers of judicial review and hands down preliminary rulings to national courts (which those courts are obliged to follow) where questions of possible conflict of law arise. Competition policy and certain other cases are delegated to the lower Court of First Instance.

Over the years the ECJ has taken every opportunity to extend its scope. As early as 1960 it described its ultimate rationale (*ultima ratio*) as being to enable 'the Community interests enshrined in the Treaty to prevail over the inertia and resistance of Member States'. It looks behind the wording of texts to the underlying objectives of the Treaties, as expressed in their preambles, with their constant refrain of progressive realisation of European Union. Where the ultimate purpose of a piece of legislation is broader than its literal meaning, the ECJ generally treats the purpose as overriding specific provisions. This subordination of Anglo-Saxon style jurisprudence to political ends has earned the ECJ considerable odium in the UK, much of which would be better directed against the Treaties themselves.

Those who value the principle of sovereignty are troubled less by the supremacy of Community law where it conflicts with national law than by its continuous encroachment and the fact that it operates outside any democratic framework. That the Court construes its principal function as the advancement of European integration is particularly at odds with the British concept of the law as the last bastion of individual protection against over-mighty authority. In that context, significant questions remain to be answered. Where would be the checks and balances if the ECJ were to exceed its lawful powers? Could it deprive a member state of its independence by setting aside an Act to repeal the terms of its accession to the EU? Given the reliance of English courts on precedent, the concern of British libertarians is that the House of Lords might one day accept that Parliament's authority had ebbed away and become subordinate to that of the EU in perpetuity. Even a written constitution may no longer afford a country protection, since the 1997 Treaty of Amsterdam appears to have set Community law above constitutions.

European Cup

The ultimate footballing crown for European clubs, played between the champions of the various national leagues and culminating in a knock-out tournament.

European Currency Unit

See ECU.

European Defence Community (EDC)

The EDC was the first major failure of the federal cause in Europe. By 1950 the Cold War was under way and the Korean War had just broken out. The UK and the USA wanted German rearmament, while the Six members of the soon-to-be-created European Coal and Steel Community (ECSC), spiritually led by Jean Monnet, wanted a European army with mixed nationality units, as a prelude to a wider economic and political unity. The project fell apart in 1954 when the French assembly, to the strains of the 'Marseillaise', rejected the EDC Treaty, which had been in abeyance since its signature in 1952. The effects of the collapse of the EDC were rapid and far-reaching. In 1954 Germany joined NATO and in 1955 Monnet retired from the presidency of the ECSC to devote himself to lobbying for a United States of Europe, playing an influential role in the events which led up to the Treaty of Rome in 1957. It would not be until the late 1990s that military unification would again creep on to the European agenda. (See also **WEU**.)

European Economic Area (EEA)

The EEA comprises the EU plus the EFTA countries (except Switzerland, whose government in 1992 signed the EEA Treaty but whose people then rejected it in a referendum). The Treaty was prompted by the entry into force of the single market and was designed to create a Europe-wide free-trade zone – albeit on terms dictated by the EU. The essence of the arrangements is that the EFTA countries accept the *acquis communautaire* and are bound by Community legislation, over which they have no influence. These features are often said to demonstrate the futility of the EFTA position. Membership of the EEA does not, however, commit the signatories to the Common Foreign and Security Policy, to co-operation in Justice and Home Affairs, to EMU, to the Common Agricultural Policy or to the Common Fisheries Policy. Moreover, the institutions of the EEA, including the EFTA Court, are expressly stated to lack the sovereign authority claimed by the institutions of the EU. Thus many of the areas which define national independence remain within the competence of those EEA states which have elected not to join the EU. At the same time they escape the most costly of the EU's policies – altogether perhaps no bad bargain for surrendering a small say in the framing of Community law.

European Economic Community (EEC)

The original term under the 1957 Treaty of Rome to describe the Common Market. Later merged with Euratom and the European Coal and Steel Community to become the European Community.

European Economic Interest Grouping

In the absence of a European Company law, companies may co-operate across European borders within the loose framework of a European Economic Interest Grouping. The best-known example is Airbus Industrie, a French, British, German and Spanish collaborative venture. A major weakness in the structure is the lack of a central decision-making body or a unified set of financial accounts.

European Economic Space

A translation of the French term for the combination of the European Free Trade Association and the European Economic Community, or what became the European Economic Area, the phrase has degenerated into a vague expression, faintly suggesting a self-contained European zone or a Fortress Europe.

European Flag

Originally the flag of the Council of Europe, the symbol of 12 gold stars on a blue background was adopted by the Commission in 1985 and is widely used as a means of promoting the European identity. Although there happened to be 12 member states at the time, the significance of the number lies elsewhere and is deeply embedded in European Christian civilisation – thus the Virgin Mary's halo is traditionally a circle of 12 gold stars; and there are 12 signs of the zodiac, 12 apostles and 12 months in the Western year.

European Free Trade Association

See **EFTA**.

European Games

The European Games for track and field athletics are held every four years, alternating at two-year intervals with the Olympic Games. During the Cold War the women's events and the strength events, such as shot-putting, were dominated by athletes from the Soviet bloc, whence came a string of androgynous amazons, who set numerous world records (as they did in swimming events). The use of performance-enhancing drugs was suspected; these were known to make the female physique more masculine, with often tragic side-effects. But it was not until German reunification that Western investigators were able to inspect the training methods that had been used in East Germany, uncovering a comprehensive system of state-organised doping. The centre for this activity was the College for Physical Culture in Leipzig, where doctors and coaches secretly drugged several thousand competitors over the years in the name of promoting the superiority of communism. With the collapse of the Soviet empire the use of drugs declined and performances reverted to normal.

European idea

Between the 1914–18 and 1939–45 wars many idealists believed that some form of European federation was necessary to prevent another conflict. The depression of the 1930s and the rise of fascism gave a socialist tinge initially to this utopianism (although Berlin and Vichy France, too, dreamed of a post-war new order with some startling similarities to the present EU). After World War II Winston Churchill, quick to see the new Soviet threat to a ruined Europe, lent his authority to sponsoring the concept of a 'kind of United States of Europe', to be built on Franco-German reconciliation. He hoped that this would stand alongside the USA and the Commonwealth as bulwarks against tyranny. Successive presidents in Washington enthusiastically embraced the idea as a central element in the policy of containment of the USSR.

Despite the collapse of the Warsaw Pact around 1990, the belief still lingers that peace is the ultimate justification for the EU. The danger of a third European war appears fanciful to most Britons, as it does to a younger Continental generation, yet Chancellor Helmut Kohl has repeatedly cited this as Germany's principal reason for seeking deeper integration. When the Bosnian crisis erupted Luxembourg's foreign minister declared 'the hour of Europe has struck', but a discordant EU was impotent as battle raged on its border until the USA intervened to call a halt – a reminder that to this day European security is not so much a product of the Community as of NATO and the American alliance.

After peace, the other central theme in the European idea is that of building a political union on a sense of cultural identity. This has ancient roots in history, traceable to Julius Caesar, Charlemagne and Napoleon. The UK shares Christianity, the Roman conquest and much else of its heritage with Europe, but it also shares language, common law, political traditions and popular culture with the USA. Mindful of battles fought beside Americans in both world wars, Britons are wary of European empire-building; and when Charles de Gaulle vetoed British entry to the EEC in the 1960s he was percipient in reading the UK as instinctively Atlanticist. Indeed, even without the striking cultural distinctions between northern Protestantism and southern Catholicism, the Anglo-Saxon dimension alone would be enough to guarantee that diversity (going beyond mere regionalism) must be the hallmark of any pan-European vision capable of winning the affections of all its peoples.

As post-war Europe evolved, two competing ideals emerged: that of a Europe of Nations co-operating voluntarily, espoused by de Gaulle and Margaret Thatcher and colouring the thinking of many ordinary voters in all the member states; and that of a supranational Europe, espoused by successive German leaders, by the Commission in Brussels and by a substantial proportion of Europe's governing elites. Although both these visions are still alive, the integrationist model created by Monnet, Adenauer and Hallstein, and further developed by Delors and Kohl, is in the ascendancy, founded on the conviction that the member states will rarely agree on a common cause without the ability of the majority to impose its will. In its extreme form, the federalist ideal is of the ending of the European nation state.

Veering between these two visions of Europe, France often speaks of a Continent under joint Franco-German hegemony. This would have for France the triple appeal of protecting its influence, neutralising a stronger rival and creating a superpower able to 'challenge' Asia and the USA. French suspicions of Germany find a surprising echo in Germany itself, which sometimes appears to embrace a federal Europe because otherwise it could not trust itself not to relapse into nationalism. A less charitable interpretation is that an integrated Europe would provide a platform for the expanded exercise of German, rather than French, power.

The UK's main contribution to European unification has been its support for the single market. Yet Britons are uneasy about full economic integration. They want free trade, but for the most part they regard EMU – not to mention political federation – with great reserve. They accept the need for certain common measures, for example on the environment and drug traffic; and they would prefer (though not at the expense of US relations) to be more frequently aligned with the EU in foreign affairs. But these limited aims fall short of anything that Continentals would recognise as genuinely *communautaire*.

Italy's and Spain's reasons for their European convictions are not dissimilar. The two countries are defined more by their artistic heritage and their flair for living than by their political traditions, of which their citizens are contemptuous. They are attracted by sound northern money and an enlarged market place. Italy has no strong sense of nationhood, and Spain's powerful regions benefit from the largesse of Community subsidies.

> *The Germans want the Union to stop them from falling into Nazi ways. The French want to be cured of an inferiority complex. The Italians want to become a nation. The Spaniards want to bury Franco … I sometimes think that the Common Market should have been founded not in Rome but in Vienna, on Dr Freud's couch.*
> Dr Pedro Schwartz, Spanish economist, 1996

Among the smaller countries, the European idea has both financial and political appeal. Portugal, Greece and Ireland are major cash beneficiaries; Belgium, lacking a national sense of identity, finds a new purpose in its unique position at the geographical centre of the Community; and for Austria, the Netherlands and Finland, escapees from the shadow of dominant neighbours, a small say in the EU's affairs may have more to offer than a somewhat anonymous independence.

From its earliest years, the realisation of the European dream required a diminution of national democracy, for which the European Parliament has proved no substitute. By contrast, the enlargement of the Community to embrace Denmark, Sweden and the UK brought into the fold robust democracies, with a vision of society accountable to the people. These alternative political ideals have yet to find their reconciliation. Until they do, the European idea, however assiduously promoted with emblems and propaganda, is destined to remain more an ambition of the elites than a reflection of popular aspirations. (See also **Founding Fathers**.)

European identity

The European identity as a political goal had been inherent from the early post-war years in the thinking of Jean Monnet, Walter Hallstein and others. It was first set out formally at a summit meeting of heads of government in 1973, shortly after the UK's accession. It envisaged a Union open to other European countries, with a common market, common institutions and a common policy in relation to third countries. It thus contained many of the central themes later enshrined in the Single European Act of 1986, the Maastricht Treaty of 1992 and the 1997 Treaty of Amsterdam.

In common parlance, the European identity has come to be associated with the various emblems and symbols by which the Commission has sought to influence ordinary people of the appeal (and the inevitability) of a United States of Europe. These include the European anthem, the European passport, the European driving licence, European citizenship, twinning, the European flag and the ubiquitous 12 stars displayed on every project part-funded by the EU, as well as the planned single currency.

European Institute of Public Administration

Founded in 1981 in Maastricht, the institute focuses on European integrationist studies for academics and administrators. The governors are drawn from representatives of the Commission and EU member states.

European Investment Bank (EIB)

With its headquarters in Luxembourg, the EIB was established in 1958 under the Treaty of Rome and is the European Community's long-term lending arm. Often operating alongside the structural funds, the EIB focuses particularly on cross-border projects and on capital investments in less prosperous regions. Some 90% of its lending is within the EU, the balance going to Eastern Europe, the Arab Mediterranean states (the Maghreb and the Mashreq) and the ACP (African, Caribbean and Pacific) countries participating in the Lomé Convention. The EIB's loans are made on a non-profit basis, its low lending rates reflecting its own ability to borrow on fine terms owing to its AAA credit rating in international markets. Of the bank's capital of over 60 billion ECUs only a small proportion has been paid up; the uncalled capital represents a claim on the shareholders (the EU's 15 member states) and is the foundation of the EIB's high standing as a borrower.

The Board of Governors consists of one minister (normally the finance minister) from each shareholder. A 24-strong part-time Board of Directors takes lending and borrowing decisions and a Management Committee (the bank's president and seven vice-presidents) runs the organisation operationally.

European Monetary Institute (EMI)

Established in 1994, the EMI, headed first by Alexandre Lamfalussy and subsequently by Wim Duisenberg, was designed under the Maastricht Treaty to be the precursor to the European Central Bank (ECB). It succeeded the Committee of Central Bank Governors and is charged with the co-ordination of monetary policy among member states and with preparation for the single currency. It also holds 20% of the official gold and foreign exchange reserves of member states to enable it to manage the European Monetary System. Its ruling Council consists of the governors of the central banks of all the EU member states.

European Monetary System (EMS)

After the collapse of previous attempts at currency union in Europe, notably the Snake, Roy Jenkins launched the EMS in his first year as president of the Commission in 1977. It came into force in 1979, accompanied by the customary fanfare of forecasts of lasting growth with stability, a progressive return to full employment and other desirable objectives. The two components of the EMS were the ECU (the embryonic single currency) and the Exchange Rate Mechanism (ERM), a revised system of fixed but adjustable exchange rates. All the EU member states participated in the EMS and the ECU, but membership of the ERM was neither mandatory nor universal. The advent of EMU in 1999 will render the EMS obsolete, replacing both the ECU and the ERM with a regime of irrevocably fixed exchange rates, leading by 2002 to the single currency.

European Monetary Union

It is a common mistake that EMU means European monetary union. In fact the initials stand for Economic and Monetary Union, a more far-reaching goal.

European Monitoring Centre for Drugs and Drug Addiction

Set up in Lisbon in 1994, the centre tracks statistical and other information on the drug problem throughout the Community.

European Movement

Founded in the flush of post-war enthusiasm, the European Movement, with Winston Churchill, Prime Minister Alcide de Gasperi of Italy and Paul-Henri Spaak of Belgium among its honorary presidents, organised the Congress of Europe in 1948, which led to the establishment of the Council of Europe in 1949. The European Movement has remained in existence as an all-party Europe-wide pressure group for integration, albeit with limited funds for publicising the causes it backs. Its current president is the former Portuguese president, Mario Soares, who succeeded the former French president, Valéry Giscard d'Estaing.

European Parliament

The European Parliament's intended purpose is to supply democratic legitimacy to the proceedings of the EU, against a background of the progressive transfer of powers from national elected governments to Brussels.

The Parliament's ineffectiveness arises from many causes. Its headquarters are in Strasbourg, but it also meets in Brussels, while its library and much of its secretarial back-up are in Luxembourg (squabbles over its location persisted for 40 years and the resultant unworkable compromise was the product of horse-trading). With its expensive buildings and its caravanserai of translators and documents it is an immensely costly operation. It is also hard to understand. Even to well-informed observers, the party lists, national lists and regional lists of elections in other EU countries are unfamiliar, as are the political groups in the Parliament, with their obscure initials (PES, EPP, ELDR, UEL, EDA and so forth) and their lack of party discipline or coherent agendas. With an average of 600,000 EU citizens per MEP, there is little sense of meaningful representation. European elections in most countries are consequently decided on domestic issues. The turnout, despite compulsory voting in several European countries, is low and has fallen at every election, demonstrating the apathy of voters.

To anyone reared on the rough and tumble of the British and other national parliaments, the proceedings of the European Parliament are tame indeed. Votes are taken electronically at fixed times and there is rarely a record of how individual MEPs voted. The subject-matter consists mainly of committee reports, presented by *rapporteurs*. The debates are dominated by unelected commissioners and by the Parliament's political groups, which have precedence to nominate speakers. Absenteeism is so rife that the president often lets voting carry on without a quorum. The extravagance of the Parliament is a byword. With travel expenses, attendance pay and office allowances, MEPs can add considerably to their basic salary. Further lucrative possibilities arise from inter-parliamentary exchanges and delegations to developing countries.

The Parliament started as an appointed Assembly in 1951, its first direct elections (for five-year terms) being in 1979. For a while, under the leadership of Altiero Spinelli, it attempted to build on its new elective status to assert itself, drafting a federalising treaty, making resolutions and inviting heads of state to address it. Finding, however, that scant attention was paid to its Opinions and the deliberations of its numerous committees, it lowered its sights to more modest increments of power. More recently, it has started to recover its confidence, seeking the right of initiative in legislation and the authority to be closely involved in the drafting of Treaties. Its powers have steadily grown in number and are no longer as token as they once were. It has the right to be informed about international negotiations and to be consulted on legislation and on key appointments. It can block the accession of a new state. It can suggest amendments to legislative proposals or defer them. Its main weapon is co-decision, the effect of which is to put the Parliament on a par with the Council of Ministers in agreeing legislation in selected areas. This right was extended by the 1997 Treaty of Amsterdam to 27 new fields, including employment and social policy.

MEPs may ask questions of the Commission and the Council; they may sue either of these institutions for failure to act, receive petitions from citizens and set up committees of inquiry into maladministration. On paper, the Parliament's most draconian power is to sack the entire Commission by a censure motion carried by a two-thirds majority, though since the Commission serves in practice as the Parliament's government this remains essentially a theoretical right. The Parliament also has certain limited financial powers, of which the most significant is its right to reject the Budget. Since, however, it has no say in either revenue-raising or so-called compulsory expenditure (that is, the bulk of budgetary spending), this amounts in reality to little more than the right to delay and seek amendments.

Although the Parliament's ambitions are limited by the fact that it has to compete for authority with the Commission, the Council of Ministers and national governments, the fact that it has gained ground despite its shortcomings reflects Europe-wide concern at the democratic deficit. Italy and Germany see in it the best hope of an eventual federal democracy. The UK, often in agreement with France, generally opposes any wide extension of its powers, seeing democratic legitimacy as stemming from national elections in which issues are put to the people in their own language by politicians known to them. Nevertheless, the probability is that the Parliament will continue inching its way forward, without achieving the radical breakthrough that could only come from a complete overhaul of the EU's institutional structure. (See also **Appendix 3**.)

European passport

The so-called European passport, with its European Community heading and its burgundy-coloured cover, is actually a national passport in a common form. It was introduced in 1985, after lengthy arguments about its design and content, and is meant to reinforce the European identity by symbolising citizenship of the Union.

European Patent Convention

A convention allowing inventors to obtain patent protection in 18 European countries by filing a single application, processed by the European Patent Office in Munich.

European Political Community

In the early 1950s ministers from the six member states of the European Coal and Steel Community drafted a constitution for a new form of democratic government to control the planned European Defence Community. The proposals were ambitious. There would be a two-chamber Parliament (the lower chamber directly elected, the Senate elected by national parliaments), a powerful appointed Executive Council, an advisory Council of National Ministers and a Court of Justice. This so-called European Political Community (EPC) would be able to levy taxes and would establish a Common Market. The collapse of the European Defence Community, voted down by France in 1954, led to the EPC being permanently shelved. Four years later the far more cautious Treaty of Rome inaugurated the European Economic Community and the long process leading to the European Union.

European political parties

See Political groups.

European Regional Development Fund (ERDF)

See Structural funds.

European Social Fund (ESF)

See Structural funds.

European Space

A vague term, with overtones of a somewhat assertive or protectionist United States of Europe.

European Space Agency (ESA)

Based in Paris, the ESA is not an EU body although it co-operates closely with the Commission. It is financed by its 15 European sponsoring states, including Switzerland, supplemented by commercial revenue from satellites launched by Ariane.

European System of Central Banks (ESCB)

The ESCB, nicknamed the Eurofed by analogy with the US Federal Reserve system, consists of the future European Central Bank (ECB) and the national central banks of the EU member states. Since it will have no independent management the ESCB is something of an abstract concept. After EMU is introduced, each national central bank will supply a member of the ECB's Governing Council. Collectively, the central banks will use their knowledge of markets and their links with traders to execute the ECB's monetary and foreign exchange policy and will make available to it by way of reserves up to 50 billion ECUs in gold and foreign exchange (the UK is exempted from this obligation through its opt-out from Stage Three of EMU). In case of need, all the reserves of the single currency participants will be callable by the ECB through the ESCB network. (See also **EMU**.)

European Union (EU)

The EU denotes the supranational institutions of the European Community together with the 'pillars' of intergovernmental co-operation between member states. In 1997, a proposal to make the EU a legal entity in the Treaty of Amsterdam was rejected. (See also **Treaty on European Union**.)

European University Institute

Founded in Florence in 1976, the Institute offers postgraduate courses in history and civilisation, economics, law and political and social sciences. The EC's archives are kept at the Institute, which is financed by the EU's member states.

Europhile

A convinced supporter of the objectives and methods of the European Union.

Europhobe

One who distrusts all the objectives and methods of the European Union, perhaps from xenophobic motives. Also used by Europhiles as a term of disparagement for Eurosceptics.

Europol

Europol, the EU's embryonic FBI, was foreshadowed in the 1992 Maastricht Treaty, which provided for police co-operation between member states to combat terrorism, drug trafficking and other international crime, including if necessary customs offences. The Europol Convention was not, however, agreed until 1995 and by 1998 only the UK, Denmark, Spain and Portugal had signed it. Pending wider ratification, Europol's activities are limited to exchanges of information and a certain amount of investigation through a staff of national police officers attached to its office in The Hague. Although the 1997 Treaty of Amsterdam attempted to promote Europol by bringing certain police work under the sway of the EU, home affairs remain for the time being mostly in the intergovernmental domain. France has not been alone in raising the alarm over the prospect of ceding control of its national police force, which appeared to be the logical outcome of Chancellor Helmut Kohl's vision of Europol as 'central to the development of the EU's security policy'. In the UK, the focus of anxiety has been more on the protection of the citizen against summary arrest and detention, areas where the country enjoys a long tradition of civil liberty not universally reflected in the behaviour of foreign police. Against the background of these concerns, Europol's development is likely to be slow and tortuous. (See also *Corpus Juris*.)

Eurosceptic

One who casts an enquiring, sceptical eye on the project of European integration and especially on EMU. Eurosceptics sometimes describe themselves as Eurorealists, to escape the false charge of Europhobia.

Eurosclerosis

Hardening of Europe's economic arteries. A term used to denote stagnation arising from rigid labour laws, high social costs, heavy taxation and over-regulation.

Eurospeak

A high-flown, ambiguous or obscurantist mode of expression used by Eurocrats to mask or put a gloss on their objectives. For example, the principle of subsidiarity, widely misunderstood in the UK as conceding increased powers to national governments, in fact means that all significant legislative authority belongs to the EU unless delegated to subsidiary national governments. Eurospeak also tends towards political correctness, as in 'the under-represented sex' for women, and officialese, as in 'cultural workers' for artists, musicians and actresses. The Maastricht Treaty's unrelieved Eurospeak disgusted even Jacques Delors, who was not to know that the Treaty of Amsterdam would be no better.

Eurostat

The Commission's statistics office, with responsibility for making sense of the reams of figures (often neither comparable nor reliable) supplied by member states. Eurostat also compiles the calculations on which eligibility for the single currency are judged. The office is a mine of information, although its credibility was somewhat dented in 1998 by its apparent acquiescence in some exercises in creative accounting designed to disguise French, Italian and even German problems in meeting the convergence criteria.

Eurotunnel

The rail tunnel linking the UK to France, jointly owned by twinned French and British companies, whose debt finally escalated to £8.5 billion, obliterating shareholders' equity but not preventing the completion of a project first started by Napoleon.

Euro-X

The informal committee of finance ministers of countries adopting the single currency, otherwise known as the Stability Council (X stands for the number of participants). In 1998 Euro-X fell into controversy before it even came into being. France wanted it to act as a political counterweight to the European Central Bank, a concept opposed by Germany, and the UK unsuccessfully demanded a seat on it, fearing that it might usurp the role of Ecofin. (See also EMU.)

Excessive deficit

The economic convergence criteria established by the 1992 Maastricht Treaty allow member states to have an annual excess of expenditure over revenue of 3% of GDP and a cumulative government debt of 60% of GDP. Member states are expected to report their deficits to the Commission. An excessive deficit meets first with Ecofin's recommendations, then with sanctions and ultimately with fines. In evaluating a deficit, the Council of Ministers can take into account trends as well as absolute figures – a necessary concession, given that Italy and Belgium both have government indebtedness of over 120% of GDP. Those countries which join EMU are more specifically bound by the Stability Pact, which covers similar ground.

Exchange Rate Mechanism (ERM) (1)

The ERM is the central feature of the European Monetary System (EMS), the two terms having become almost interchangeable in common usage. It was introduced in 1979 at the initiative of the Commission president, Roy Jenkins, as a renewed attempt to create a zone of currency stability in Europe – long seen by integrationists not only as an end in itself, but also as a step towards ultimate political unification. Two previous attempts (the Snake and the Snake in the Tunnel) had ended in failure, but the collapse of the dollar-based Bretton Woods system in the early 1970s had left many Europeans with the conviction that the EC should take its monetary destiny into its own hands.

The original participants in the ERM were the Benelux currencies, the French franc, the D-Mark, the guilder, the lira, the Danish krone and the Irish pound. Of the then member states of the EC, the UK alone did not initially participate; nor did Greece when it joined the Community in 1981. The Spanish peseta entered the ERM in 1989 and the Portuguese escudo in 1992, respectively three and six years after the accession of Spain and Portugal. The pound sterling finally joined the ERM in October 1990, after nearly a decade of political controversy in which Margaret Thatcher became isolated from some of her senior cabinet colleagues, who considered that the UK's detachment was lessening its influence in the Community.

The mechanics of the ERM provided that the participating currencies were given a central exchange rate against the ECU, from which they derived central cross-rates against each other. Each currency was allowed a limited degree of deviation from these rates. If a currency threatened to approach its upper or lower limit, central banks would intervene and corrective domestic measures would be taken, such as the adjustment of interest rates. But if a fundamental imbalance emerged in a currency's parity, a realignment could be negotiated through Ecofin. The permitted fluctuation was not identical for each currency. The majority (many of them natural members of the D-Mark bloc) were given a narrow band margin of 2.25% on either side of their central rates, whereas the peseta, the pound and the escudo were allowed a broad band of 6%. The purpose of the wider margin for these currencies was to provide more flexibility and so to deter speculation – on the principle that the ideal target for a speculator is a currency which is on the brink of a limit which the market considers indefensible, but which is nevertheless being defended by central banks with heavy purchases or sales.

The UK's entry to the ERM came at a particularly unfortunate time. The country was in a recession, which called for an accommodating domestic monetary stance; but the Bundesbank, having been commanded to supply D-Marks on an inflated one-for-one basis in exchange for Ostmarks so as to ease German reunification, was compensating with a tight monetary policy. To stay within its ERM band, the UK had to raise interest rates, thereby deepening its recession. There was no easy escape through realignment. The Commission president, Jacques Delors, was preparing the ground for the Maastricht Treaty and full-blown economic and monetary union. As a result the ERM was changing in character from a fixed but flexible system into a rigid straitjacket.

In September 1992 massive currency speculation broke apart the ERM. The peseta was devalued by 5% and the pound sterling and the lira were both driven out of the system. There was, at the time, widespread recrimination. Thatcher had been ousted. Her successor, John Major, had made membership of the ERM a central plank of his economic policy and blamed Germany for failing to support the pound as wholeheartedly as the French franc. A well-known Wall Street investor, George Soros, admitted to having made a killing by short-selling sterling, which Germany considered to have entered the ERM at too high a parity. It was in any event clear that the rejection of the Maastricht Treaty by Denmark in June, combined with the possibility that France also would vote against the Treaty in its impending referendum, had given the market objective reasons to be alarmed about the durability of the ERM.

Renewed speculation in August 1993 concentrated on the French franc and led to the fluctuation band being increased to 15% for all the remaining currencies within the ERM except the D-Mark and the guilder, which kept their narrow bilateral link. For the time being, it seemed that the ERM had gone the way of the Community's previous failed efforts to achieve stability. Gradually, however, equilibrium was restored. As the belief grew that EMU would go ahead in 1999, speculators became nervous that they might get their fingers burned if they launched unsuccessful forays in the exchange markets. The lira returned to the ERM in 1996, Finland, Austria and Greece (but not Sweden) also joined and all the participating currencies except that of Greece came back unofficially to the narrow band. Sterling stayed outside, but confounded the pundits. The Europhiles had predicted that its expulsion would lead to a sharp depreciation (or competitive devaluation, as some in France bizarrely termed the pound's unwilling fall), together with higher interest rates and a prolongation of the UK's recession. In reality British interest rates declined, the economy recovered and by 1998 the pound had climbed back above the level which had once been regarded as unrealistically high.

The 1992 Maastricht Treaty had specified observance of the 'normal fluctuation margins' within the ERM for at least two years as one of the convergence criteria, upon which qualification for the single currency would be judged. Much, however, had happened since the Treaty was signed and it was not altogether clear whether a country could meet this test by *de facto* stability without formally being inside the ERM – a point of particular significance to the UK. For the other countries that wished to adopt the euro, a few years of calm had seen to it that this clause no longer posed a problem. (See also **EMU**.)

Exchange Rate Mechanism (ERM) (2)

By 1999 the work of the original ERM will have been completed with Stage Three of EMU and the irrevocable fixing of parities. At that point a new ERM will come into existence, in which 'pre-ins' will be allowed a fluctuation margin of 15% either side of the euro, or a lesser margin if mutually agreed. A country with a derogation from the single currency will not be formally obliged to participate in the new ERM but will be expected to do so, and will in any event be bound to treat the stability of its own exchange rate as a matter of common interest under the Treaty of Rome. It is an open question whether the UK, as a country intending 'in principle' to adopt the euro, will have to pre-qualify by joining the new ERM.

F

Factortame

Few law cases have so jolted British opinion as the Factortame case. Factortame was a one-ship shelf company, Spanish-owned but registered in the UK to enable its owner to exploit the British fishing quota in the Atlantic under the Common Fisheries Policy (CFP). This practice, known as quota-hopping, was outlawed by Parliament in 1988 under a new Merchant Shipping Act, but Factortame sought to set aside the Act, claiming that it was suffering discrimination, contrary to the Treaty of Rome.

The Divisional Court suspended the Act temporarily. The Court of Appeal reversed that decision, backed by the House of Lords, which observed that no English court could set aside 'Parliament's sovereign will' on the mere grounds that Parliament might subsequently be overruled by the European Court of Justice (ECJ). The Lords did, however, refer the question to the ECJ, which reversed the Appeal Court's ruling, whereupon the Lords suspended the Merchant Shipping Act, pending a final decision by the ECJ on the substantive issue.

Subsequently, the ECJ ruled again in favour of the Spanish, dismissing the argument that the intent of the CFP was to permit discrimination to protect the livelihood of fishermen. Both decisions of the ECJ caused distress and surprise in the UK, where the public had been lulled by facile assurances. The effect on the British fishing industry gave rise to considerable ill feeling, and the revelation that an Act of Parliament could be so lightly set aside opened the eyes of many Britons for the first time to how far their sovereignty had already been surrendered.

Failure to act

The concept of failure to act as a misdemeanour arises in the EU from the lack of an executive branch armed with the backing of an elected central government. The Treaty of Rome allows member states or Community institutions to bring proceedings before the Court of Justice if the European Parliament, the Council of Ministers or the Commission infringe the Treaty by failing to carry out any of its provisions. If the complaint is upheld, the Court may require the institution concerned to take remedial measures. The best-known case was that bought by the Parliament in 1983 against the Council for failing to give legal force to a common transport policy (the Court was sympathetic, but deemed the policy too vague to form the base of an action at law). The same principle is applied to a member state's failure to transpose a Directive into national law. The 1990 Francovich case established that a citizen who suffers damages from a government's non-fulfilment of such an obligation is entitled to compensation.

Federalism

To opponents of a European superstate federalism denotes a political system dominated by supranational bodies or by the majority will of European governments, at the expense of the individual nation state. In deference to this fear, expressed most cogently by the UK and Denmark, the F-word was eliminated from the Maastricht Treaty, a concession rated highly by Prime Minister John Major but regarded with amused contempt by President François Mitterrand, Chancellor Helmut Kohl and Commission President Jacques Delors.

The day of the nation state is over.
Roman Herzog, president of Germany, September 1996

To those accustomed to a federal structure, federalism denotes the sharing of power between the constituent parts and the centre – that is, the converse of a fully centralised political system. Many Germans therefore affect puzzlement at British concerns, some going so far as to say that, far from resisting it, the UK ought logically to make federalism its objective.

Although federation is too ill-defined a concept to bear the weight of close analysis, it clearly implies a national union of some sort. Quebec, Scotland, California and Bavaria, for example, each has autonomy in varying degree, but they are not considered sovereign states since the superior authority rests with government in Ottawa, London, Washington and Bonn (or Berlin). A confederation is looser than a federation, allowing more power to the subordinate political units, yet even in confederate Switzerland the ultimate right of decision belongs to Berne.

The powers traditionally allocated to the federal authorities cover defence, foreign policy, the currency, central taxation, the supreme court of appeal, the signing of treaties, nationwide legislation, immigration, policing and citizenship. The EU has already taken over many of these areas from the member states and has ambitions towards the remainder. Against that background, semantic quibbles about the meaning of federalism are trivial compared with substantive discussion of the EU's treaties, laws and institutional arrangements. (See also **Europe of Nations, Sovereignty** and **Treaty on European Union**.)

FEOGA

See **Common Agricultural Policy**.

Finland

An independent state only since the 1917 Russian revolution, Finland was under effective Soviet domination from the end of World War II until the end of the Cold War, a term of its retention of some autonomy being its adoption of neutrality. Finland joined the Nordic Council and the United Nations in 1995, EFTA (of which it had previously been an associate) in 1986 and the Council of Europe in 1989, in each case deterred from more timely membership by fear of its eastern neighbour.

On the collapse of Soviet communism Finland applied in 1992 for membership of what was about to become the European Union, obtaining admittance in 1995. The economy, which had previously depended partly on barter trade with the Soviet Union, suffered badly in the early 1990s but has since started to recover. The country is a member of the ERM, with a 15% fluctuation band, and will participate in the first wave of the single currency.

Fiscal dumping

The charge of attracting inward investment by virtue of lower taxes. Like competitive devaluation and social dumping, the phrase suggests a desire on the part of Europe's high-cost economies to level up costs within the EU. The chief targets include Ireland, Spain, Belgium and the Netherlands, which give special tax incentives to international companies, and Luxembourg, which is a comprehensive tax haven. The UK, too, as a country with a relatively benign tax regime, may not be immune from attack.

The Community's competence in the fiscal area had hitherto been regarded as covering only VAT and other indirect taxes, but in 1997 the Commission drew up plans for a voluntary code of conduct aimed at countries with a 'significantly lower than average' business tax rate. This move was seen as the thin end of the wedge for intervention by Brussels in a field previously reserved for national governments. (See also **Harmonisation**.)

Fischler, Franz (1946–)

An Austrian politician and a lifelong agriculturalist, Franz Fischler became the EC Commissioner for Agriculture in 1995, inheriting the intractable problems of CAP reform and soon walking into the 'mad cow disease' crisis.

Flexibility

The 1997 Treaty of Amsterdam disappointed some integrationists (and encouraged others) by endorsing the principle that the Community's institutions could occasionally be used by a majority of member states to achieve their objectives without involving all the remaining member states. The Treaty does not, however, provide much comfort for sceptics, since such flexibility, or closer co-operation, is available only as a last resort and on the basis that the *acquis communautaire* is unaffected. (See also **Two-speed Europe**.)

Fontainebleau Agreement

In 1984, frustrated at the EC's lack of progress, François Mitterrand determined to use the French presidency to resolve a number of outstanding issues at the Fontainebleau meeting of heads of government. Spain's and Portugal's accession was pushed forward, the budget resources were augmented, the rise in agricultural spending was to be moderated and studies were initiated for creating a political union and a People's Europe. Above all, the long-running problem of the excessive British contribution to the budget was solved. The Fontainebleau Agreement gave the UK its abatement, known also as the British rebate, thereby terminating a dispute originated by Margaret Thatcher in 1979.

Football

The most popular spectator sport in Europe, football has seen the emergence of outstanding club and national teams in all the leading EU countries. The 1995 Bosman ruling of the Court of Justice (named after a Belgian footballer) held that professional football, as an economic activity, was subject to Treaty law on free movement of services and banned quotas limiting the number of players from other member states eligible to play in club competitions. The ruling also enabled players to negotiate their own terms of transfer, breaking the ability of clubs to collect large transfer fees on players whose contracts had expired. The resulting increase in the remuneration of star players helped to widen the gap between rich and poor clubs.

Fortress Europe

The defence of Europe's economic interests through protectionism rather than adaptation to the global market. In reality the Fortress Europe approach is more or less confined to the CAP and to the intermittent mercantilism of France, since Germany and the UK are essentially free traders.

Fouchet Plan

The name of Fouchet, a French diplomat, would doubtless have languished in obscurity for ever had he not been made the mouthpiece of Charles de Gaulle's designs for Europe in 1961 and 1962. De Gaulle had two aims: to sever Europe's dependence for military security on the Atlantic Alliance and the USA; and to restructure the Community by turning it into a voluntary union of independent states, based in Paris, with extensive national veto powers over all common policies. The Fouchet proposals envisaged the emasculation of the Commission and the Council of Ministers and the subjection of Community law to national law.

The five other member states of the Common Market rejected Fouchet's plan, prompting a violent attack by de Gaulle on Commission President Walter Hallstein; this in turn led to widespread ministerial resignations in France. There followed the vetoing of the UK's application to join the Community in 1963, the French boycott of Community institutions in 1965 (the empty chair crisis), the Luxembourg Compromise in 1966 and finally a decade and a half of institutional paralysis in Europe, lasting for a dozen years after de Gaulle's death. To this day the spectre of Fouchet's plan is evoked in Brussels whenever a proposal surfaces that smacks too much of national autonomy.

Founding Fathers

The EU has a pantheon of prophets and heroes, who are endowed in retrospect with special foresight of the European destiny. The first of these in modern times was Count Coudenhove-Kalergi (1894–1972), who convened a series of pan-European congresses shortly after World War I and remained an advocate of a United States of Europe until well after World War II. Although an intimate of statesmen from many countries, he never managed to create an enduring institution, perhaps hindered by his own statelessness (his mother was Japanese, his father a part-Flemish, part-Greek Austro-Hungarian diplomat).

The socialist Aristide Briand (1862–1932), 11 times premier of the French Third Republic, who helped to negotiate the 1925 Locarno pacts on European frontiers, is claimed by his countrymen as a European pioneer. In 1929 he advocated a European Federal Union within the framework of the League of Nations, his real motivation being the containment of Germany. His German opposite number, Gustav Stresemann, embraced Briand's proposal not for reasons of Europeanism but in the hope of exploiting it to restore German hegemony in Central Europe.

The 1939-45 war years saw the birth of various different strands of Europeanism. A yearning for peace inspired models of a new world government – if freedom survived – more effective than the League of Nations had been after World War I. Failing world government, a United States of Europe might be a more attainable aim. Nor was such thinking confined to idealists – several German and Vichy French planners conceived a post-war order based on a European Economic Area with a single currency and a customs union. It is, however, politically incorrect to mention this latter phenomenon, and the names of Alfred Six, Walther Funk, Werner Daitz and Alphonse de Château-briant have been consigned to oblivion.

Federalists were also to be found among neutralists and in the active Resistance movements. Of politicians from this era, the Belgian socialist grandee Paul-Henri Spaak, who spent most of the war in the UK and later rose to prominence in the United Nations and NATO, has a strong claim to prophet status, based on his presidency of the Assembly of the Council of Europe from 1949 to 1951 and his chairmanship of the committee which authored the report leading to the 1957 Treaty of Rome.

The first universally acknowledged Founding Fathers, however, were Jean Monnet and Robert Schuman. The 1950 plan to pool the German and French coal and steel industries was named after Schuman, premier and subsequently foreign minister of France soon after World War II. This was the forerunner of the Treaty of Paris in 1951, which established the European Coal and Steel Community, which in turn was the forerunner of the later European Community.

---

*The amazing progress of technology, the shrinking of distances thanks to
modern communications ... and the present-day tendency to form wider
associations and larger areas for joint economic development ...
all these compel Europe to unite more closely. Europe has become too small
for ... self-contained sovereignties.*
Departmental memorandum to von Ribbentrop, Berlin, 1943

The brain behind the Schuman Plan was that of Jean Monnet, who, like Altiero Spinelli and Walter Hallstein, devoted the best years of his life to the cause of European unity. Together these three (Monnet and Hallstein technocrats, Spinelli a romantic communist in the Italian resistance) constitute the Holy Trinity of the early faith, the precursors of Jacques Delors. Each in his own way had a consistent vision of a single European state, in which recalcitrant nation states would progressively be transformed into colourful regions.

Among national politicians, Alcide de Gasperi of Italy, Valéry Giscard d'Estaing and François Mitterrand of France and Konrad Adenauer and Helmut Schmidt of West Germany were noted Europeanists. So, too, in his very different way, was Charles de Gaulle. None, however, has surpassed Helmut Kohl, whose single-minded dedication was the driving force behind EMU and the Maastricht Treaty in the 1990s.

It is to be noted that none of the accredited European heroes is British. Winston Churchill believed in a Community led by a reconciled France and Germany, to which the UK would be but loosely linked. Harold Macmillan and

Harold Wilson applied to join the Common Market out of weakness, not conviction. Edward Heath and Roy Jenkins have the strongest claims, but the first is insufficiently regarded at home and the second a touch too bonhomous and epicurean to qualify for the top table of visionaries. (See also **European idea**.)

Four freedoms

The 1957 Treaty of Rome sets out four freedoms which should characterise the internal market and lay the foundations of an ever closer union among the peoples of Europe – the free movement of goods, persons, services and capital.

France

France's relationship with the Community falls into three phases. Initially, through Jean Monnet and the Schuman Plan, France built on ideas with roots in the inter-war years and in the Vichy period, the crucial element being that France was now the victor, not the vanquished. The overriding aim was political: to contain Germany by co-mingling the French and German basic industries of coal and steel, so as to ensure that there could be no repeat of the three wars, initiated by Bismarck, the Kaiser and Hitler, which had devastated France in 1870, 1914–18 and 1939–45. As Monnet developed his federalising vision he found his ideal bureaucratic counterpart in the German Walter Hallstein, the energetic first president of the European Commission, while at the governmental level Konrad Adenauer went so far in 1950 as to propose the union of France and Germany. In economic terms, France's objective was to foster its countryside by agricultural protection in exchange for allowing Germany a freer market in industrial goods.

Italy and Benelux were also founder signatories to the Treaties of Paris and Rome, in which Alcide de Gasperi and Paul-Henri Spaak played important roles, but the Franco-German *entente* was the bedrock of the European Community, and even when Charles de Gaulle inaugurated a new phase of French policy, with his hostility to the Anglo-Saxons and his insistence on a Europe of Nations, the expression of German dismay was muted. In 1963, at the height of his ten-year battle with the Commission, de Gaulle signed the Treaty of the Elysée with Adenauer, which was to set the pattern for the alliance of France and Germany through thick and thin until the present day. Meanwhile, the outcome of the struggle over the direction of the Community was a temporary stalemate. De Gaulle's plans to restore authority to the member states were frustrated, but in the Luxembourg Compromise he won an enhanced role for the national veto, which effectively intimidated the Commission into paralysis for years to come.

On de Gaulle's retirement in 1969, successive French governments, starting with Georges Pompidou's, returned to federalism, albeit never without that tinge of nationalism that distinguishes the French approach from that of Germany, Italy, Benelux and the Commission itself. It is one of Europe's ironies that France's instincts for independence are similar to the UK's. Yet France has retained its reputation as a good European by always in the end choosing the federal path, confident in its ability to lever German economic might into French diplomatic power and doubtless mistrustful of the permanence of any understanding with the UK. Pompidou's successor, Valéry Giscard d'Estaing, was characteristic of French attitudes. In 1974 he established the summitry of the European Council as an instrument to bolster the influence of member states and in 1977 he vehemently opposed Roy Jenkins' initiative to elevate the presidency of the Commission into *pari passu* status with heads of government.

By the early 1980s President François Mitterrand was willing to make a dead letter of the Luxembourg Compromise. Nevertheless, he continued the policy of European integration *à la Française*, resisting German reunification in 1989, opposing an increase in the number of German MEPs, taking a cavalier approach to Community rules on state subsidies and coming within an inch of wrecking the GATT negotiations in 1993. In each case, a deal, not always of the most appetising nature, saved the day. Most of his term of office coincided with the Commission presidency of his fellow French Socialist, Jacques Delors. Together they saw through the Single European Act of 1986 and the Maastricht Treaty of 1992, the latter often seen as a way of enabling France to dilute German monetary hegemony in return for not blocking German reunification.

> *Europe is the way for France to become what she has ceased to be since*
> *Waterloo: the leading power in the world.*
> General de Gaulle to Alain Peyrefitte, 1962

Economically, France is a rich and successful country, by most measurements the world's fourth largest (behind Germany and slightly in front of the UK). But to foreign eyes, some of its triumphs seem Pyrrhic. Since 1987 the government's *franc fort* policy of keeping parity with the D-Mark has brought a heavy cost in unemployment. That French public opinion has doubts about EMU was shown by Mitterrand's desperately narrow victory in the Maastricht referendum; and although the economy began a strong recovery in 1998, the strikes and government cave-ins of 1997 showed the fragility of civil consensus in times of difficulty.

There are even signs of strain in the hitherto unshakeable Franco-German alliance. France's protectionist and anti-American stance in trade negotiations is at odds with Germany's liberal, Atlanticist approach. Moreover, as EMU approaches, Mitterrand's Gaullist successor, Jacques Chirac, and his Socialist premier, Lionel Jospin, have advocated some political influence over the euro, fearing a deflationary Bundesbank-style management of the currency that might fuel unemployment. Chancellor Helmut Kohl, by contrast, having invested so much political capital in EMU, is reluctant to ask his people to exchange their strong D-Mark for a less stable currency. These differences have been heightened by the at times frosty relationship between Chirac and Kohl and by disputes over foreign policy and nuclear testing. In 1998 the impasse caused by Chirac's unsuccessful attempt to place a Frenchman at the head of the new European Central Bank added another source of tension.

So long as Germany still hesitates to assert itself 50 years after World War II, the alliance will no doubt survive such disagreements intact. The *pensée unique*, or sole consideration of French policy, places judicious friendship with Germany at the centre of the government's strategy. Thus Europe edges towards statehood in accordance with German wishes while France enjoys the illusion, or the reality, of leadership of the Continent. Were this arrangement ever to run its course, for example if other countries' voices were to become more authoritative or if the next generation in Germany were to feel less insecure politically, French nationalism, never far beneath the surface, might gain strength, with incalculable consequences for the future of Europe.

Francovich ruling

Francovich, an employee of an insolvent Italian company, claimed that he would have received greater financial protection if Italy had transposed into law a 1980 Directive on the treatment of employees in cases of bankruptcy. In 1990 the European Court of Justice held that Francovich was entitled to compensation from the Italian government for its failure to enact the necessary enabling legislation. This was a landmark ruling, which established that an individual citizen could have rights under Community Directives even before they had been implemented domestically.

Fraud

The amount of Community-specific fraud is unknowable. That it is 'huge', 'continuing' and 'a public scandal' (House of Lords Select Committee report, 1994) is clear, and it has been estimated by the Court of Auditors at up to £6,000 million per year. Most of this fraud is related to the Common Agricultural Policy and to the disbursement of subsidies, a recurrent problem being that member states (especially those which benefit most from Community payments) have little interest in detection, since this would result in them having to make repayments.

The same Lords report noted 'a worrying absence of indignation' about a situation which merited 'the collective outrage of European taxpayers'. An element in this apparent indifference is the attitude of the Commission, which uses the problem as an excuse to seek legal harmonisation and to extend the Community's powers of investigation and prosecution, but otherwise downplays it.

Among colourful examples of malpractice have been the £3,400 million of levies misappropriated from the Community by Italy and Spain from 1989 to 1993 by cheating on milk quotas (the fine – reimbursement – was reduced by £800 million under threat by the two countries to block the EU budget and veto the admission of new member states to the Community); £1,000 million worth of wheat reported by the Court of Auditors in 1994 as mysteriously missing; the painting of fake olive trees by Greek farmers to fool satellite photography and boost subsidies; the Irish 'cattle carousel', whereby cattle cross and recross the Ulster border, collecting export subsidy as they pass; and some spectacular abuse of the structural funds, especially, it is alleged, by Italian business (said to have collected some £5,000 million of regional aid improperly over three years).

Over 80% of Union funds is disbursed by member states; and the reluctance of countries to encourage greater Commission participation in detection must to some extent absolve it from blame. Nevertheless, the December 31st 1996 Statement of Assurance of the Court of Auditors, referring to the Community's 1995 financial year, was a damning indictment. The Court was 'unable to express any opinion' on 2.3% of Community payments (approximately £1,300 million); the 'probable cumulative amount for the very numerous substantial errors' arising from irregular transactions amounted to approximately £3,300 million, though there were 'too many errors' for the Court to be able to give 'overall assurance'; many of the defective systems had been in operation 'for many years'; and the best the Court could say in conclusion was that 'it is probably reasonable to conclude that around nine-tenths of Community payments' are properly disbursed 'except to the extent that they might be affected by concealed deliberate irregularities'.

The Court's report on the 1996 year was little better. For the third year running no assurance could be given as to the propriety of the Community's payments. The Commission was 'unable to properly assume its role in managing the budget'. Between £2.2 and £2.9 billion had been wasted in excessive CAP subsidies. Within the Economic and Social Committee and the Committee of the Regions, abuse of travel allowances had become the norm. In the Court's opinion, the Commission's accounting and systems had failed to keep pace with the expansion of its activities, and this was largely responsible for opening up the possibilities of large-scale undetected fraud.

Free movement of capital

One of the four freedoms which laid the foundations of the Common Market, the free movement of capital between member states was not fully accomplished until nearly 40 years after the signing of the Treaty of Rome in 1957. Sporadic upheavals in foreign exchange markets, combined with variations in the strength of individual EU economies, served as reasons for delay in the case of Spain, Portugal, Greece and Ireland and for allowing the exceptional use of protective measures in the event of a financial emergency. The 1992 Maastricht Treaty, however, set Europe on the path to EMU, a goal incompatible with any remaining restrictions; and the resultant fiscal discipline imposed on member states aspiring to join the single currency has enabled them to enjoy freedom of capital movement not only within the Community but also in their external economic relations.

Free movement of goods

The first of the Treaty of Rome's four freedoms which laid the foundations of the Common Market, the free movement of goods between member states was characterised initially by the complete abolition of internal customs duties and quotas. This was accomplished by 1968. There are, however, other methods of favouring domestic producers, such as discriminatory product specification, VAT, nationalistic public purchasing policy and unreasonable bureaucratic barriers. Each of these has been tackled progressively by the Commission, the major breakthrough being the Single European Act of 1986, which extended qualified majority voting to single market legislation, enabling the Commission to sweep away a host of restrictions. (See also **Cassis de Dijon case**.)

Free movement of persons

The free movement of persons, the second of the four freedoms enshrined in the Treaty of Rome, has ramifications well beyond the economic sphere. Initially, because it had been framed in the context of laying the foundations of the Common Market, freedom of personal movement was construed as an objective applying to workers. But with the Community's growing integration a wider interpretation came to prevail. Various Directives established rights of residence for students and retirees, while the Court of Justice held that individual EU citizens have the right of free movement throughout the Community, provided they can show that they will not be a financial burden on the host member state. The dismantling of border controls as part of the single market programme in the late 1980s was followed by the Schengen Agreement, the 1992 Maastricht Treaty and the 1997 Treaty of Amsterdam, each marking stages of a process designed ultimately to abolish all internal European frontiers.

Unlike the goals of free movement of goods, services and capital, which were directed solely at easing the operation of the Common Market, freedom of movement of persons raises fundamental sovereignty issues connected with citizenship, immigration, terrorism and organised crime. For the time being, therefore, its full accomplishment is subject to the national veto and is likely to remain a sensitive matter.

Free movement of services

One of the Treaty of Rome's four freedoms which laid the foundations of the Common Market, the free movement of services allows professionals to practise anywhere in the EU (except as a public official). Although the principle of free movement of services was established early, it took over 15 years before mutual recognition of qualifications was achieved, enabling lawyers, architects, doctors and others to surmount national barriers. Even then, subtle ways were found to inhibit foreigners from providing domestic services. (See also **Discrimination**.)

Free trade area

A free trade area differs from a customs union in that each of the member countries may have its own individual tariffs or other trading arrangements with third party states, whereas in a customs union there is a uniform external trade regime. Another feature of a free trade area, such as that constituted by NAFTA (the North American Free Trade Agreement), is that it carries no federal political implications.

A free trade zone – precisely what we have been trying to avoid for the last 25 years.
Yves-Thibault de Silguy, commissioner for economic and monetary affairs, on the consequences of a delay in EMU, 1997

Freedom of establishment

Part of the wider four freedoms laid down by the Treaty of Rome, freedom of establishment is the right to set up in business or as a professional service provider anywhere within the EU without discrimination.

G

G-3

The idea, sometimes bruited by the Commission and other federalists, of a Group of Three – the EU, the USA and Japan – to replace the existing Group of Seven leading economic powers as the principal forum for global financial discussions.

G-7 and G-8

See **Group of Seven**.

G-10

The monthly meeting of ten central bank governors from leading economies (all but three of them European), namely Belgium, Canada, France, Germany, Italy, Japan, the Netherlands, Sweden, the UK and the USA.

Gaitskell, Hugh (1906–63)

Hugh Gaitskell became leader of the Labour Party in 1955, but died suddenly in 1963, opening the way for Harold Wilson to win the 1964 general election. Gaitskell's speech to the party conference in 1962 remains a seminal text on Europe. After giving a balanced account of the pros and cons of the UK joining the EEC, including the cost of abandoning Commonwealth preference, he turned in famous words to federalism: 'We would be foolish to deny ... the desire of those who created the Economic Community for political federation.' Likening the UK's destination within the EEC to 'no more than a state in the United States of Europe, such as Texas and California', he said that federation would mean 'the end of the UK as an independent European state'.

Gaitskell went on to criticise Harold Macmillan's duplicity in enthusing about political union in Brussels while denying it in the House of Commons, and entered a passionate plea for the UK not to dishonour its pledges to safeguard Commonwealth trade. His premature death deprived the country of a potential prime minister who might have altered the course of the UK's relationship with Continental Europe.

GATT (General Agreement on Tariffs and Trade)

Superseded in 1995 by the World Trade Organisation (WTO), the GATT was established in 1948, as an adjunct of the UN, for the regulation of international trade. Technically an agreement rather than a chartered body, the GATT evolved a life of its own, with a secretariat in Geneva, the backing of the USA and a list of signatories accounting for some 90% of world trade. From the outset it was dedicated to the elimination of discrimination and the reduction of barriers to trade, and perhaps more than any other institution it was responsible for the almost uninterrupted growth in prosperity among developed countries since World War II. At the end of the last round of negotiations in 1994 (the Uruguay Round) average duties on manufactured goods, which had been over 40% in the 1940s, were scheduled to fall to 3% by 2002.

The GATT rules cover all aspects of trade, including dumping, dispute resolution, retaliation, rules of origin, intellectual property rights and the administration of certain specially permitted discriminatory agreements (known as multilateral agreements) in such areas as textiles and agriculture. As a regional trading arrangement the EC is excepted from the most favoured nation requirement, which in principle bars states from giving preferential tariff treatment to each other.

Although the individual countries of the EU are members of the WTO and signatories to the GATT in their own right, the Commission negotiates on their joint behalf in matters of international trade – no easy task given the divergence of attitudes, ranging from France's protectionism to the UK's free trading traditions. On more than one occasion during the Uruguay Round it seemed that an impasse had been reached on agricultural levies, with the EU feuding with the USA and both the Council of Ministers and the Commission splitting over France's intransigence, which threatened to provoke a global trade war. In 1994, after a last-ditch compromise had been achieved, the Commission sought clarification from the Court of Justice as to where the authority for ratification lay. The Court ruled that the Commission had exclusive competence over trade negotiations between the EU and the future WTO, and that the member states and the Commission had shared competence over intellectual property and some services.

German Europe

The containment of Germany has been an objective of other European states, especially France, for at least 75 years. In 1951 Jean Monnet and Robert Schuman designed the European Coal and Steel Community expressly to prevent German industrial hegemony. Fearful of stirring mistrust, Germans have acquiesced enthusiastically in their own absorption. Whether that would result in Germany dominating the EU or merely playing a proportionate supporting role has been succinctly posed in the question: 'A German Europe or a European Germany?'

Partitioned and demilitarised after World War II, Germany's recovery has depended on exercising collective influence in NATO and the EU. It rejects the idea of the national veto, attributing Europe's past conflicts to the nation state. For democratic legitimacy it seeks to build up the European Parliament, in which after reunification it commands more seats than any other country. Germany is the driving force for further European integration, culminating in its support for EMU.

In many ways the EU has already been shaped along German lines. The social dimension of the Maastricht Treaty reflects the Rhine model rather than the Anglo-Saxon free-market approach, and the D-Mark dominates a currency zone which includes France, Benelux and Austria. The structure of the future European Central Bank in Frankfurt and the party lists and coalitions of the Parliament mirror German institutional arrangements. The very idea of a federal Europe is based on the Federal Republic of Germany.

On the other hand, Germany is a stable democracy, the EU's chief paymaster and the epitome of prosperity, peacefulness and sensible bourgeois virtues. A less Europeanised Germany would not have been able to contribute to the collapse of the Soviet satellite empire by acting as such a powerful magnet to the neighbouring peoples of Central Europe.

The paradox of Germany's position, then, is that having earned by its responsible behaviour the right to be called the most European of nations, it has nevertheless stamped its image so firmly on the EU's institutions as to have converted part of Europe into something approaching a German dominion.

The more European our foreign policy is, the more national it is.
Hans-Dietrich Genscher, German foreign minister, Vienna 1989

Germany

After the country's defeat in World War II, Germany was divided into four occupied zones – US, British, French and Soviet. Berlin, itself divided into the same four zones, lay in the Soviet sector, and in 1949 East Berlin became the capital of a grim new Soviet satellite state, the German Democratic Republic, known as East Germany. At the same time the Federal Republic of Germany, or West Germany, was formed from the three western zones, with Bonn as its capital. For a year in 1948/49, Berlin was blockaded by the Soviet Union but rescued from starvation by an allied airlift, thus preserving a lone beacon of freedom behind what Winston Churchill in 1946 had called the Iron Curtain lowered on Europe by Stalin. In 1961, to stem the westward flow of refugees, the communists built the Berlin Wall, which was not torn down until the collapse of the Soviet empire in 1989 paved the way to the reunification of the country and the demise of East Germany.

Against this background, the German story over the last 50 years is one of great achievement. It is principally that of a few strong men, Konrad Adenauer, Ludwig Erhard, Walter Hallstein, Willy Brandt, Helmut Schmidt and Helmut Kohl, and their complex relationship to their country's troubled past and to their neighbours.

Germany's war guilt still casts its shadow. No 'good German' speaks of nationalism without a shudder (the contrast of the UK's positive historical consciousness of nationhood and German recollections of National Socialism bedevils discussion of sovereignty between the two countries). Germany's response to its own legacy has been to seek rehabilitation through integration with a federal Europe, although whether the main result of this policy has been to dilute Germany's power or to extend its reach remains a matter of lively debate (see **German Europe**).

Some of the ideas that came to shape the modern Europe have a long history in German thought. In the Third Reich and Vichy France German conquest was rationalised as the beginning of a vigorous new European order capable of standing up to Bolshevism and challenging the Asian and Anglo-Saxon worlds. Earlier still, World War I planners in Berlin had nurtured visions of a customs union stretching across *Mitteleuropa* from France to the Russian frontier. Defeat, partition and the communist threat wrought a transformation in these ideas, which were now inherited by a peaceful new generation wedded to democracy and determined to anchor itself in friendly alliances: with NATO and the USA against the Soviet Union; with France as an assurance against another Western war; and with the EEC as a stepping stone to stability and prosperity. These efforts were rewarded with astonishing success. A reunified Germany is today free from threats on either border. It is rich and highly regarded as a reliable ally. If doubts about excessive power remain, they are as often the self-doubts of Germans as the misgivings of its neighbours.

West Germany's yearning to be reaccepted as a civilised nation after World War II coincided with Churchill's vision of Franco-German reconciliation within some form of united Europe. West Germany was established with a new constitution in 1949, entering the Council of Europe in 1950. Meanwhile, Chancellor Adenauer was pursuing friendship with France and unsuccessfully proposed complete union of the two countries in 1950. His policy of integration continued with the signing of the Treaty of Paris in 1951, the North Atlantic Treaty in 1955 and the Treaty of Rome in 1957. Germany's Francophile strategy, sealed by the 1963 Treaty of the Elysée, did not, however, blind it to other priorities, some of which were anathema to Charles de Gaulle. Adenauer was pro-American and favoured British membership of the EEC; Erhard spearheaded economic recovery along free-market lines and was opposed to French-style protectionism, even to a customs union; and Hallstein was an ardent federalist, a policy continued under Adenauer's successors, Brandt, Schmidt and, since 1982, Kohl.

Overhanging all post-war German questions was the issue of reunification. Brandt had instituted *Ostpolitik*, or détente with the East, a policy greeted with caution, even suspicion, in anti-communist circles. When the Berlin Wall came down in 1990 François Mitterrand and Margaret Thatcher reacted to the potential enlargement of Germany with visceral alarm, as did Italy's premier Andreotti, but Kohl pushed ahead resolutely. Mitterrand, recognising the inevitable, switched tack, accepting reunification in exchange for the Maastricht Treaty, which he saw as a new version of France's longstanding policy of German containment.

The future will belong to the Germans ... when we build the house of Europe.
Helmut Kohl

Reunification presented the Community with severe technical obstacles, relating chiefly to the *acquis communautaire*, Russian troops and East Germany's treaties. East-West German trade was already free, however, and transitional arrangements were soon agreed. The united Germany was incorporated into NATO and in 1994 the last of Russia's 350,000 soldiers departed. The cost of reunification was incalculable. On top of some DM13 billion paid to the Russians, there was the expense of cleaning up East Germany's pollution, the cost of building an infrastructure and the disguised cost of exchanging the D-Mark for the worthless Ostmark on a 1-for-1 basis. Priced out of the labour market, East Germans migrated westwards in search of jobs, while high interest rates, designed to forestall inflation, fed through into Europe-wide recession and volatile foreign exchange markets.

Reunification added 17 million to Germany's population and 30% to its land area. Already Europe's largest country, it was now even more dominant. Germany's number of MEPs was consequently increased from 81 to 99, though its weight in qualified majority voting in the Council of Ministers remained unchanged. Impotent in the 1991 Gulf War and the Bosnian crisis, Germany reflected its maturing political status by amending its constitution in 1994 to allow German troops to be deployed outside its own borders on UN-backed operations.

1998 marked Kohl's 15th year as chancellor, by which time he had progressively realised his mission of a united Germany in a united Europe. He has staked his reputation on the single currency, against the advice of the prestigious Bundesbank and seemingly against the wishes of the majority of his fellow citizens. Years of weak and divided coalition opposition, however, combined with German abhorrence of any action that could be construed as a reversion to nationalism, have ensured that EMU has gone surprisingly unchallenged. Political indecision has also been responsible for the country's inability to undertake tax and labour market reforms in the face of mass unemployment. Further problems as the millennium approaches are the influx of refugees from Eastern Europe and the trend of manufacturing industry to invest abroad rather than incur Germany's excessive social and regulatory costs. Many would have preferred Kohl to concentrate on solving such domestic difficulties; thus the extent to which Germany's European policy will survive his eventual re-placement by a younger political generation is a great imponderable.

Gibraltar

See **Small countries**.

Giscard d'Estaing, Valéry (1926–)

Vain, patrician, intelligent and condescending, Valéry Giscard d'Estaing became president of France in 1974, having previously been finance minister under Charles de Gaulle and Georges Pompidou. His presidency was marked by the oil crisis, when soaring petroleum prices stifled growth and caused inflation and unemployment. During the seven-year period when their leadership of their respective countries coincided, Giscard's friendship with Helmut Schmidt ensured that France and Germany together determined all major EC policies – an echo of de Gaulle's relationship with Konrad Adenauer and a forerunner of François Mitterrand's with Helmut Kohl.

Giscard initiated the replacement of intermittent summits by regular meetings of the European Council. More importantly, he teamed up with Schmidt to support Roy Jenkins' revival of the cause of Economic and Monetary Union. He was, however, sufficiently Gaullist to resist strongly (if unsuccessfully) the idea that Jenkins, as Commission president, should be treated on a par with heads of government; and when Margaret Thatcher became prime minister he fought her hard over the issue of the British contribution to the European budget.

Defeated by Mitterrand in 1981, Giscard later briefly became an MEP and for many years continued to champion the European cause as president of the European Movement.

Globalisation

The ability to supply goods or services globally and to acquire them from the most competitive source in the world. This is a growing phenomenon, resulting from falling tariffs, the spread of technology and the mobility of international capital.

Blamed by protectionists for Europe's economic underperformance and by developing countries for exchange rate instability, globalisation has led to calls for import or capital controls, depending on the standpoint of the complainant.

Goldsmith, Sir James (1933–97)

Wealthy Anglo-French entrepreneur, who personally financed the British Referendum Party; author of *The Trap*, advocating protectionism in developed economies against low-cost, chiefly Asian, competition; French MEP (1994–97); and dedicated opponent of faceless bureaucracy.

González, Felipe (1942–)

As Spain's Socialist prime minister for nearly 14 years until his defeat in the 1996 general election, Felipe González steered his country into the European Community in 1986 and presided over its emergence from the aftermath of dictatorship into its current standing as a robust democracy. A strong and popular character, González remains a candidate for high office within the EU, provided that he escapes contamination from the 'dirty war' once waged by his government against the Basque separatist ETA guerrillas.

Greece

The cradle of Western civilisation and democracy, Greece traces its history back more than 4,000 years. Within a span of some 150 years from 480 BC to 330 BC, Greeks created the cultural and intellectual framework for the empires of Alexander the Great and Rome. After many subsequent vicissitudes, Greece fell under Turkish rule for nearly 400 years, regaining its independence in 1829. The next 100 years saw intermittent armed conflict with Turkey. In World War II Greece was occupied by Italy and Germany, succumbing to virulent civil strife between Marxists and right-wing militarists, which continued after the war. A prolonged effort to unite with Cyprus ended in 1974 with the partition of the island following a failed Greek coup and a Turkish invasion. The monarchy was abolished the same year and elections were reintroduced after seven years of rule by colonels.

Greece was admitted to the EU in 1981, becoming its poorest and least harmonious member. The country is one of the main beneficiaries of European subsidies, but pays little heed to Community policies, preoccupying itself with its ageless vendetta against Turkey, including vetoing the Turkish application for EU membership. Greece is also hostile to the former Yugoslav republic of Macedonia, on the grounds of its alleged territorial ambitions over Greek Macedonia. The country has been making efforts to prepare for the single currency by strengthening its financial controls and joining the Exchange Rate Mechanism, but will not qualify for the first wave of participants.

Green currencies

Green currencies represent an artificial common exchange rate for farm products, designed to equalise prices regardless of currency fluctuations. A country with a strong currency, which would otherwise have suffered from selling produce at the less valuable common exchange rate, used until 1992 to be recompensed by monetary compensation amounts; the opposite applied for a country with a weak currency. The single currency will render obsolete this system, which was modified in 1993, having over many years protected German farmers from the consequences of the rising D-Mark. The timing of the sharp increase in the value of the pound in 1997–98 was thus particularly unfortunate for British farmers. (See also **Common Agricultural Policy**.)

Green parties

At the national level, European concern about the environment has been reflected in the emergence of Green political parties, especially in Germany and Sweden. The German Greens, divided between pragmatic 'realos' and fundamentalist 'fundis', are potentially powerful enough to act as kingmakers in domestic coalition governments, and also comprise a sizeable minority among German MEPs. In the European Parliament, some of the Greens are allied with the far left.

Greenland

Greenland is chiefly remarkable in European circles for being the only country to have withdrawn from the EC. This it achieved in 1985, having gained a substantial measure of independence from Denmark in 1979 (before 1953 it was a Danish colony; between 1953 and 1979 it was an integral part of Denmark, in which capacity it joined the Community in 1973). Greenland is paid by the EU for access to its fish and continues to qualify for structural funds.

Group of Seven (G-7)

The seven leading developed countries – the USA, Japan, Germany, France, the UK, Italy and Canada – which meet regularly at head of government and finance minister level, with the president of the EU in attendance, to discuss economic issues. The occasion is also generally used to add discussions of international political affairs, in which case the foreign ministers are present. The G-7 will become the G-8 if Russia (currently an observer) becomes a full member.

H

Hallstein, Walter (1901–82)

A law professor who had been West Germany's foreign minister under Konrad Adenauer, Walter Hallstein was the author of the doctrine of refusing diplomatic relations to any country that recognised East Germany. In 1958 he became the first president of the European Commission, an office which he held for nine years (barely less than Jacques Delors). Hallstein's independent ideas, which clashed sharply with those of Charles de Gaulle, were aimed at increasing the Commission's authority; more fundamentally, he believed that economic integration naturally led towards political union. He stood his ground so effectively as to cause France to boycott the EC and the European Parliament for the last six months of 1965. (See also the **Empty chair crisis**.)

Hard core

Germany, France, Benelux and Austria, the countries which already form a *de facto* hard currency bloc based on the D-Mark and are regarded as the bedrock of EMU, in contrast with the supposedly less austere Club Med countries.

Hard écu

The idea that the EC should adopt a non-exclusive common currency, instead of a single currency, was floated by the British government in 1990, but rejected by the other member states as insufficiently *communautaire*. The proposal was to create a 'hard écu', that is, one that could not be devalued against any national European currency. The difference between the hard écu and the discredited ECU was that the latter, being a basket of currencies, had suffered from the extreme weakness throughout the 1980s of some of its components such as the drachma and the escudo.

Harmonisation

Harmonisation (referred to in the Treaty of Rome as approximation) is the legal process of standardisation implicit in the creation of the single market. If carried too far harmonisation can also represent levelling down, with the effect of ironing out comparative advantages and so reducing the global competitiveness of EU firms. An interesting test case in 1998 was that of the London art market, which with New York had long ranked as the world's two leading international art trading centres. VAT (introduced in 1995 at the Commission's insistence on works imported from outside the EU) reduced imports to the UK by 40% between 1994 and 1997, driving London's business to New York, Geneva and Hong Kong. The Commission, which had set the VAT rate at an experimentally low level of 2.5%, plans to increase it to 5% in 1999, while at the same time imposing *droit de suite* (a royalty to artists or their descendants) on modern art. These rules, which apply in many of the unsuccessful art markets of Europe, would indeed harmonise the UK with the rest of the EU, but at the expense of fatally damaging one of London's – and Europe's – more glamorous businesses, together with its many ancillary trades.

A less intrusive approach to harmonisation had been made possible by the 1979 Cassis de Dijon case, in which the Court of Justice forbade Germany to ban the marketing of a French liqueur which met French requirements but did not match German standards of alcoholic content. This decision established the principle of mutual recognition, making it unnecessary to enforce detailed legislation to ensure that European products could be sold across borders (before the Cassis de Dijon judgment, the Commission had been obliged to redefine the carrot as a fruit to allow Portuguese carrot jam to be marketed in the Community).

With the growing integration of the EU, however, the pendulum has swung back towards a more activist approach, in which new forms of harmonisation are being turned to the service of the federal cause. Some degree of alignment of indirect tax levels has always been accepted within the Community, albeit modified by cultural differences, such as the Greek preference for relying on direct tax and the north European puritanical leaning towards high duties on spirits. But direct tax is the prerogative of the nation state, so that any attempt to insert the EU into this field is sensitive. Nevertheless, prompted by Continental unemployment and mindful of the ability of Ireland, the UK and the Netherlands to create jobs with their low-tax regimes, some in Europe have suggested harmonisation of corporate tax rates. This proposal would, in its authors' eyes, achieve several objectives simultaneously: it would eliminate the unfair advantage of 'fiscal dumping'; it would contribute to a more socially oriented society (for the harmonisation would doubtless be upwards, to a level designed to finance improved welfare); and it would establish the EU's right to occupy another part of the battlefield previously reserved to the member states. Against this it was argued that the proposals were anti-competitive and likely in the long run to destroy jobs, as well as being an infringement of national competence.

The 1997 Treaty of Amsterdam broadened the scope of harmonisation into the field of criminal law, proposing a strengthening of Europol to combat Community fraud and foreshadowing the eventual alignment of police and judicial methods of detection, arrest and trial throughout the EU. EMU will also have a harmonising effect. The stability pact will reduce governments' freedom of fiscal manoeuvre, and the single currency will dispose of exchange rate variations. Further standardisation of indirect and direct taxation would leave the management of member states' economies almost entirely in the hands of Brussels. Yet although this macroeconomic process is being conducted largely in the name of completing the single market, there is still much to be done before harmonisation achieves its aims in the world of day-to-day business, where many forms of national protectionism survive.

Overall, the verdict on harmonisation must remain ambivalent. Under the control of interventionists it is a powerful weapon for working towards a unitary European state; but under a minimalist system organised on free-market principles, it would be an indispensable tool for raising transparency and eliminating restrictive practices.

Heath, Sir Edward (1916–)

Allegedly converted to the Europhile cause as a young officer during World War II, Edward Heath was in good company in attempting, as part of Harold Macmillan's Conservative government, to negotiate the UK's entry in 1961 into the then Common Market, an attempt brought to an abrupt halt in 1963 by the veto of Charles de Gaulle. In 1970, as prime minister, he completed the negotiations started by his Labour predecessor, Harold Wilson, and in 1972 the UK signed the Treaty of Rome. The terms which Heath obtained were controversial, and when he lost power in 1974 the incoming Labour government sought to amend them. But it was too late. Heath had accepted the Common Fisheries Policy, which caused Norway to vote against joining the EEC. His pledge that the UK would not turn its back on the Commonwealth was barely compatible with the Common Agricultural Policy, and his re-assurances that British sovereignty would not be impaired were at odds with the advice of government legal officers about the supremacy of Community law. Doubtless his objectivity, like his negotiating stance, was undermined by the sincerity of his belief in the UK joining the Community. In his later years he claimed to have been a long-standing federalist.

Helsinki Final Act (Helsinki Accords, Helsinki Agreement)

In 1975, 35 countries (the USA, Canada and all the European countries except Albania, which after Stalin's death had allied itself to China) signed the Helsinki Final Act on human rights and security, the centrepiece of what are known as the Helsinki Accords. To the West, as to thousands of oppressed dissidents, the Helsinki Agreement signalled acceptance by communist regimes of individual entitlement to civil liberties in return for the settlement of frontiers. Among the Iron Curtain dictatorships, the Agreement was regarded as principally a propaganda exercise to weaken Western resolve to oppose communism militarily and politically; indeed, for a citizen in the Soviet bloc to cite it in aid of human rights was to invite severe reprisals. The Brezhnev Doctrine, to the effect that the Soviet Union had the right to intervene in the affairs of its satellite states, was in contravention of several clauses in the Final Act establishing the principles of non-interference and renunciation of force. But the West allowed the Brezhnev Doctrine to continue unchallenged until it was terminated at the end of the 1980s with the disintegration of the Soviet empire. (See also **OSCE**.)

Herzog, Roman (1934–)

President of Germany since 1994, Roman Herzog is given to forthright pronouncements on the German malaise and European stagnation, which he has attributed to the dead hand of over-regulating government and the consequent dearth of innovation.

History of the European Union

Readers looking for a historical perspective of the Union can use the chronology table in Appendix 1 as a framework. For the early origins, see Founding Fathers. For the later history, see especially Common Agricultural Policy, Council of Ministers, EMU, European Commission, the European idea, the European Parliament, France, Germany and The UK and Europe. Of the entries on individuals, those on Churchill, Monnet, Adenauer, de Gaulle, Delors, Mitterrand, Thatcher and Kohl cover much of the Union's historical evolution.

Hungary

Hungary fought on the German side in World War II and after defeat in 1945 was pulled under the domination of the Soviet Union. By 1952 the entire economy had been redrawn along communist lines. An uprising in 1956, the consequence of popular demands for Soviet troop withdrawals and free elections, was violently crushed and a new Soviet-backed puppet administration under Janos Kadar was put in place. Kadar remained in power until 1989, having in the meantime been compelled by declining living standards and growing foreign debt to introduce some economic reforms. In 1989, as the Soviet empire collapsed, the formation of political parties in Hungary was finally allowed, and late in the year the national Assembly declared the country an independent democratic state.

The advent of economic liberalisation in Hungary proved traumatic. Despite the privatisation of almost half of the country's state businesses, greater trade with the West could not immediately compensate for the severing of links with the Soviet Union and the disruption of trade with Yugoslavia occasioned by the Bosnian crisis. Disillusionment with the conservatives led to the victory in the 1994 elections of the refashioned Communist Party, renamed the Hungarian Socialist Party, under a former Stalinist, Gyula Horn, who prudently formed a coalition government to mark his transformation into a social democrat.

A debt crisis in 1995 prompted a round of market-oriented reforms, with dramatic effects. The influx of foreign capital rose, the overseas debt was reduced and GDP turned upwards. Hungary applied for membership of the EU in 1994 and voted to join NATO in a 1997 referendum, albeit on a turnout of under 50%. About 60% of the country's external trade is with the EU, which has accepted Hungary among the next group of favoured candidates. Nevertheless, the country's still difficult economic situation, with high inflation and a GDP per head of some 25% of the EU average, leaves a number of hurdles to overcome.

Hurd, Douglas (1930–)

As foreign secretary from 1989 to 1995, Douglas Hurd presided over the UK's Maastricht Treaty negotiations and played a leading role in the EU's ultimately ineffectual policy during the Bosnian crisis. With Chancellor Kenneth Clarke, Hurd was widely believed to have been responsible for dissuading John Major from taking a more robust stand against British membership of the single currency.

I

Iceland

A member of the European Free Trade Association since 1970 and the European Economic Area since 1992, Iceland is strongly opposed to membership of the European Union, since that would mean accepting the Common Fisheries Policy, which would effectively destroy Iceland's all-important fishing industry.

IGC (Intergovernmental Conference)

IGCs are summoned whenever a new Community treaty is in the offing, the participants being the EU member states, in the person of ministers and senior civil servants, with the Commission in attendance. The calling of an IGC creates a climate in which greater integration is taken for granted, only the degree of progress being left open for negotiation. Up to and including the 1992 Maastricht Treaty an obsessive secrecy was always observed in the pre-meetings, on the grounds that diplomatic bargaining positions would be prejudiced by transparency. The IGC preceding the 1997 Treaty of Amsterdam was less secretive, but many key points were not exposed to democratic debate. When the draft text emerged, its obscurantist wording, like that of Maastricht, showed a notable disregard of the need for comprehension by national parliamentarians, let alone the general public.

Information

The stated policy of the Commission is to supply objective information about the EU. This is not, however, a neutral activity, for the Commission's devotion to federalism often causes it to go beyond the facts and construe its task as leading citizens to 'think along European lines'. The estimated $300 million or more per year spent by the Community in this field, combined with the fact that there is no formal opposition to the Commission's political standpoint, makes it appropriate, if perhaps a little harsh, to deal with the subject under the heading propaganda. For the period 1998–2002, the main emphasis is on persuading people to accept the euro in place of their national currencies.

Intergovernmental

Between (sovereign) governments – an adjective used to describe relationships in Europe which are not subject to Community law or governed by supranational EU institutions. For example, defence policy is intergovernmental, that is, decided by member states working voluntarily together, whereas the Common Agricultural Policy is a Community policy, decided by majority voting under regulations designed by the Commission and enforced by the European Court of Justice.

Internal market

Another term for the single market; also known as the common market, although that expression has wider connotations.

Internet (1)

Attempts to make the European Union more accessible have not always been productive. The documentation that arrives daily at the European Documentation Centres is too voluminous to be successfully catalogued, and the blank spines of the *Official Journal* make finding the relevant issue a tedious business. The EU Internet site goes some way to rectifying the problem. Situated at http://europa.eu.int, the site provides recent news, information on the EU's institutions, an ABC (or citizens' guide) to the supposed benefits of European integration and summaries of Community policies. The site gives access to Rapid, a database which offers up-to-date press releases and texts of speeches, and to Eurostat, which provides sample statistics on such issues as convergence. There is also the facility to view official publications, such as the treaties and the Court of Auditors' Reports. For an alternative view, the *Daily Telegraph* offers a free Euronet site at its own web site http://www.telegraph. co.uk, providing comment on current affairs and rapid access to recent treaties. Links to connected web sites make this a useful place to start a search for European information.

Internet (2)

Internet usage in the EU is less than half that of the USA, but it is growing rapidly, incidentally reinforcing the ascendancy of the English language in Europe. Commercial revenue generated by European web sites is projected to rise from 2 billion ECUs in 1997 to some 50 billion ECUs by 2001.

Intervention

The purchase of unsold agricultural produce by the Community for storage – an expensive feature of the Common Agricultural Policy, which has the effect of propping up prices and creating surplus supply.

Ireland

A founder member of the Council of Europe, but never a member of EFTA, the

Republic of Ireland applied to join the EEC in 1961, encountering the same vetoes from Charles de Gaulle as the UK. De Gaulle's successor, Georges Pompidou, lifted France's objections and Ireland acceded to the Community simultaneously with the UK in 1973. In a referendum held before accession, over 80% of the votes were favourable, principally because of the prospect of generous agricultural subsidies.

Catholic, neutral in World War II, with a leaning to the German side and a long history of feuding with the UK, the Irish were further attracted by the expectation of emerging from the shadow of their Protestant neighbour to *pari passu* rank as a European state. In 1979 Ireland joined the Exchange Rate Mechanism, thereby breaking the 58-year link between the punt and the pound sterling.

The country is a strong supporter of the EU, a natural result of being the largest net recipient per head of Community cash (EU subsidies account for over 5% of Ireland's GDP). The Republic's constitution necessitated a protocol to the Maastricht Treaty condoning the prohibiting of abortion but asserting the right of Irish citizens to information on clinics abroad. Another difficulty is Irish neutrality, given the prospect of an eventual common EU defence policy. This, however, has not been a bar to the accession of Austria, Sweden and Finland and an extensive cosmetic discussion is in progress to redesign the meaning of neutrality. A second referendum in 1992 resulted in a two-thirds majority in favour of ratifying Maastricht.

The Irish experience of life in the EU has been positive. The Republic's economy has consistently outpaced its European neighbours. At the cost of being accused of fiscal dumping, it has attracted foreign capital by offering generous tax breaks to business. It is enjoying net immigration for the first time for centuries and it anticipates growth for the next decade at a rate normally associated with emerging market economies. Ireland hopes to reach the average EU standard of living by 2005, and with tight fiscal controls and continuing Community subsidies it not only qualified to join the single currency in the first wave but was even able to achieve a modest revaluation of the punt.

Iron Curtain

Winston Churchill's prophetic 1946 description of the Soviet Union's oppressive clampdown on Eastern Europe, leading to the Cold War. The original Iron Curtain countries were Albania, Bulgaria, Czechoslovakia, East Germany, Hungary, Poland and Romania (the Warsaw Pact signatories), with Yugoslavia on the sidelines, communist but independent. Albania defected to an alliance with Maoist China in 1968, while Romania, under the dictator Ceausescu, pretended in the 1970s and 1980s to a degree of autonomy that it did not possess.

Isle of Man

See **Small countries** under **Channel Islands**.

Isoglucose case

In the 1979 isoglucose case (the details of which are of no importance) the European Court of Justice established that the Council of Ministers was not entitled to treat consultation of the European Parliament as a trivial formality. Failure to consult properly, where the Treaty of Rome prescribed a certain procedure, could result in Community legislation being declared void.

Italy

Never deeply blamed for its part in World War II or taken over-seriously as a belligerent, Italy found peace-time reconciliation relatively easy. Under Alcide de Gasperi, a former member of the Resistance who founded the Italian Christian Democratic Party and served as prime minister from 1945 to 1953, Italy joined NATO and signed the Treaty of Paris. After de Gasperi came a long succession of weak coalition governments (more than one a year on average since 1945), which followed his policy of becoming a founder member of each institution of the European Community, but left the active shaping of Europe's destiny to France, Germany and the Commission. Italy contented itself with unswerving support for federal initiatives – doubtless mainly because of cynicism on the part of Italians about the quality of their own political administration, which they saw as corrupt and chaotic, although another factor will have been an undeveloped sense of nationhood. In 1989 Italians voted by a large majority in a consultative referendum for the principle of being governed by the European Parliament.

The size of Italy's black economy is a matter as much of pride as of shame (it was the basis of the claim in the 1980s to have overtaken the British economy); and the country's disappointing record of compliance with Community Regulations and Directives (not to mention imaginative exploitation of Community subsidies) is greeted with a shrug of the shoulders. Over the years, financial indiscipline has resulted in frequent devaluations and an exorbitant national debt. Nevertheless, despite these shortcomings, Italy has been one of Europe's outstanding success stories. Its economy has grown rapidly, based largely on the vigour and design skills of its small and medium-sized enterprises in the north, so that from impoverished post-war beginnings the country has become as prosperous as the average EU member state.

After the 1992 Maastricht Treaty, Italy set its heart on acquiring a reputation for financial rectitude in order to become one of the first wave participants in the single currency. It has made considerable progress in fiscal consolidation, though its debt legacy from the spendthrift years will take decades to shrink and it is a source of concern that since the 1996 elections the centre-left coalition government of Romano Prodi has sometimes had to rely on the support of the Communist Refoundation Party. Nevertheless, when the choice of participants was made by heads of government in 1998, Italy was deemed to have done enough to qualify for immediate membership, despite residual German doubts about the durability of the country's anti-inflationary policies. France was not alone in wishing to dilute Germany's hyper-orthodox influence over the euro by admitting Italy, a reward merited not only by the country's loyalty to the EU but also by its unique contribution to European civilisation.

J

Jenkins, Roy (1920–)

Roy Jenkins held high office in Harold Wilson's Labour government between 1965 and 1970, a period which included Charles de Gaulle's veto of the UK's application for membership of the EEC. In 1971 Labour, now in opposition, voted against the terms of accession negotiated by Edward Heath, but Jenkins defied the party whip to support the Conservatives. By 1974 Wilson was back in power, and after a trivial renegotiation the issue of the UK's membership of the Community was put to a referendum in 1975. The active part played by Jenkins in the pro-European campaign helped cost him the leadership of the Labour Party on Wilson's retirement, and in 1976 he left domestic politics to become the UK's first and only president of the Commission.

The urbane and sybaritic son of a Welsh coalminer, Jenkins was ideally suited to Brussels, taking easily to the mandarin life. He observed his fellow Eurocrats amusedly, with a biographer's perceptive eye, and pleased the smaller countries by procuring for the Commission president a permanent seat alongside heads of government at the top table of summit meetings. His principal European initiative was a renewed attempt to launch EMU in 1977 (a previous attempt in the early 1970s had collapsed). This led to the European Monetary System in 1979, whose grandiose aims of 'lasting growth with stability' and 'a progressive return to full employment' were made to seem empty by the ensuing period of instability, stagnation and joblessness. Jenkins returned to the UK to found the Social Democratic Party, which later merged to become the Liberal Democrats, the only national party which has been consistently and wholeheartedly committed to the EU.

Always advance along the line of least resistance provided that it leads in approximately the right direction.

Advice given to Roy Jenkins by Jean Monnet

JET (Joint European Torus)

Based near Oxford, JET's research objective is the development of nuclear fusion as a safer energy source than nuclear fission. The siting of JET was the subject of a notorious dispute between the UK and Germany, eventually settled in 1977 at head of government level as part of a characteristic EC trade-off involving more important, but unconnected, policy issues. To date, JET has produced no useful results.

Joint Action

Unanimously agreed action by member states in the field of foreign affairs or home affairs. Under the Maastricht Treaty the implementation of any joint action would normally be governed by qualified majority voting.

Jospin, Lionel (1937–)

Elected prime minister of France in 1997, Lionel Jospin proclaimed traditional socialist policies during his campaign, raising the prospect that he would put economic reflation at the top of the political agenda, even if that meant jeopardising France's participation in EMU. Within weeks of becoming premier, however, he abandoned many of his pre-election pledges and set about reducing France's budget deficit – albeit through tax increases rather than President Jacques Chirac's preferred conservative method of expenditure cuts. These steps towards fiscal consolidation, together with an economic upturn, emboldened Jospin to reassert belief in the single currency.

Justice and Home Affairs (JHA)

One of the three pillars of the EU formalised by the Maastricht Treaty, JHA refers to the anticipated integration of member states' operations in various fields of common interest, including fraud and organised crime, asylum and immigration, customs, civil and criminal judicial co-operation and the creation of a European Police Office, Europol. The Maastricht Treaty only requires member states to inform and consult each other in these areas, with action essentially limited to joint positions and voluntary joint actions, subject to national veto. But the Treaty of Amsterdam goes further, bringing border control into the *acquis communautaire*, creating new civil rights and foreshadowing the ultimate harmonisation of national laws and criminal procedures. As a result the JHA name was changed at Amsterdam to Police and Judicial Co-operation in Criminal Matters.

These developments have given rise to concern in several countries, particularly the UK, with its common law evolved by precedent over centuries and its concept of the law as a bastion of protection for the individual – traditions very different from the processes and presumptions of the European civil codes descended from Napoleonic law. Although intergovernmental co-operation in JHA has some modest achievements to its credit, such as simplifying extradition and improving the exchange of police intelligence, these cannot be attributed to the Treaties; and the 'full association' of the European Commission in judicial affairs prescribed at Maastricht and Amsterdam suggests that civil liberties may be on their way to falling under the sway of bureaucracy.

The approach of the Commission towards JHA has been pragmatic. Where a specific opportunity presents itself, such as combating Community fraud, integration is pushed forward vigorously with the aim of making the remedies enforceable at the EU level through the Court of Justice; but where the Commission encounters resistance, it resorts to general principles in the form of Declarations or Treaty Articles. A particularly sensitive area is that of border controls. French unhappiness over the Schengen Agreement to abolish European frontiers, caused by Dutch laxity over drug trafficking, led to France reintroducing passport checks in 1995. In 1997, however, the Treaty of Amsterdam substantially incorporated Schengen into Community law. (The UK, which was opposed to any weakening of its defences against terrorism or unwanted immigration, obtained an opt-out from that section of the Treaty.)

Towards the end of 1997, fears arose throughout the EU that illegal immigrants might exploit internal freedom of movement within the Community to circumvent European asylum law. Fleeing Kurds from Turkey, Moroccans and Algerians from North Africa and Albanians and others from Eastern Europe alerted many countries, especially Germany, to the ease of entry to the EU through slack control or inadequately monitored coastlines. Italy and Greece were singled out as particularly negligent and the beginning of 1998 saw a flurry of emergency meetings of interior ministers, amid fears that the Schengen Agreement (and, with it, elements of the Treaty of Amsterdam) might unravel.

As with the other intergovernmental pillar, the Common Foreign and Security Policy, JHA raises the issue of sovereignty. Having conceded the supremacy of Community law, and being for the most part about to surrender their currencies and control over their economies, member states have little left of the distinguishing marks of autonomy other than defence, foreign policy and home affairs. If these areas, too, are to become the province of the EU, the nation state will effectively cease to exist. For this reason, France's Constitutional Council has ruled that the Treaty of Amsterdam will require an amendment to the French constitution, and Denmark is true to its own robust and independent traditions in putting the Treaty to a referendum. (See also *Corpus Juris*.)

K

Karlsruhe (German Constitutional Court)

Karlsruhe is the home of the German Federal Constitutional Court. In 1993 anti-Maastricht campaigners led by Manfred Brunner, a former *chef de cabinet* to a German commissioner, Martin Bangemann, challenged the compatibility of the Treaty with the Basic Law of the Federal Republic. At issue was whether the Basic Law, which allows the transfer of sovereign powers to intergovernmental institutions, would also allow the transfer of such powers (including the management of the currency) to the EU, which was supranational. The Court ruled that since two of its pillars were intergovernmental, the EU was not a genuine state; the Treaty could therefore be ratified. In the Court's view, the EU was a confederation, not a federal state. On a second issue, the Court held that the democratic guarantees of the Basic Law were protected by the supervisory powers of the European Parliament.

The alleged manipulation of national accounts in the run-up to EMU led in 1998 to a renewed challenge in the Constitutional Court, on the grounds that the safeguards contained in the Maastricht Treaty had been evaded. The Court, however, declined to accept the case, doubtless reluctant to overturn a decision of the Bundestag and the Bundesrat (Germany's lower and upper houses), despite the expressed reservations of the Bundesbank and the apparent unpopularity of the euro among voters. (See also **Ratification**.)

Kohl, Helmut (1930–)

A man of vast physical bulk and uncomplicated political beliefs, Helmut Kohl has for some years been a dominating figure in Europe, though perhaps underrated in Germany, where the demise of his career has been frequently predicted and as frequently falsified by events.

As a boy Kohl saw at first hand the final throes of a war in which his brother was killed and which he attributed simplistically to nationalism. During his formative years the idea of a natural connection between the nation state and political confrontation – even armed conflict – became fixed in the German consciousness, informing Kohl's lifelong approach to the development of the EU and leading to repeated clashes with Margaret Thatcher and John Major, both of whom saw national sovereignty, expressed through elected parliaments, as the bastion of democratic legitimacy.

Kohl joined the Christian Democratic Union (CDU) at 17, serving his political apprenticeship as a centrist conservative in the Rhineland–Palatinate *Land* and becoming the party leader in 1973. In 1982 he became chancellor of the Federal Republic when the Free Democrats switched coalition allegiance from the Socialists to the CDU. He has remained chancellor ever since, winning four elections and becoming the longest-serving German head of government since Bismarck. He owes his political longevity partly to the weakness of his opposition and partly to his skill and indefatigability in behind-the-scenes bargaining, an essential feature of any coalition administration.

In foreign affairs, Kohl has been a strong supporter both of NATO and of the Franco-German alliance. He has never wavered in pushing forward European integration, a cause in which he found his staunchest allies in the socialists Jacques Delors and François Mitterrand. He was one of the architects, and the most vehement proponent, of EMU, which he saw as a milepost on the road to European political union. He did not allow the occasional disagreement with France (for example, over French protectionism or nuclear testing) to overshadow a relationship which he conceived, like his predecessors Konrad Adenauer and Helmut Schmidt, as the power-house of European progress.

The fall of the Berlin Wall in 1989 was a defining moment for Kohl. His single-minded determination to seize the opportunity to achieve German reunification was rewarded in 1990 when, despite the misgivings of Mitterrand, Thatcher and Italy's Giulio Andreotti, he incorporated the former communist German Democratic Republic first into the Federal Republic and then into the EC. This triumph, however, carried with it the seeds of future problems. The poverty of the new eastern *Lander* of Germany became a severe financial burden, exacerbated by Kohl's decision to overrule the Bundesbank and exchange the Ostmark at parity with the D-Mark. The run-up to EMU also created economic difficulties, and Kohl's obsessive concentration on European affairs, combined with the virtual paralysis of decision-making within the coalition, led to postponement of much needed domestic reforms in tax and labour markets.

Kohl did not share with President Jacques Chirac the same sense of common purpose he had enjoyed with Mitterrand. Moreover, the French National Assembly elections of 1997, which brought the Socialists to power, heightened concern in Bonn that France might lack the stomach for the strong euro which Kohl had promised German voters so as to induce them to abandon the D-Mark. Meanwhile, with unemployment in Germany rising to some 4.5 million, a level not seen since Hitler's years, the country's once unquestioned European industrial supremacy looked less assured. As the 1998 federal election approached, commentators once again were predicting that Kohl's position was on the verge of being untenable, although the arithmetic of coalition politics made the outcome far from certain.

L

Languages

The EU has 11 working languages, requiring both translation and simultaneous interpretation, and a 12th official language, Irish Gaelic, into which the Union's treaties and certain other key documents are translated (Austria, Belgium and Luxembourg share official languages with other member states). Currently, the most troublesome language is Finnish, which among European tongues is related only to Hungarian and Estonian. The number of EU linguistic combinations, already 110, will more than double when the next round of enlargement is completed early in the 21st century, bringing with it a crop of new and generally unfamiliar Slavonic languages.

Approximately one-third of the Commission's staff are interpreters or translators. Despite the assistance of machine translation, the ever-expanding volume of paperwork represents a heavy burden. Accordingly, proposals have been made from time to time to reduce the number of working languages to three or four, which would particularly ease the problems of the European Parliament, where language skills are low and the output of amendments, reports and draft legislation prolific. But fear of offending small member states – and of frightening off new applicants – has so far been enough to prevent reform.

Latin Monetary Union

In a rare (perhaps unique) previous attempt to achieve monetary union without political union, France, Belgium, Italy and Switzerland, soon joined by the Papal States and Greece, determined in 1865 to use the French franc as their common unit of account, while nominally retaining their own national currencies, each with silver coins of identical weight and value. The system came under pressure almost immediately when Italy and France printed paper money to finance wars. Later it disintegrated when the silver price collapsed to below its value as legal tender. The resultant rush to mint silver coins and exchange them for hard currency led to unsuccessful demands for France to guarantee unconditionally the gold value of the other countries' reserves. The Union finally collapsed some 30 years after its inception.

Some have suggested a parallel between the Latin Monetary Union and EMU, with speculation against, for example, the lira leading to demands for a German guarantee of value. Striking as the similarities are, however, the dissimilarities are too important to enable such conclusions to be drawn.

Latvia

Dominated by Russia with little interruption since 1795, Latvia was annexed by the Soviet Union in 1940 under the infamous Molotov-Ribbentrop pact, invaded by Nazi Germany in 1941, recaptured by the Soviet Union in 1944 and finally liberated in 1991, after clashes with Soviet troops. Having been forcibly integrated into the USSR's command economy, Latvia has found the transition to free markets difficult and its application for early membership of the EU has not been recommended by the Commission.

League of Nations

The League of Nations, founded in 1920 after World War I, was the precursor of the United Nations. Idealistic and ineffective, it operated by unanimity and failed to cope with Mussolini's aggression in Abyssinia or Hitler's invasions of Austria, Czechoslovakia and Poland. Germany, which had been admitted in 1926, withdrew in 1933, as did Italy in 1937. The USA never became a member. Jean Monnet was a senior official in the League, from which he doubtless drew the lesson that voluntary co-operation alone was not enough to prevent nationalism and war.

Legal instruments

The EC's principal legal instruments are Directives, Regulations and Decisions, each of which takes precedence over national laws. These all derive, some loosely, from clauses or general principles in the Treaty of Rome, the Maastricht Treaty, the Single European Act and the various national Accession Treaties. The choice of instrument, unless specified in a Treaty, is largely at the discretion of the Commission. (For the volume of legislation see **Directives** and for a general description see **Community law**.)

Level playing field

The seemingly high-minded ideal that all member states should be treated equally. Sometimes, as when attempts are made to prevent fraud or the evasion of Directives, the term lives up to its promise. Often, however, it is used to justify protectionism or excessive harmonisation. The Social Chapter, from which the former British prime minister, John Major, negotiated an opt-out, but which the Labour government has adopted, invokes the level playing field principle to foreshadow the imposition of rules and legislation over a wide range of social and employment issues. The intrinsic harm of the concept is that it is generally based on levelling down; by seeking to achieve equality of outcome it attacks the principle of comparative advantage, thereby striking a blow at the free-market system on which the global competitiveness of European companies is based. (See also **Fiscal dumping** and **Social dumping**.)

Liberalism

A word with two clear but opposite meanings and a hazy intermediate meaning.

1 As used by Continental commentators (often pejoratively), liberalism denotes the Anglo-American model of free-market economics, in contrast to the European welfarist system generally known as social democracy.
2 As used by American commentators, liberalism denotes left-wing political and economic ideas, in contrast to free-market principles.
3 In the UK, liberalism generally refers to centrist, libertarian or progressive values, but is also used in senses (1) and (2).

Liechtenstein

See **Small countries**.

Lithuania

Long a buffer state between Germans and Asiatics, Lithuania was under Russian domination from the late 18th century, was annexed by the Soviet Union in 1940 under the infamous Molotov-Ribbentrop pact, invaded by Nazi Germany in 1941, recaptured by the Soviet Union in 1944 and finally liberated in 1991, after clashes with Soviet troops. The country was industrialised by the Soviet Union and forcibly integrated into the USSR's command economy, making the subsequent transition to a free-market economy very difficult, and its application for early membership of the EU has not been recommended by the Commission.

Lobbyists

Despite the rapid growth of all forms of lobbying in Brussels, there is not as yet a register of professional lobbyists or pressure groups. Approximately 13,000 people are believed to be engaged in 'interest representation' in the city.

Lomé Convention

The Lomé Convention (named after the capital of Togo, where the Convention was first concluded in 1975) is a three times renewed trade and aid agreement between the EU and 70 African, Caribbean and Pacific (ACP) states. These ACP countries, mainly former colonial territories of EU member states, enjoy duty-free access to the Community on almost all their exports, as well as grants from the European Development Fund (financed by member states but administered by the Commission) and soft loans from the European Investment

Bank. The Fourth Lomé Convention of 1989 covers the years from 1990 to 2000. Under its terms the EU contributes development aid totalling 26 billion ECUs over the ten-year period; in return it gains secure access to raw materials. A key feature of the Convention is its stabilisation fund to offset fluctuations in commodity prices. This includes the purchase of cane sugar at the EU's artificially high internal market price, so as to assist the former British Caribbean states whose livelihoods were threatened by the end of Commonwealth preference when the UK joined the EEC in 1973. The Lomé agreement also contains less explicit agendas – it is a lucrative source of contracts for French industry selling into Africa – and it is intended to support political stability in some of the most volatile parts of the world.

By 1995 it was clear that the Lomé strategy required an overhaul to de-emphasise subsidies and give priority to education, business promotion and infrastructure projects. Growing realism about the counter-productive effects of ill-targeted aid prompted the Commission to mount a review of resource allocation in advance of the forthcoming Fifth Lomé Convention. Meanwhile, the prospect of expensive new commitments closer to home, particularly in Eastern Europe, was giving rise to concern whether the EU budget, already under severe constraint, would be able after 2000 to sustain the same level of assistance to the ACP countries as before.

Luxembourg

The smallest and richest member state of the EU and one of the founders of the Community, the Grand Duchy of Luxembourg derives its prosperity partly from its status as a tax haven and partly because many of the institutions of the EU are located there.

Luxembourg Compromise

A loose arrangement which was never recognised by the Commission or the European Court of Justice, the 1966 Luxembourg Compromise effectively extended the life of the national veto beyond the transitional period allowed in the Treaty of Rome. Its genesis was the impasse known as the empty chair crisis, when France boycotted Council meetings for the last six months of 1965 in protest against bureaucratic supranationalism and the advent of qualified majority voting, thereby immobilising the Community. President Charles de Gaulle took the line that the Treaty of Rome was ambiguous or flawed, and that it was unthinkable that France should be outvoted by foreigners. Under the Luxembourg Compromise any decision which affected 'a very important national interest' would be deferred until a unanimously acceptable solution could be found, regardless of whether the Treaty prescribed majority voting.

There were various interpretations of what counted as a vital interest and of the situation that would arise if agreement could not be reached, but the practical effect of the Compromise was to paralyse Community decision-making for the next 17 years.

Although the Compromise had no legal status and was seldom formally invoked, the spectre of another debilitating row killed off many Commission initiatives without a vote being taken. Unpassed draft regulations piled up and the single market programme stagnated, but fears that the imposition of laws by majority verdict might cause the EC to fragment delayed any serious re-examination. Gradually, however, the mood changed. A British attempt to block the CAP prices settlement in 1982 stiffened the resolve of the other member states (not least France, whose attitude had changed after François Mitterrand became president in 1981) to restrict the veto to matters of genuine national importance. The Stuttgart Declaration of 1983 sounded the death knell of the Compromise, accompanied by a flurry of explanatory minutes from all ten member states.

If the Luxembourg Compromise had continued in use, the single market would not have come into existence and the Maastricht and Amsterdam Treaties would not even have reached the drafting stage. It remains, some say, as a theoretical weapon of last resort, but most national interests of importance are covered by the unanimity principle or by opt-outs, and the Community's affairs are now so extensive that the invocation of the Compromise on an issue of middling significance would invite painful retaliation. For practical purposes, therefore, the Compromise has been consigned to history.

M

MacDougall Report

The 1977 MacDougall Report, named after its chairman, an economic adviser to the CBI, was produced at the request of the Commission. It studied public finance in the context of the EEC's move towards great integration, concluding that the Community should be spending 2–2.5% of member states' total GDP in a pre-federal stage; 5–7% in a federal small public-sector stage; and up to 25% in a federal large public-sector stage. The EU currently spends some 1.2% of the aggregate GDP of its members. Thus the MacDougall Report recommended something between a doubling and a 20-fold increase in Community spending, depending on the degree of Europe's federal ambition.

Although MacDougall's budgetary conclusions, which were aimed at redistribution and economic adjustment, have been conveniently shelved, they had an uncomfortable logic; and both the structural funds and the concept of convergence owe much to his report.

Maastricht Treaty

The Maastricht Treaty, signed in 1992 and officially known as the Treaty on European Union, introduced several important amendments to the existing Treaties and signalled the largest advance in European integration since the 1957 Treaty of Rome. Its central features were EMU and the establishment of the European Union by the addition of two new fields of policy co-operation: the Common Foreign and Security Policy (CFSP) and Justice and Home Affairs (JHA). These new areas were formulated as intergovernmental responsibilities, rather than responsibilities of the Community, an arrangement which was to a limited extent modified subsequently in the 1997 Treaty of Amsterdam, where the Community was given more of a role in providing policy guidelines. Together with the Community itself, the CFSP and JHA constituted the three pillars of the EU.

The ratification of the Treaty came near to disaster on several occasions, notably when it was rejected in a Danish referendum in 1992, accepted by the narrowest of margins in a French referendum the same year and only passed by the UK's House of Commons after unprecedented pressure by the whips in 1993. Nevertheless, it survived a second Danish referendum and a ruling by the German Constitutional Court to pass eventually into law, its obscure phraseology reflecting an uneasy compromise between integrationists and those who favoured a Community of voluntarily co-operating nation states. A notorious example was subsidiarity, a concept explained by the British government as recognising the vital role of national lawmakers and simultaneously explained by Continental politicians as recognising the superior role of the Community.

The main legislative part of the Treaty concerned the implementation in progressive stages of economic and monetary union. There would be a fixed timetable, leading to the adoption of the single currency by those member states which were able to meet the convergence criteria. The British government accepted participation up to the preparatory Stage Two, but arranged an opt-out from Stage Three, when exchange rates would be irrevocably locked, the euro would come into being and national currencies would be abolished.

Other features of the Treaty included the expansion of the structural funds to supply aid to the poorer EU regions; the widening of the competence of the Commission to cover new areas such as education, culture, public health, consumer protection, trans-European networks, industry and the environment; the creation of the position of Ombudsman; and the formal introduction of the concept of citizenship of the Union.

A significant intention at Maastricht was to expand the Community's social dimension by introducing policies covering such aspects as workers' health and safety, workplace conditions, equal pay and the consultation of employees. These aspects were to be included in a separate section of the Treaty, called the Social Chapter. The British government refused to agree to this section being incorporated in the body of the Treaty and insisted on an opt-out. The 11 other members who supported the Chapter agreed to make it a protocol to the Treaty, which was not binding on the UK. In 1997 the incoming British Labour government cancelled the opt-out and agreed to sign the Social Chapter, which was thereupon put back into the main text as revised by the Treaty of Amsterdam.

After the Maastricht Treaty had been signed, such was the complexity of the drafting and so great the exhaustion of the negotiators that many of the protagonists had little clear idea of its meaning. The British team was temporarily proud that the word federal appeared nowhere in this most federalising of documents. The public throughout Europe was baffled, and the unemployment that ensued in the mid to late 1990s did nothing to endear voters to a Treaty that they mistrusted and suspected of being at least partly responsible for the recession.

In 1997 the Treaty would undergo substantial amendment in the Treaty of Amsterdam. To distinguish between the original text and the later version, it is sometimes convenient to call the first one the Maastricht Treaty, reserving the technically correct Treaty on European Union for the amended and consolidated text. Likewise, those parts of the Treaty of Rome that were amended at Maastricht may be referred to equally correctly as being contained in the Treaty of Rome, the Maastricht Treaty or the consolidated Treaty establishing the European Community.

Macmillan, Harold (1894–1986)

As Conservative prime minister, Harold Macmillan applied to join the EC in 1961, prompted by his own world-weary pessimism born of the UK's relative lack of economic success, its weakening Commonwealth ties and its declining post-imperial influence in the world. There was also pressure from the USA, which supported a united Europe. President Charles de Gaulle vetoed the UK's application, fearing a rival for political leadership of the Community.

Major, John (1943–)

As prime minister from 1990 to 1997, John Major entered the scene as a pro-European, bent on being at the heart of Europe, in contrast to his predecessor Margaret Thatcher. He negotiated the Maastricht Treaty in 1992, his proud claim being to have obtained opt-outs from the final stage of EMU and from the Social Chapter. Indeed, at the time little more could have been achieved to protect the UK's position, which differed for good reason from that of its Continental partners.

All the quaintness of a rain dance and about the same potency.
John Major when prime minister, misreading the prospects for EMU,
The Economist, September 1993

Circumstances changed when Denmark rejected the Treaty by referendum in June 1992, for the Treaty of Rome can only be amended by the unanimous consent of the member states, and Maastricht was an amending Treaty. Three months later the European exchange rate system collapsed. There was intense speculation that France, too, would reject Maastricht and monetary union. Meanwhile the UK, in the grip of recession, could not sustain the high interest rates resulting from German reunification. A costly attempt to keep the pound locked to the D-Mark ended in failure and the pound was forced to devalue. It was Major, as Thatcher's chancellor, who had brought the UK into the Exchange Rate Mechanism (ERM), but it was his successor in that post, Norman Lamont, who paid the price by resignation.

When the Maastricht Treaty came to be ratified in 1993 the parliamentary arithmetic was on a knife-edge. The ERM fiasco was seen as a warning of the consequences of fixed exchange rates, and a few backbenchers risked their

---

careers to vote against the constitutional implications of the Treaty. Only merciless whipping and a threat to dissolve Parliament enabled the bill to be passed. From that moment onwards, Major was a victim of events. His *communautaire* reputation dissolved in the beef crisis, but the British economy recovered strongly, benefiting from the pound's unsought freedom of manoeuvre. The 'bastards' (as Major imprudently described his dissident fellow Conservatives), who opposed the UK joining the single currency, proved to speak for a majority of the party. But they were outmanoeuvred by a group of senior cabinet ministers, led by Chancellor Kenneth Clarke, Foreign Secretary Douglas Hurd and Deputy Prime Minister Michael Heseltine, who considered that scepticism over EMU would damage the UK's wider European interests.

Major was defeated by Tony Blair's Labour Party in the 1997 general election, bequeathing him a sound economy in which the secret of rising employment and growth without inflation appeared to have been unlocked by Conservative reforms. To the end even those closest to Major could not fathom his own position on EMU; and his equivocation on European matters doubtless contributed something to his undoing.

Malta

See **Small countries**.

Marshall Plan (Marshall Aid)

The Marshall Plan, named after General Marshall, a US army chief of staff in World War II, was a unique act of American generosity and enlightened self-interest. Under the Plan, which was overseen by what later became the OECD, the USA distributed some $12,500 million over three years, starting in 1947, to 16 European states, on condition that they set about dismantling trade barriers and systematically organising their own recovery. The instigator of Marshall Aid, as it became known, was President Truman, who perceived clearly the Soviet threat to a weakened Europe. Under pressure from Stalin the East European satellite countries refused to accept any Marshall Aid; the USSR also attempted, not without success, to raise fears in leftist circles in the West over German revanchism and American imperialism. Together with NATO, the Plan signalled the emergence of the USA as a European power and set Europe on a path to freedom and prosperity on a hitherto undreamed of scale, creating a debt of honour which France alone has sometimes been reluctant to acknowledge.

MECUs

Million ECUs, sometimes written mecus.

MEP

Elected member of the European Parliament.

Mergers

See **Competition and merger policy**.

Messina Conference

In 1954 plans to create a European Defence Community (to replace the national armies of Germany, France, Italy and the Benelux countries with a common defence force) collapsed when France refused to ratify the Treaty. The Six thereupon turned their attention to the idea of a customs union, meeting at Messina in 1955 to entrust Paul-Henri Spaak of Belgium with the production of the report which led to the 1957 Treaty of Rome and the formation of the EEC, or Common Market.

The UK sent an emissary to the Messina Conference to argue the case for a free trade area, but did not attend the Conference officially, an omission to which British Europhiles attribute many of their country's subsequent difficulties with Europe. The diagnosis appears flawed. The Six paid no attention to the British position. Nor could the UK have lightly abandoned Commonwealth trade, cheap food and the Anglo-American nuclear alliance in favour of expensive French farm produce, a protectionist Community and Euratom. Thus Charles de Gaulle, who saw the incompatibility clearsightedly, had good reason to veto the UK's entry throughout the 1960s, even if he was also motivated by the wish to avoid having a rival for European leadership.

Mittelstand

The German name for the small and medium-sized company sector, generally family-owned manufacturing firms, which have been substantially credited with Germany's post-war economic success. The same sector has been largely responsible for northern Italy's rise to prosperity and for the revival of the UK economy (where services play an important part), a fact often obscured by the virtual monopoly of media opinion by big business.

Mitterrand, François (1916–96)

Few more subtle politicians than François Mitterrand have held centre stage in Europe. A Vichyite until the war turned against Germany, thereafter a devotee of the Resistance, he was twice defeated in French presidential elections before finally becoming president in 1981, a position he held until the year before his death.

Mitterrand's tenure of office was marked initially by nationalisations of

French companies and other manifestations of socialism, followed by a retreat to the centre ground and reprivatisation in response to electoral setbacks to his Socialist Party in the Assembly. With Chancellor Helmut Kohl and Commission President Jacques Delors, who were his political contemporaries and closest allies, he was one of the architects of the Maastricht Treaty. Viscerally hostile to German reunification, he conceived the Treaty as a bargain. Germany would be allowed to reunite; in return, France would dilute the power of the Bundesbank by incorporating the D-Mark into an EU-wide monetary system. Together, France and Germany would continue to decide the fate of Europe, as they had under his and Kohl's predecessors, first Charles de Gaulle and Konrad Adenauer and subsequently Valéry Giscard d'Estaing and Helmut Schmidt.

Mitterrand's political position was progressively eroded by domestic problems. His policy of matching the strength of the D-Mark at any cost led to an overvalued franc and was one of the causes of growing unemployment. Scandal followed scandal in political and business circles, undermining popular faith in the French elites. Obsessed with grandeur, Mitterrand lavished public money on prestige projects, but did little to modernise the economy and equip it to meet the challenge of globalisation. In 1992 he put the Maastricht Treaty to a referendum, in expectation of a ringing endorsement, but won approval by the narrowest of margins.

His attitude to Margaret Thatcher was one of mingled fascination and confrontation. Although he supported her in the Falklands War and it was under his presidency that the British rebate was finally agreed, they opposed each other over the EU at every turn. He was an integrationist; she believed in a Europe of sovereign nations. He was protectionist; she was a free trader. He (with Kohl) created the Franco-German Eurocorps; she was convinced that security rested solely on NATO and the Atlantic alliance. He was a complex intriguer, capable of considerable deviousness, whereas she was not averse to taking her opponents head on.

Mitterrand's declining years were spent trying to create a legend of his own life story to pre-empt the possibly chillier judgement of historians. In Europe, he will be remembered chiefly for his political adroitness and his calculated devotion to the Franco-German relationship.

Monaco

See **Small countries**.

Monnet, Jean (1888–1979)

A French technocrat, Jean Monnet, even more than Walter Hallstein and Jacques Delors, was the authentic architect of what became the EU. Starting as a cognac salesman, he soon graduated to financial planning, spending his World War I years in London and moving on to the League of Nations. World War II found him in Washington as an adopted British official, after his dramatic proposal to unite the UK and France into a single country had been agreed by Winston Churchill and Charles de Gaulle, but had failed to prevent his country's surrender. Returning to France, and charged with designing French economic recovery, he was the brains behind the 1950 Schuman Plan and the European Coal and Steel Community, of which he was the first president. When his other great project, the European Defence Community, failed, Monnet withdrew from public office in 1955 to form the Action Committee for the United States of Europe, a lobby group which played an influential part in the Messina Conference and the subsequent creation of the EEC.

Never a member of any party, he was convinced that a united Europe was essential to peace and could only come about through supranational institutions capable of overriding sovereign democracies – a view sharply at odds with that of de Gaulle, with whom he was in constant conflict during the 1960s. A pragmatist, though with a consistent vision of Europe's destiny, Monnet hoped that the UK would play a full part in the Community once the British saw that its institutions were actually working.

Monti, Mario (1943–)

An EC Commissioner since 1995, with responsibility for the internal market, Mario Monti has led the drive for Community fiscal harmonisation and for the involvement of the EU in corporate and withholding taxes, areas hitherto left to national governments.

Morocco

Morocco applied to join the Community in 1987 but was rejected as not being a European country.

Multi-fibre Arrangement (MFA)

The MFA is a tariff and quota arrangement between the EU, the USA and developing countries to protect the declining textiles industries of the advanced nations against low-cost imports. Under the 1994 GATT negotiations, the MFA is supposed to be phased out by 2004.

Mutual recognition

The principle of mutual recognition, whether of product standards or professional qualifications, is central to the operation of the single market. If each member state were to accept goods and services from the other member states as freely as domestic goods and services, the need for excessive harmonisation would fall away, and with it much of the apparatus of integration. In 1979 the Cassis de Dijon judgment of the European Court of Justice established that a product lawfully made and sold in one EC country could not be prohibited, except on public health grounds, from sale in another (important though this case was, it did not, however, stem the flow of harmonising legislation that followed in the late 1980s and the 1990s).

Professional services proved more difficult, since not only were national qualifications jealously guarded but the regulatory systems differed from one country to the next. Nevertheless, after negotiations which in some cases, such as that of architects, took 15 years or more to complete, by 1987 doctors, vets, dentists and midwives were able, at least in theory, to practise throughout the EU, as were lawyers, architects and pharmacists. Subsequent Directives further eased the mutual recognition of all qualifications acquired after not less than three years' training. Such discrimination as remains is generally based on creative interpretation of the exceptions permitted under Community law.

N

Nationalism

Originally the name for a version of self-determination, namely that a state's boundaries should be decided by the indigenous population, nationalism has acquired unpleasant connotations and now suggests xenophobia or worse (Nazi being derived from National Socialism). Thus while federalism has a positive ring, there is no satisfactory word to denote support for the abstract idea of the sovereign nation (patriotism being defined as loyalty to a single state). This accident of language goes some way to explaining the mutual incomprehension with which Britons and Germans, in particular, debate their visions of the future of Europe.

National parliaments

The EU story is one of progressive reduction of the influence of national parliaments. Hence the democratic deficit, for which the Council of Ministers provides scant compensation, since the accountability of ministers to their own parliaments in respect of their Council deliberations rarely goes beyond reporting after the event (with the notable exception of Denmark, which requires its ministers to consult a parliamentary committee before agreeing to significant Council proposals – an example followed to a more limited extent by other countries).

The residual powers of national parliaments in respect of Union affairs are not, however, trifling. They can ratify or reject Treaty changes, accession treaties and modifications of the Community's budgetary financing. They have some scope for manoeuvre in the manner in which they implement Community Directives, although the 1997 Treaty of Amsterdam envisages that this will be diminished. Where there are opt-outs, as with the UK for EMU, or where policy still rests with individual governments, as with Justice and Home Affairs and the Common Foreign and Security Policy, national parliaments retain much of their traditional role. A strong parliament can also set broad parameters to the negotiating freedom of its government ministers in the Council.

British ministers are in theory barred from agreeing to any Community legislation until the House of Commons Scrutiny Committee has examined and passed it. In practice, however, the effectiveness of such scrutiny is greatly reduced by the unmanageable volume of Community law. The level of debate and the mastery of detail has generally been higher in the House of Lords than in the Commons, with the Lords European Select Committee distinguishing itself by a series of authoritative reports which have commanded attention throughout the Union. In most of the member states, however, scrutiny is perfunctory and debate apathetic.

In the early days of the Community, the European Parliament was composed exclusively of national MPs, a state of affairs which effectively came to an end with the advent of directly elected MEPs in 1979. The subsequent proliferation of interparliamentary committees has done little to engage domestically elected representatives in the European legislative process. Thus the source of genuine democratic legitimacy is separated from the decision-making arena – a failing for which various solutions have been suggested, including the creation of a European 'Senate' drawn from national MPs. No such suggestion, however, has found favour within an EU which already has a confusing number of institutions.

Parliament must ... resign itself to becoming a rubber stamp.
Lord Kilmuir, advice to Edward Heath, December 1960

National representations

See **Permanent representations**.

NATO (North Atlantic Treaty Organisation)

A model of brevity, the North Atlantic Treaty of 1949 contains 14 Articles committing the participants to collective security. Its pivotal clause is Article 5, stating that 'an attack against any signatory in Europe or North America shall be considered an attack against them all' and will result in a concerted response to restore security, including the use of armed force if necessary. In 1948 the Treaty of Brussels had committed the UK, France and the Benelux countries to a mutual defence pact; to these countries the North Atlantic Treaty added the USA, Canada, Denmark, Iceland, Italy, Norway and Portugal. The key to NATO's credibility was the USA, with its conventional forces and its nuclear deterrent, whose involvement was a consequence of its growing appreciation of the Soviet military threat, highlighted by the 1948–49 blockade of Berlin. Greece and Turkey joined in 1952 and West Germany (following the collapse of the proposed European Defence Community) in 1955.

NATO's defence capability was one of the determining factors in maintaining peace during the Cold War era, placing the USA at the heart of European security. With its North Atlantic Council of foreign ministers, its regional commands, its Defence and Nuclear Planning Committees and its Military

Committee, composed of national chiefs of staff, all supported by research teams, NATO constituted a formidable politico-military machine. France, irritated by American predominance, withdrew from the integrated command in 1966, as did Spain within years of joining in 1982, but despite these hitches and constant undermining by peace groups and communist fronts, a united policy was quite easy to maintain in the face of Soviet repression and belligerence.

For 40 years NATO's field of operations was limited both geographically and by reference to the alliance's defensive character. With the collapse of the Warsaw Pact in 1991 a new rationale was needed, and NATO's first shots fired in anger came in 1994 while supporting an international peacekeeping mission in Bosnia. The polarities of the Cold War had possessed the merit of simplicity; now a web of conflicting interests and legal questions surrounded the application of military force in a case of internal aggression in the former Yugoslavia, which lay outside the NATO area (defined as the territory of the signatories). It was eventually under the aegis of the United Nations – after the EU had shown itself impotent – that NATO forces carried out air strikes against Serb positions; and since the conclusion of the US-brokered peace accord in December 1995, NATO has organised its invigilation.

No sooner had Poland, Czechoslovakia and Hungary rid themselves of their communist regimes than they moved in the early 1990s to cement their integration into Western civilisation, announcing their candidature for the EU and NATO. This caused friction with Russia, impinging on its traditional sphere of influence and raising an old spectre of encirclement. An agreement in 1997 providing for a joint council between NATO and Russia went some way to answering the Russian government's concerns, and the three applicants seemed likely to be accepted. But there were doubts among existing NATO members over the wisdom of any further enlargement. It was important not to dilute the credibility of Article 5. The Baltic states, for example, being isolated from the main ground forces, would be impossible to defend in an emergency. The extension of NATO would also entail costly improvement of the military infrastructure of any new entrants at a time of cuts in national defence budgets. In the context of French-led calls for a greater European military role, centred on the reactivation of the moribund WEU (Western European Union), US willingness to meet the bulk of these expenses was no longer assured, but the EU economies had themselves embarked on austerity programmes in the run-up to the single currency.

In 1991 NATO had issued a Declaration of Peace and Co-operation, aimed at the former Soviet bloc, simultaneously announcing a 30% force reduction. Its Partnership for Peace programme, launched in 1994, gives a form of associate status to some 37 countries from Albania to Kazakhstan, encouraging joint exercises, democratic control of the military and a commitment to humanitarian missions. Since 1997 the activities of the Partnership for Peace have been co-ordinated by the Euro-Atlantic Partnership Council. Reflecting European sensitivities, a framework has also been created for NATO operations without US involvement, although the rejection by the EU of Turkey, a vital NATO partner, is a complicating factor. These developments have brought signs of a renewed French interest, albeit sometimes on conditions (including the surrender of NATO's Southern Command to a French officer) which the USA has found too presumptuous to accept.

As NATO approached its 50th anniversary, its world had changed. In place of a single enemy the new danger was of brushfire wars, ethnic conflict and deranged but well-funded dictators with access to chemical, biological or nuclear weapons. Most of the potential flashpoints were out of area and likely to need a speedy response – the speed applying as much to political decisions as to military logistics. Against this background the EU was increasingly assertive, but barely more capable than before of concerted or decisive action, as the Bosnian fiasco, and before it the 1991 Gulf War, had cruelly demonstrated. The UK in particular was sceptical about the effectiveness of the WEU, preferring to rely on NATO's new Rapid Reaction Corps and the tried and tested Anglo-American alliance, preferably operating under a UN mandate. For the former Warsaw Pact countries, heartened by President Clinton's promise to keep 100,000 American troops in Europe, NATO remained an emblem of security. To itself, and to the EU, NATO was becoming a source as much of questions as of answers.

Near abroad

Former Soviet states with Russian populations, over which Russia harbours ambitions of influence, if not hegemony.

The Netherlands

The EU's sixth largest state and a founder signatory of Benelux and NATO as well as the Treaty of Paris and the Treaty of Rome, the Netherlands has concentrated on its own affairs, content to take something of a back seat in the conduct of the Community. It has supplied only one president of the Commission, a former agricultural commissioner, Sicco Mansholt, author of the Mansholt Plan to reform the CAP, who took over briefly in 1972 on Malfatti's resignation. None of the EU's principal institutions are located in the Netherlands.

Known for its egalitarianism and the trading acumen of its business community, the Netherlands is well attuned to the social consciousness and employer–union consultative methods of the EU. Since the mid-1980s its economy has become the envy of its neighbour, Germany, as successive centrist coalition governments have restored the health of state finances and reduced nominal unemployment, achievements mainly attributable to a pared-down welfare state, wage moderation, part-time jobs (a remarkable 38% of all employment), early retirement and increased disability leave. The currency has been in effective union with the D–Mark for some years and will be one of the first wave members of the planned single currency. The guilder's apparent stability does, however, disguise a depreciation in real terms over the last 15 years as a result of falling inflation–adjusted wages, doubtless an important factor in the country's above-average growth rate.

Neutrality

Neutrality, although carefully defined by the 1907 Hague Convention, has proved a conveniently elastic concept in the context of the EU. Austria, Finland, Ireland, Sweden and Switzerland are all neutral countries, some by constitution, others by tradition. Yet each has felt able to apply for membership of the Union and none has been rejected by the Commission or by the other member states, despite the Maastricht Treaty's vision of a Common Foreign and Security Policy 'including the eventual framing of a common defence policy, which might in time lead to a common defence'. Thus although subtle minds are currently at work redefining neutrality, it is evident that the status is in reality incompatible with one of the key pillars of the EU. (See also **WEU**.)

Nordic Council

The Nordic Council is a body of parliamentarians from Denmark, Finland, Iceland, Norway and Sweden which meets twice a year to review and co-ordinate policy on matters of common interest. Unlike Benelux, the Nordic Council has no tangible economic arrangements, these being subsumed within EFTA and the EEA. It does, however, have a passport-free zone which is in negotiations with the EU over the Schengen Agreement.

Despite their many shared characteristics, the Nordic bloc countries have parted company over the European dimension of their military, political and economic affairs. Denmark, Iceland and Norway are in NATO, whereas Finland and Sweden are neutral; and Iceland and Norway are associates of the WEU, whereas the other Nordic states are observers (Scandinavia therefore supplies no full members to this embryonic European defence force). Iceland and Norway are outside the EU, whereas Denmark and Sweden are in, but distinctly Eurosceptic. Iceland and Norway are automatically outside EMU; Denmark has an opt-out; Sweden has elected to stay out for the time being; and Finland alone is favourably inclined (in government circles, if not in the opinion polls).

The reasons for these differences are historical. Finland has a 750-mile border with Russia and attaches great importance to aligning itself with its West European neighbours. Sweden has benefited from remaining independent of alliances for nearly 200 years. And Denmark, Iceland and Norway are essentially Atlanticist in outlook.

Norway

A founder member of NATO, EFTA, the EEA, the Nordic Council and the Council of Europe, Norway has twice applied successfully for membership of the Community and twice (in 1972 and in 1994) narrowly rejected by referendum its own Accession Treaty. Both rejections were fuelled by a strong grass-roots sense of independence and Scandinavian solidarity, allied to a legitimate concern over the Common Fisheries Policy and some suspicion of the sophisticated mores and political horse-trading of more southerly European capitals.

In the light of the conventional wisdom that exclusion from the Community spells painful economic isolation, it is ironic that Norway, despite high social spending, shares with Switzerland the distinction of being the wealthiest country in Europe. This is, however, mainly because of cheap hydroelectric power and the country's North Sea oil resources, which have enabled it to extinguish its external debt and to establish a fund (forecast at $60 billion in 2001) for future obligations, including pensions.

O

Occupied field

The EU doctrine of the occupied field asserts the precedence of the Union's authority over that of national legislatures in a given policy area. The term is particularly used to denote a currently unregulated field of activity in which, by reserving its right to exercise its powers at some future time, the EU effectively frustrates the ability of national governments to legislate, lest their laws be subsequently overruled by Community law.

Official Journal (OJ)

The *Official Journal of the European Communities* contains the EU's legislative texts, parliamentary proceedings, Court cases, Commission proposals, Opinions, appointments, currency data, invitations to tender for contracts and other such information. It is published continuously in all the official languages.

OECD (Organisation for Economic Co-operation and Development)

Originally an organisation to promote European economic co-operation, known as the OEEC, in which guise it supervised the administration of the post-war Marshall Plan, the OECD reinvented itself as an international think-tank of the richest nations in 1960, after the Six and the Seven had respectively formed the EEC and EFTA. Based in Paris, it focuses on broad policy issues, publishing authoritative reports with a free-market orientation, to the occasional irritation of socialist opinion among its backers. Apart from the EU countries, the OECD's membership also includes the USA, Canada, Japan, Australia, New Zealand, Switzerland and Norway.

Ombudsman

The role of the Ombudsman – a 19th century Scandinavian invention – is to investigate complaints made by individual citizens against the authorities. The Maastricht Treaty required the European Parliament to appoint an Ombudsman with powers to investigate maladministration (that is, malpractice or incompetence) on the part of any EU institution except the Courts of Justice. The first appointment was made in 1995 when a Finn, Jacob Soderman, was elected for a five-year term.

By the end of 1997 Soderman's office had received 2,321 complaints, 1,920 of which he judged to be outside his remit as they involved matters partly or wholly the responsibility of the member states, a fact which reflects the confusion of national and supranational powers within the EU. The Ombudsman cannot penalise offenders; his sole right of redress is to forward a critical report to the Parliament and to the institution against which a complaint was made.

Opinion

The powerlessness of many EU bodies, especially in the Community's early years, made it useful to give them some formal influence by authorising them to give Opinions (or *avis* in French), which the decision-making institutions were obliged to note, but not necessarily to follow. The most significant Opinions are those given by the European Parliament on draft legislation and those given by the Commission on applications for membership of the EU. The selection of countries to join the single currency was preceded by Opinions from a number of bodies, including the Commission and the European Monetary Institute.

Optimal currency area

A large area, generally covering more than one country, where the advantages of having a single currency outweigh the disadvantages, for example because of proximity, labour mobility and cultural and economic homogeneity. The UK and Germany are often said not to constitute an optimal currency zone, due to the structural differences in their economies. For instance, the UK trades and invests predominantly in dollars; the British business cycle is more in tune with the US cycle than with the German one; and Germany is less sensitive than the UK to movements in short-term interest rates and stockmarkets. Proponents of the single currency reply that these points, though true, are of secondary importance and that EMU would itself help to produce closer economic alignment.

Opt-out

Concerned about the threats to independence implicit in the 1992 Maastricht Treaty, the UK and Denmark negotiated opt-outs from the final single currency stage of EMU. Denmark also obtained an opt-out on measures affecting defence, and the UK obtained an exemption from the Social Chapter, which it feared would be used as a basis for old-fashioned socialist measures which would damage competitiveness.

Early experience of the effectiveness of these opt-outs, which are contained in protocols to the Treaty, has been mixed. The Community's Working Time Directive, limiting certain employees' hours and specifying their rest periods, was introduced in 1993 not under the Social Chapter but as a health and safety provision under the Treaty of Rome. The Labour government elected in 1997 has signed up to the Social Chapter, but has stated that this will not be allowed to become a source of reduced competitiveness – a promise which may prove hard to deliver under qualified majority voting.

The EMU opt-outs appear to be retaining their validity. Several clauses in the Treaty of Rome, however, arguably clash with the Maastricht protocol. These include an Article which enjoins 'the establishment of economic and monetary union, ultimately including a single currency'. Moreover, Maastricht established the principle that exchange rate policy is a matter of 'common interest'. Thus the British and Danish exemptions might come under threat if a majority of the other member states decided to challenge them.

The 1997 Treaty of Amsterdam also contains opt-outs exempting the UK (and therefore Ireland) from its provisions abolishing internal borders. These were initially criticised as non-*communautaire*. Within months, however, the UK's caution appeared justified, as the EU faced a growing influx of refugees from Turkey, North Africa and Eastern Europe, who, once inside the Community's frontiers, were able to choose their destination at will. (See also **Closer co-operation**.)

OSCE (Organisation for Security and Co-operation in Europe)

The OSCE is the name given since 1994 to the collective official peace, security and human rights movement of 54 states (originally 35), as reflected in the 1975 Helsinki Final Act and several subsequent conferences. Originally known as the CSCE (Conference on Security and Co-operation in Europe), its purpose was to reduce tensions in Europe between NATO and the Warsaw Pact countries and to establish human rights principles behind the Iron Curtain – an endeavour viewed idealistically in the West, if cynically by the Soviet bloc. The Charter of Paris for a New Europe, signed in 1990, reaffirmed the Helsinki agreement, committed the participants to democracy and free markets and signalled the impending transformation of the CSCE into a structured institution, with a council, a committee, a secretariat, a parliamentary assembly, a Conflict Prevention Centre and other such bureaucratic appurtenances (all with headquarters in European cities). The EU is not strictly speaking a member of the OSCE, although Jacques Delors signed the Charter of Paris; of the participants all but two (the USA and Canada) are European states or former Soviet republics.

Ostpolitik

The West German policy of conciliation with the Soviet bloc during the Cold War, of which the chief exponent was Chancellor Willy Brandt in the early 1970s. The policy was in direct contrast to the previous Hallstein doctrine of refusing diplomatic relations with any country which recognised East Germany. *Ostpolitik* should be seen in the wider context of détente, or the reduction of East-West tensions, principally through unilateral concessions by the Western powers.

Own resources

See **Budget**.

P

Partnership for Peace

See NATO.

Party list

The system, common on the Continent, for choosing election candidates from a list approved by the relevant party, as opposed to the UK system of constituency-appointed candidates. Party lists, which ensure a high degree of obedience to the leadership's line, are proposed for the first time in the UK for a proportion of the candidates for any future Scottish or Welsh post-devolution elections, as well as for elections to the European Parliament.

La pensée unique

The notion that the sole objective of French policy is solidarity with Germany.

Pensions

Most state pensions in Europe are on a pay-as-you-go basis, whereby current payments are met from contributions, tax and other current income. As populations age, fewer wage-earners will be supporting more people in retirement and the affordability of state pensions will deteriorate, leaving governments with harsh options: to reduce benefits; to increase contributions or taxes; or to raise the retirement age. The exception is the UK, where state pensions are extensively supplemented by private funded schemes – the value of funds set aside and invested to meet future British pension commitments exceeds that of all the other EU member countries combined.

It has been estimated that if the pension obligations of Europe's major economies were to be fully funded, it would cost Germany, France and Italy the equivalent of about 100% of each country's GDP, whereas the cost to the UK would be under 20%. This hidden liability is known as the net present value of underfunded pensions. Although the actuarial assumptions and methods of calculation differ slightly from one source to another, the order of magnitude is broadly agreed by the OECD, the International Monetary Fund and the European Commission. Another way of expressing the same deficiency is to say that Germany and France should be allocating about 3% more of their GDP each year for pension provision if they are to meet, without extra borrowing, the promises of generous index-linked retirement benefits given to voters during the last 30 years.

The size of the shortfall is such that if it were included in the calculations used to judge which large European countries should qualify on a sustainable basis for the single currency, only the UK would pass the test. The problem appears to be containable for a few more years, but by 2005 it will worsen and after 2010, when the baby-boom generation retires, EU member states may not be able to afford their pension commitments. At that stage, some in the UK fear that a unified European balance sheet or tax harmonisation might be invoked to make the UK pay for imprudence elsewhere; and that the clause in the Maastricht Treaty shielding countries from being forced to bail each other out will be nullified by the common obligation of member states to protect the integrity of EMU.

The terms of pensions in Europe inhibit the mobility of labour by depriving employees of their acquired rights when they cross borders, a feature which is contrary to the principles of the Treaty of Rome and an impediment to the single market. The Commission's idea of a portability Directive appears well conceived. It has, however, been blocked by countries which regard pensions as a loyalty bonus rather than an independent entitlement, still less an adjunct to flexible markets.

People's Europe

The term People's Europe was coined in 1984 by the European Council, which set up a committee presided over by an Italian, Pietro Adonnino, to explore ways to strengthen the European identity. Among the Adonnino Committee's recommendations were a Euro-lottery (an idea scotched at the time by the British, but now expected to be revived), European citizenship, the European passport, the European flag, a uniform electoral procedure, mutual recognition of qualifications, common postage stamps, an Ombudsman and proposals to improve the workings of the single market. Many of these suggestions were adopted. When the UK assumed the presidency in 1998 the phrase People's Europe was revived, reflecting the ambition of Prime Minister Tony Blair for a more user-friendly Community and mirroring the People's Britain image on which the Labour Party had successfully campaigned in the British elections.

Permanent representatives

The purpose of the EU legations of the member states in Brussels, which are often known as permanent or national representations, is to support their parent country's negotiating stance, resolve differences with other member states and supply comprehensive information on EU affairs to policy-makers at home. They are thus intended to act as a counterweight to the integrationist tendencies of the Commission.

The station heads, or permanent representatives, with senior ambassadorial rank, meet collectively as COREPER, the influential committee which prepares the meetings of the Council of Ministers and presides over the behind-the-scenes bargaining process which underlies all Community legislation. The British representation, known as UKREP, is led by a Foreign Office appointee, supported by a deputy and a number of senior technical officials, many seconded from Whitehall. UKREP's reporting line to London is also to the Foreign Office, which ensures the predominance of that department's way of thinking. It is, indeed, a characteristic of the national representations that domestic opinion often regards them as overly susceptible to the blandishments and compromises of the Brussels milieu. (See also **Community method**.)

Pillars

The EU is said to stand like a temple on three pillars: the Community; the Common Foreign and Security Policy; and co-operation in the field of Justice and Home Affairs (recast in the 1997 Treaty of Amsterdam as Police and Judicial Co-operation in Criminal Matters). These pillars are of unequal strength. The Community (essentially the supranational institutions and policies created by the Treaty of Rome as amended by the Single European Act, the Maastricht Treaty and the Treaty of Amsterdam) dominates the life of the Union. By contrast, the other two pillars (essentially the intergovernmental policies created by the Maastricht and Amsterdam Treaties) represent areas of loose co-operation between national governments. The temple metaphor doubtless symbolises the vision of Europe as a stately building whose architecture is ultimately destined to belong entirely to the Union. (See also **Community method**.)

Poland

The Polish national anthem, 'Poland has not yet been destroyed', bears witness to the extent of foreign oppression over the centuries. Split between Austria, Prussia and Russia in 1795, Poland regained independence in 1918, only to be redivided between Nazi Germany and the Soviet Union following Hitler's invasion which precipitated World War II. Under Stalin the Soviet Union betrayed the Polish wartime resistance to Germany, overran the country and imposed a puppet government after the war, a process completed in 1952 with the adoption of a Soviet-model constitution following the earlier merger of the socialist and communist parties to form the Polish United Workers' Party (PUWP). Strikes in 1980, caused by price rises, involved 300,000 workers and forced the PUWP to allow independent trade unions, including Lech Walesa's Solidarity movement, which continued to exist underground after the declaration of martial law in 1981. Further concessions made by the government during the 1980s, in which political prisoners were freed and a referendum on reforms held, failed to arrest the growth of Solidarity. More strikes in 1989 culminated in talks between Lech Walesa and the PUWP. The resultant package of reforms included elections in the summer of 1989, in which the PUWP was defeated.

Succeeding post-communist coalition governments instituted market liberalisation, but the initial outcome was higher prices, rising unemployment and a breach of internationally agreed budgetary limits, leading to a prescription of shock therapy from the IMF in 1992 and 1993. The medicine was efficacious. GDP growth running at 6% has started to bring down unemployment and privatisation has transformed industrial competitiveness. Inflation, too, declined modestly in 1997, although it remained high at some 15%. In the September elections of that year the Solidarity Party made a comeback, winning a coalition majority.

Poland's invitation to join NATO in 1997 perhaps owed something to the country's historical position as a buffer state (Russia, at least, construed the event negatively), but from Poland's standpoint it stood alongside an application for membership of the EU as evidence of the national determination to be accepted into the mainstream of Western civilisation. Poland's accession, which has been recommended by the Commission, will have a major impact on the EU. It will add a Catholic population of approximately the same size as that of Spain, and agricultural land about equal to that of the UK or Italy. With GDP per head about one-third of the level reached by Portugal and Greece, the EU's poorest current members, Poland will require structural funds and CAP subsidies far beyond the compass of the EU budget as it now stands. Already the prospect is causing distress and pre-emptive protest from the main recipients of Community largesse, since Germany, while strongly supporting the eastward enlargement of the Union, has stated that it has no intention of paying for it.

Police and Judicial Co-operation in Criminal Matters

This is the new heading, introduced in the 1997 Treaty of Amsterdam, of the Maastricht Treaty's Justice and Home Affairs pillar. The change of name reflects a sharper focus on crime, the abolition of frontier controls having become part of the *acquis communautaire* by the incorporation of the Schengen Agreement into the main Treaty.

The object of the policy is to pave the way to legal harmonisation and to increase co-operation between the judicial, police and customs authorities of the member states in matters concerning organised crime, terrorism, fraud and arms and drug trafficking. The Maastricht wording has been largely rewritten to emphasise the guiding role of the Community (including a strengthened Europol) at the expense of the member states. (See also **Corpus Juris**.)

Political co-operation

Eurospeak for foreign policy co-operation.

Political groups

The European Parliament contains some nine loose political groupings, of which the largest are the Party of European Socialists (PES) and the European People's Party (EPP), the latter dominated by German Christian Democrats and Spanish Partido Popular members, in coalition with British Conservatives. The other groups include Liberals of various hues, Greens, Independents, anti-Maastrichtites, Regional parties, Nationalists (including Gaullists and Forza Italia) and a Communist-Nordic Left alliance.

The two big groups, with well over half the votes, control the Parliament and collude over all major decisions. The others are for the most part a shifting sand of unstable membership, sometimes held together by little more than the desire to obtain office and parliamentary funds, both of which are dispersed according to the number of affiliated MEPs.

Certain of these groups, notably the Socialists, the EPP, the Liberal federation, the Greens and the Alliance of regional parties, have made efforts to turn themselves into real European parties. These efforts have not been re-warded with success, although the Maastricht Treaty welcomed the emergence of cross-border parties as a 'factor for integration contributing to European awareness'.

Among many obstacles to further progress are media and voter indifference, the unsatisfactory nature of the Parliament itself, the ceiling on personal advancement and the contrast between the cut-and-thrust of national politics and the consensual nature of European-level political discourse. (See Appendix 3.)

Pompidou, Georges (1911–74)

Georges Pompidou's political career began when he became acquainted with Charles de Gaulle in 1944. His rise from the directorship of the French Rothschild bank to prime minister (1962–68) and then president (1969–74), without any previous experience of elective office, was characteristic of the presidential style of government initiated by de Gaulle. When de Gaulle returned to power in 1958, Pompidou helped draft the constitution of the Fifth Republic; he became premier after playing a part in negotiating an end to the Algerian war of independence. De Gaulle dismissed Pompidou following the unrest and student rioting which paralysed France in 1968, but his own political position had been fatally damaged and when he stepped down in 1969 Pompidou stood for, and was elected to, the presidency. Pompidou maintained

French links with the Soviet Union and controversially expanded arms exports to the Middle East to secure the oil on which France was dependent. In these, as in many other policies, he remained a Gaullist. In Community affairs, however, he distanced himself from some of his predecessor's nationalist ways, lifting the veto on British membership of the EEC and, with the German chancellor, Willy Brandt, launching monetary union – the latter initiative soon collapsing in the wake of the Arab–Israeli war and the resulting oil crisis.

Portugal

A founder member of NATO and EFTA, Portugal applied to join the EC in 1977, the same year as Spain, and the two countries were admitted together in 1986. Previously, Portugal had been disqualified, having had an authoritarian government for 50 years (36 of them under the dictator Salazar), which ended only when a Marxist coup failed and democracy was restored in 1976. As one of the poorest member states Portugal is a major recipient of structural funds from the Community, which has helped it to achieve above average growth, and its budgetary discipline has been sufficient for it to have been invited in 1998 to join the first group of participants in the single currency.

Portugal has a common interest with Spain, Italy and Greece over the Common Fisheries Policy. Together they command 28 votes in the Council of Ministers, sufficient for a blocking minority under qualified majority voting. More generally, Portugal relies on the larger Club Med countries to bear the brunt of any negotiations to maximise the share of Community resources allocated to the south European coastal states.

Portugal's economy has continued to expand in the late 1990s, based partly on infrastructure investment stimulated by the hosting of Expo in 1998 to mark the 500th anniversary of Vasco da Gama's discovery of the sea route to India. Questions remain, however, about the future. Portugal now provides universal free education and a burgeoning social security system, but the standard of education has dropped and the country risks remaining dependent for competitiveness on low wages. The funding of the welfare state will be affected by the low birth rate, and when the EU's enlargement brings in states with an even more pressing need for subsidies, the grants which Portugal has enjoyed may fall. It is therefore recognised that reform of the country's existing structures may be needed if it is to sustain its momentum.

Preamble

The introductory Resolutions and Affirmations by the heads of state at the beginning of the EU's key Treaties were written after the Treaties had been formulated and serve to describe, in general terms, the issues agreed. Like the

Declarations attached to the end of the Treaties, these Preambles are not legally binding. They are, however, important in that they are intended to express the common political will among the contracting parties and to define the intentions of the Community. They therefore form the basis of interpretation of the Treaties and the justification for any resultant legislation.

Pre-in

A country which intends to join EMU but either is unwilling to join or is barred from immediate entry because it fails to meet the Maastricht convergence criteria. For example, when Gordon Brown announced in 1997 that the UK would not adopt the euro in the first wave but was in principle in favour of EMU, the country moved from being an 'out' to being a 'pre-in'.

Preliminary ruling

A ruling on a point of Community law given by the European Court of Justice to a national court of law.

Presidency

The six-monthly presidency of the Council of Ministers and the European Council rotates between member states and is occupied by the appropriate minister for the subject under discussion (prime minister for the European Council, agriculture minister for the CAP, finance minister for Ecofin, and so on). The member state occupying the presidency is in addition entitled to its regular national seat at the Council of Ministers.

The presidency sets the agenda, mediates differences (or settles them by qualified majority voting), answers to the European Parliament, speaks for the EU in international circles and under the draft Treaty of Amsterdam is responsible for foreign, but not defence, policy. Such an aggregation of powers can be almost comically incongruous during the presidency of a small country with self-important ministers.

As the Union is enlarged and the presidency of each country comes round at longer intervals, it is probable that the larger powers will increasingly settle the important issues privately, as France and Germany have done in the past. Alternatively, pressure will mount for reform of the system to give more votes to the leading member states. (See also **Troika**.)

Primacy

The doctrine that Community law is superior to national law. The 1957 Treaty of Amsterdam goes further, stating that Community law is also superior to national constitutions, a doctrine previously rejected by a number of EU member states, including Germany, France and Denmark. The view taken (or, in the words of the Treaty, 'developed') by the European Court of Justice is that the Treaty of Rome and the other seminal European treaties have created a new legal order which has precedence over all pre-existing or subsequent laws in the member states.

Prodi, Romano (1939–)

Romano Prodi became Italian prime minister in 1996 as head of the broad left-of-centre 'olive tree' coalition. A former Christian Democrat, Prodi has to rely for a majority on the votes of the Reconstructed Communist Party and occasionally on the votes of opposition parties. He has made participation in the first wave of member states adopting the euro the cornerstone of Italian policy, for which he has demanded an austerity programme that has often seemed on the verge of bringing down his government. Initially, Italy's creative accounting to meet the Maastricht convergence criteria reinforced German doubts about the country's suitability for EMU, the suspicion being that once its vast national debt could be more cheaply serviced by being denominated in euros, Italy might revert to financial indiscipline, thereby undermining the single currency. In the end, however, Prodi's intensive lobbying, supported by France, overcame all resistance and in spring 1998 Italy was admitted to founder membership of the euro club.

Propaganda

Different authorities give different accounts of the amount spent by the Community on information. A former special adviser to the Commission has estimated it (how reliably is hard to judge) at over $750 million per year, of which some $300 million is attributable to the Directorate-General for Audiovisual Information, Communication and Culture. The budget for just three information campaigns in 1996/97 (Let Us Construct Europe Together, Citizens First and a third on monetary union) amounted to $60 million, and in 1998 the European Parliament approved a $75 million campaign to promote the euro. In addition to Commission spending, each Community institution has its own public relations activities, and of the numerous pro-European lobbying organisations in member states some are part-funded from official sources. The true overall expenditure figures are, however, impossible to establish, given the multiplicity of institutions and the slim dividing lines between normal information, public relations and propaganda, lines made hazier by the absence of any formal opposition to the Community's policies.

From the outset the Community's strategy has been to spare no expense to place itself in a favourable light as the defender of the citizen against exploitation and the purveyor of peace and prosperity to member states. Emphasis is given to the success of regional programmes, the key role of subsidiarity, the supposedly overwhelming support for the EU among ordinary voters and the bright prospects for growth and jobs. As an inducement to think positively, many of the more than 750 journalists accredited to Brussels are paid for helpful reports, recruited to compose articles for Commission publications or given grants for writing books. By such means they can double their regular salaries.

Information policy is focused, with advice from experts in psychology. A 1993 report advocated targeting young people 'where resistance is weakest' and women, as more 'intuitively inclined ... to recognise the advantages of a better future'. As early as 1954 the European Coal and Steel Community commissioned a study which concluded 'it is necessary to play on sentiments and appeal to beliefs held without judgement, in short to everything which constitutes the psychological temperament of the crowd'. Although lip service is paid to transparency, journalists seeking factual information are met with the ruling of the Court of Justice that the Commission may 'regulate the right of public access' to relevant documents.

The British people must be led slowly and unconsciously into the abandonment of their traditional economic defences, not asked.
Peter Thorneycroft, a member of Harold Macmillan's cabinet which applied to join the EEC in 1961

Proportionality

Proportionality is the principle, as much honoured in the breach as in the observance, that Community legislation should be the minimum necessary to achieve its purpose.

Protocol

An annex to a treaty, having legal force and generally containing an amplification or exception to the main text, such as an opt-out or the statute of a new institution.

Public purchasing

Successive Directives since the early 1970s have established that contracts placed by public bodies in the Community should be advertised in the *Official Journal* for open tender throughout the EU. The system operates unevenly and gives rise to a fair amount of unnecessary paperwork on small contracts.

Q

Qualified majority voting (QMV)

Designed by the Treaty of Rome to be the principal EU method of reaching decisions in the Council of Ministers, qualified majority voting allocates votes to member states according to their population, although it is weighted in favour of the smaller states. The allocation in 1998 is set out in Appendix 4, from which it can be seen that the weighting becomes higher as the size of the population declines. Thus Germany has one vote for every 8.1 million inhabitants whereas Luxembourg has one for every 200,000.

Few Council decisions require unanimity. The rest need 62 votes in favour out of 87, with 26 constituting a blocking minority. In practice, issues rarely go to the vote, as the EU's predilection for consensus has fostered a barter culture, in which support is traded for concessions on matters unrelated to the subject under discussion. Nevertheless, the over-representation of the smaller states gives them great bargaining power. For example, Greece, Portugal, Spain and Italy, with 28 votes, are able to protect the southern sunbelt interests without any other allies, and Ireland, Portugal, Greece and Spain, with 21 votes, need only one five-vote deal to secure their position as the Community's largest recipients of subsidies. Another way of expressing the point is that Germany, the UK and France, with over 53% of the EU's population, have only just enough votes to block a Commission proposal. With the addition of Italy and Spain, the five leading members have 79% of the population, but their 48 votes are still well short of the 62 needed to force a measure through the Council.

In the Common Market's early years, these discrepancies were overshadowed by a dispute which for a time nearly destroyed the Community. President Charles de Gaulle viewed the voting arrangements in the Treaty of Rome as an assault on sovereignty, imposed on France when it was weak, that is, before his time. In 1965, in protest against majority voting, France mounted a boycott on all Community business, lifting it only when the national right of veto was restored by the Luxembourg Compromise. Although the Compromise was, strictly speaking, a breach of the Treaty, it held for over 15 years, paralysing all decision-making. In the early 1980s, however, Community law was reasserted, and the veto lapsed back into its Treaty role as a device for the more important issues, with QMV resuming its status as the day-to-day mechanism for legislation and regulation.

The Single European Act of 1986 extended QMV across the whole single market programme, and the Maastricht Treaty of 1992 incorporated it into education, health, the environment, economic and monetary policy and the implementation of certain joint decisions in home affairs. The 1997 Treaty of Amsterdam continued the process, introducing QMV into such new areas as employment, equal opportunities, social policy, statistics and the implementation of joint decisions in foreign policy. By now its justification as a necessary device to complete the internal market had been superseded by the broader purpose of generally eroding the national veto.

These developments, however, raised a question mark over the sustainability of an inequitable voting system. In 1995 three more small states (Austria, Finland and Sweden) had joined the EU, further weakening the power of the largest countries. For a decade, Germany and France had adopted a somewhat superior attitude to such matters as the size of the blocking minority, confident that whatever the formal institutional arrangements the Franco-German alliance would be able to attain its purposes. But the impending accession of five former communist countries, all poor and four of them with small populations, would make the EU more unmanageable. Germany was also beginning to be concerned about its position as chief paymaster. It is now, therefore, widely accepted that institutional reform is inevitable, to redress the voting bias. A much canvassed approach is the double majority system, under which a majority (say, 75%) both of states and of the populations represented by those states would be required for most types of decision, with either unanimity or flexibility being reserved for matters of fundamental national importance. The smaller countries, which are also over-represented in the European Parliament, the Commission and the Board of the embryonic European Central Bank, are entitled to object that the Treaty of Rome enshrined the principle of disproportion from the outset, based on the concept of the Common Market as a pact between sovereign, and therefore equal, nations. But that was a system for six countries, not 20 or more; in the end the Community's search for greater legitimacy is bound to lead to a closer alignment of votes with populations.

Quota-hopping

The practice of registering a fishing vessel in another EU member state in order to take advantage of that state's quota – that is, its catch permitted under the Common Fisheries Policy. Quota-hopping, although legal under Community law, was banned in the UK by Act of Parliament in 1988. The overruling of the Act by the European Court of Justice gave rise to heart-searching in the UK, where the implications of the primacy of EU law had not previously been grasped. (See also **Factortame**.)

R

Rapporteur

Literally a reporter, the *rapporteur* is the spokesperson of a committee or presenter of a committee's report. *Rapporteurs* play a significant part in the European Parliament's deliberations, where the cut and thrust of debate is rare.

Ratification

The Treaty of Rome set a precedent for later EU Treaties by stipulating that it would not enter into force until all the signatory states had ratified it according to their 'respective constitutional requirements'. This would normally entail parliamentary approval (and in the UK's case royal assent), but some countries also require a referendum, while in other instances a referendum has been voluntarily undertaken. The 1992 Maastricht Treaty, for example, was submitted for political reasons to a referendum in France, but its ratification necessitated a referendum in Ireland, because it involved a change in the constitution, and in Denmark, because the *Folketing* passed it by an insufficient majority. The unanimity rule for ratifying Treaties meant that the Danish rejection which followed would have prevented Maastricht from entering into force, had not the country been persuaded to hold a second referendum, this time voting in favour.

The best-known cases of non-ratification by plebiscite were those of Norway, which twice rejected a Treaty of Accession in 1972 and 1994, and Switzerland, which in 1992 voted against the EEA agreement negotiated by its government. In theory, the law courts may also block a treaty if they consider that it breaches a national constitution, especially a written constitution. The German ratification of Maastricht was in the end dependent on the ruling of the Constitutional Court in Karlsruhe, following a private action by objectors. A similar legal challenge by individuals was mounted in Denmark; and more than one European court is likely to be called upon to rule on the constitutionality both of ratifying the 1997 Treaty of Amsterdam and of abolishing national currencies. In France, the Amsterdam Treaty, like the Maastricht Treaty, was submitted to the Constitutional Council and held not to conform to the French constitution, the remedy being to amend the constitution.

Referendum

Referendums are widely used in Europe to ratify constitutional change.

Ratification by referendum was sought for various European Treaties by Denmark, France, Ireland and Switzerland; and Sweden, Norway, Finland and Austria held votes in 1994 to determine whether to enter the EU. The British referendum of June 1975 – the first national plebiscite in the country's history – was intended to terminate uncertainty over the UK's continuing membership of the Community. At the time the concept was thought alien to the spirit of parliamentary democracy. As the years went by, however, parliamentary opposition began to weaken as it became apparent that EMU raised fundamental issues that cut across party lines. In 1997 both the UK's main parties agreed to call a referendum if the government of the day decided to apply to join the single currency.

Referendum Party

Uniquely in British electoral history, Sir James Goldsmith's Referendum Party ran in the 1997 general election on the platform that if elected it would hold a referendum on the UK's relationship with the EU and then disband itself. Backed by £20 million from its leader, the party sent some 5 million videos to householders and succeeded in raising public awareness of the European question. Fielding some candidates who were markedly more colourful than the conventional domestic politician, it did not come near to winning a seat but polled over 800,000 votes, a fair level of support in a country not given to personality cult politics.

Regionalism

Regionalism is a significant element in Belgian, German, Italian and Spanish political administration; it is an unresolved issue in the UK, where it relates specifically to the Celtic fringe; and it is of lesser interest in the more unitary states of France, Greece, Ireland, Portugal and Scandinavia. These differences stem from ethnic, religious or political features of the past, with consequences varying in extremity from the terrorism of ETA and the IRA to the virtual partition of Belgium and the ordered federalism of Germany. At its mildest, regionalism is merely folkloric, or an occasion to attract structural funds from the EU. At its strongest it represents an alternative to the nation state. The Basque country, Catalonia, Scotland, Flanders, Ulster, Bavaria and Italy's Northern League all present different aspects of the regional phenomenon.

The influence of Germany in European affairs has led to a presumption in favour of the German style of government as a constitutional model for the EU, with a multiplicity of regional governments and bureaucracies taking responsibility for administration, including such areas as education, health and much of the spending budget. Justice, monetary policy, defence and foreign policy are always left to the federal centre. This model is well suited to the Commission's ambition to transfer power progressively from national governments to the supranational bodies of the EU.

European regionalism finds its main institutional outlets in the Committee of the Regions, a consultative quango established by the Maastricht Treaty, and the European Regional Development Fund, set up on a small scale in 1975 but subsequently much boosted. There are also various bodies attached to the EU which occupy themselves with regional, municipal or local government agendas oriented either to the solicitation of subsidies or to propaganda. For instance, twinning is arranged by the Council of European Municipalities and Regions; and the promotion of regionalism and federalism is the mission of the Assembly of European Regions.

Regulation

Regulations rank with Decisions and the better known Directives as the key legal instruments of the EU. The difference between them is that Directives have force only when passed into law by each member state, whereas Regulations and Decisions have direct effect, that is, they become law throughout the Union as soon as they have been issued. Historically, Regulations have been the means of implementing the Common Agricultural and Common Fisheries Policies. The Commission intends in future to use Regulations more widely instead of Directives, since it can do so with the easily obtained assent of the Council of Ministers (and, within limits, on its own authority), avoiding the delays and closer scrutiny associated with national parliamentary legislation. (For the volume of Community legislation see **Directives** and for a general description see **Community law**.)

Religion

Of the EU's most populous nations, France, Italy, Spain, Belgium and Portugal are Catholic, as is Poland, which is due to join the Union early in the next century. Greece is Orthodox and the Netherlands is somewhat more Catholic than Protestant. South Germany and Austria are Catholic, but North Germany is Protestant. The UK is predominantly Protestant, though with a significant Catholic minority (as well as a sizeable Muslim minority), and Scandinavia as a bloc is Lutheran Protestant. Europe is thus divided into a Nordic, Germanic, Anglo-Saxon Protestant vein, accounting for approximately one-third of the population, and a Latin and central European Catholic vein, accounting for approximately twice as many. Some detect a deeper cultural significance in these historical divisions, going beyond theological beliefs to reflect ethical, social and even political attitudes, such as the independent-mindedness of the UK,

Norway and Denmark. There is perhaps, for example, less resistance in southern Europe to the collectivism of the EU, and less tolerance in northern Europe for wayward attitudes towards compliance. On a minor scale, support for this type of analysis is to be found also in the mutual hostility and incomprehension of Catholic republicans and Protestant loyalists in Northern Ireland. There are, however, too many exceptions for any generalisation along these lines to yield reliable inferences.

Christian Democracy, the largest centre-right political movement in Europe, is a relic of a more religious age, owing its origins – at least in Germany – to the late 19th century *Kulturkampf*, or struggle between beliefs, when Prussia's Bismarck tried to drive the Catholic Church out of politics. After World War II the descendants of the old Church party found a unifying cause in moderate Christian conservatism, in opposition to the more secular social democracy of the centre left and the atheistic Marxism of the extreme left. In Bavaria the movement remained Catholic and is embodied in the Christian Social Union party; elsewhere in Germany it is represented by the CDU, or Christian Democratic Union. The other major affiliated parties in Europe are Democrazia Cristiana in Italy, the Christian Democrats in the Netherlands and the two Christian parties in Belgium.

With the passing of time, increasing secularisation, together with the inevitable compromises and shifting alliances of politics, have substantially drained Christian Democracy of its religious content, and when Turkey, stung by the blocking of its accession to the EU, accused Europe in 1997 of being an exclusive Christian society, it was anachronistically wide of the mark. There is indeed bias against Muslims (including Turkish, Pakistani and North African immigrants) in several European countries, but this is as much racial, or inspired by fear of competition for scarce jobs, as religious; and although the defining EU Treaties ban such discrimination, they cannot prevent it.

Renegotiation

British politicians not infrequently cite as their aim the renegotiation of one or more unwanted aspects of EU legislation, or even the wholesale renegotiation of the UK's relationship with the Community. Such declarations generally amount to empty rhetoric. Renegotiation of significant Treaty obligations would require unanimity among the member states and would not be possible without the use of the veto to block other EU business in return for concessions to the UK. Across-the-board renegotiation could not be achieved without a credible threat of withdrawal from the Community or a constitutional convention which reshaped the EU's Treaties.

Research

The Treaty of Rome reflects the Commission's belief in a Community policy to make European industry more competitive in high technology by stimulating research. There was no greater enthusiast for spending money on such activity than Jacques Delors, and no greater sceptic than the UK government of Margaret Thatcher. The current 1994–98 programme, amounting to some 13 billion ECUs over four years, focuses mainly on information and communication technology, energy (including the JET nuclear fusion project), biotechnology and environmental research. Other well-known Europe-wide research projects include the European Space Agency and the CERN nuclear physics facility, both of which are funded by individual governments, including non-members of the EU, and so strictly speaking fall outside the ambit of the Community.

Residui passivi

Residui passivi, or residual liabilities, are Italian state funds voted by parliament for government departments but withheld by the Treasury under its programme to meet the convergence criteria for the single currency. It is not clear to what extent these obligations will eventually have to be met. By the end of 1997 they amounted to some 15% of Italy's GDP, and were causing concern abroad about the sustainability of the country's new-found financial rectitude.

Resolution

A decision by the Council of Ministers or the European Council, having no status in law, but expressing a political agreement to take legislative action. In the context of the European Parliament, a Resolution is a statement of views, akin to an Opinion, which may or may not be taken seriously by higher authority.

Rhine model

The consensus-based German-Austrian economic structure, often known as the social market economy and contrasted with the more free-wheeling British and American system. (For a fuller comparison, see **Anglo-American model**.)

Rights

There are two forms of rights: those which assert the right to protection from intrusion or oppression; and those which assert a claim on others to provide benefits such as welfare, employment or positive discrimination. The former type is libertarian; the latter, to which the Commission, the traditional left and the politically correct are drawn, depends on tax or legal compulsion. The

Maastricht Treaty endorses a number of social claims in the name of fundamental rights. The Treaty of Amsterdam goes further, adding new entitlements and permitting the punishment of a state which, in the opinion of the other member states, persistently breaches the principles of 'respect for human rights and fundamental freedoms'. (See also **European Convention on Human Rights**.)

Right of initiative

The right to initiate legislation is the closely guarded privilege of the Commission, setting it apart from conventional bureaucracies and paralleling the power of its commissioners to intervene in European political affairs. This prerogative stems from the ambition of the EU's Founding Fathers that the Commission should in time become the government of Europe.

Romania

Recognised as an independent kingdom since the late 19th century, Romania underwent significant territorial changes in 1918 and again in 1940. It collaborated with Germany in World War II until it was overrun by the Soviet army in 1944. The forced abdication of King Michael in 1947 presaged over 40 years of communist oppression, the last 24 under the dictator Nicolae Ceausescu, whose professed opposition to interference from Moscow provided some cover for a reign of terror and cultural destruction. After Ceausescu's summary execution in 1989 President Iliescu conducted affairs on neo-communist principles, with hyperinflation and minimal reform. The election of President Emil Constantinescu in 1996 gave Romania its first glimpse of genuine liberalisation, but the country is starting from an impoverished base and its application for early membership of the EU was not recommended by the Commission. Its application for membership of NATO was also rebuffed. Constantinescu's suggestion of an annual review of the progress of EU candidates has been well received.

Russia

Part European, part Asian, Russia casts a long shadow over Europe. When Stalin's Iron Curtain descended on Eastern Europe after World War II, most of the countries of free Europe received Marshall Aid and successively coalesced into what eventually became the EU – a democratic prosperity zone reliant on NATO for military security. With the fall of the Berlin Wall in 1989 and the collapse of the Soviet empire in 1991, a half century of confrontation ended. The Warsaw Pact was dissolved and most of its former members applied to join the EU and NATO. The Soviet Union also disintegrated, as its constituent parts declared their independence. Of these, the Baltic states, which had been annexed in the 1940s, progressed towards EU membership. Russia itself, together with the former Soviet republics of Ukraine, Belarus, Kazakhstan, Kyrgyzstan and Moldova, signed co-operation agreements with the EU which explicitly ruled out membership.

Struggling against a background of gangsterism and economic collapse to retain the vestiges of superpower status and to earn acceptance as a civilised democracy, Russia has become a member of the Council of Europe, an observer (and future participant) at the Group of Seven summit meetings and a member of the UN Security Council, where it inherited the seat of the Soviet Union. Russia coordinates policies with the former Soviet republics and addresses problems relating to the break-up of the Soviet Union through the Commonwealth of Independent States, established in 1991. Fearful of encirclement, Russia has tried without success to block NATO's eastward expansion. But armed hostility has been replaced by friendlier exchanges, and in 1997 (to the evident surprise of the UK and Italy) France, Germany and Russia announced that they had agreed to meet annually 'to review the state of the Continent'.

Ryder Cup

A biennial golf contest between teams from the USA and Europe, the Ryder Cup is perhaps unique in stirring spontaneous European emotions among ordinary sports fans, a feat not matched by official attempts to create a European identity.

S

Saarland

The coal-rich German Saarland, governed by the League of Nations after World War I, restored by plebiscite to Germany in 1935 and situated in the French occupied zone after World War II, was finally restored again to Germany in 1959. This was due to Konrad Adenauer's patient negotiation and the pooling of the French and German coal and steel industries in 1952 within the Monnet-inspired European Coal and Steel Community. So ended a bitter dispute which had long poisoned Franco–German relations.

Santer, Jacques (1937–)

Jacques Santer succeeded Jacques Delors as president of the European Commission in 1995, the second Luxemburger to hold this high office. Chosen as a compromise candidate, he follows the conventional EU line, without ever matching his controversial predecessor's driving sense of purpose.

Schengen Agreement

An accord to abolish border controls, first signed in 1985, and fleshed out in 1990 into a detailed Convention, the Schengen Agreement was an inter-governmental instrument. As such it was not originally part of Community law. The initial signatories were Belgium, France, Germany, Luxembourg and the Netherlands, but by the time the Convention came into force in 1995 Portugal and Spain had signed up, followed by Austria and Italy, the latter two anticipating full compliance in 1998. The Nordic Council is negotiating to merge its own passport-free zone with the Schengen area, bringing Denmark, Finland, Sweden, Norway and Iceland into the Convention, and Greece also hopes to become a full member soon.

The Schengen Agreement did not have an untroubled passage. The UK (with which Ireland has a passport pact) stood aloof, anxious about terrorism, organised crime and illegal immigration. France reimposed border controls with Belgium in 1995 to guard against alleged Dutch laxity over drug traffic. In addition, libertarians and law enforcement agencies, from their differing standpoints, raised questions over asylum, extradition, exchange of personal data, hot pursuit, visa control, tax evasion and the policing of external frontiers.

The meshing of the Agreement with the Justice and Home Affairs pillar of the Maastricht Treaty, reflecting the free movement of persons provisions of the

Treaty of Rome, was largely dealt with by the 1997 Treaty of Amsterdam, which promises to bring Schengen within the *acquis communautaire* through abolishing internal borders and transferring powers over immigration to the Community. The UK (again with Ireland) has an opt-out from this section of the Treaty, but France will lose the flexibility which it enjoyed under the Schengen Agreement.

At the beginning of 1998 a massive influx of refugees, many of them Kurds escaping Turkish oppression, but others from Albania, Algeria and other parts of Europe and North Africa, led to criticism of the inadequacy of frontier controls throughout the EU, especially in Greece and Italy. There were fears that these countries would prove soft entry points to illegal immigrants transiting to countries with generous welfare systems, such as Germany, France and (despite its opt-out) the UK. Amid calls for emergency meetings of interior ministers, there were even suggestions that the Schengen Agreement might have to be partially suspended. (See also **Asylum**.)

Schmidt, Helmut (1918–)

Helmut Schmidt became German chancellor in 1974 as head of a centre-left coalition in which his own party, the Social Democrats, was the senior partner. His friendship with Valéry Giscard d'Estaing (who also became French president in 1974) formed the bedrock of Community policy-making for the remainder of the decade, a period made difficult by the oil crisis after the 1973 Yom Kippur War, which slowed European economies and caused widespread inflation.

The collapse of the dollar during Carter's US presidency (1977–81) converted Schmidt to the plan of the Commission's president, Roy Jenkins, to revive EMU. From their deliberations was born the ultimately ill-fated European Monetary System. Gloomy, introspective and formidable, Schmidt was pessimistic about the global political and economic scene. He was nevertheless an enthusiast for the enlargement of the Community, strongly supporting the applications of Greece, Portugal and Spain. Margaret Thatcher's advent in 1979 heralded a prolonged confrontation between the UK and the other member states over the British contribution to the European budget, during which Schmidt managed to remain equally trusted and respected by Jenkins, Giscard and Thatcher. In 1982 he lost power to Helmut Kohl when the Free Democrats switched coalition sides.

Schroder, Gerhard (1944–)

By winning the Lower Saxony election in March 1998, Gerhard Schroder established himself as the Social Democrat candidate to challenge Chancellor Helmut Kohl in Germany's September 1998 federal election. Schroder's vaguely centrist position cast him in the modernising mould of British Prime Minister Tony Blair and his popularity gave him the hope, denied to his leftist Social Democrat rival Oskar Lafontaine, of ending Kohl's 16-year domination of German politics. Difficult to pin down, Schroder gives the impression of being mildly Eurosceptic, at least by German standards, but his main preoccupation in the election period was to avoid any substantive policy stance.

Schuman Plan

See **European Coal and Steel Community**.

SEA

See **Single European Act**.

That night gave us the final proof that a Europe of sovereign States was incapable of reaching the sensible decisions that were needed for the common good.

Jean Monnet on a squabble in 1953 over the location of the EC's institutions.

Seat of the EU's institutions

Unseemly squabbles have marked the choice of location for many of the EU's institutions – none more so than for the European Parliament, which meets in Strasbourg and Brussels, with its secretariat in Luxembourg. Of the other institutions, Luxembourg plays host to the European Court of Justice, the European Investment Bank and the Court of Auditors; Frankfurt will house the future European Central Bank; Brussels is the seat for the Commission and the Council of Ministers; and other lesser offices or agencies are spread around various cities.

Seigniorage

The profits earned by central banks on interest-free liabilities, chiefly banknotes. Countries with hard currencies, such as Germany and the USA, gain significantly from seigniorage, since individual citizens (especially law-breakers) in weak currency areas, including Eastern Europe, often hold large cash sums in D–Mark notes and dollar bills. The advent of the euro will reduce Germany's seigniorage to its share in the profits of the European Central Bank (ECB). The ECB's plan to issue large denomination (500 euro) notes will be particularly welcome to the black market.

Set-aside

Detested by farmers for the paperwork it begets, and by free-marketeers for its self-contradictions, set-aside is a Common Agricultural Policy measure, introduced in 1988, for cutting production by compensating farmers for taking part of their land out of crop.

The Seven

Austria, Denmark, Norway, Portugal, Sweden, Switzerland and the UK – the seven original members of the European Free Trade Association (EFTA). The Seven was a term used to distinguish EFTA from the six founder members of the European Community.

Single currency

The single currency is part of the wider project for Economic and Monetary Union, the central objective of the 1992 Maastricht Treaty. Under the Treaty, 1999 is the latest date for introducing the new currency, initially through irrevocably fixed exchange rates and finally, by 2002, through the replacement of national currencies by the euro. The participating countries were finally chosen and the conversion rates set in the spring of 1998. From January 1st 1999, the national currencies that are to be abolished will legally represent non-integral subdivisions of the euro. On the same date the ECU will be converted into the euro on a 1-for-1 basis. Between January 1999 and the end of 2001 the euro and national currencies will operate in tandem. By January 2002 banknotes and coin will have been issued to the public, contracts will be converted into euros and new contracts must be denominated in euros. By the end of June 2002 the national currencies of participating member states will cease to be legal tender.

> *The coining of money is in all states the act of sovereign power.*
> William Blackstone, c. 1765

The single currency will be managed by the future European Central Bank (ECB) in Frankfurt. The Maastricht Treaty stipulates that the Board and Governing Council of the ECB are to be bankers, free from interference from elected politicians and with internal price stability as their priority. This provision substantially follows the German system, but has caused unease in France, which has sought to establish a ministerial level political counterweight, excluding those member states which have retained their own currencies. This inner group of finance ministers is variously known as the Stability Council or the Euro-X club (X standing for the number of members), depending on whether the emphasis is on the German concept that its function is to assure permanent fiscal discipline or the French concept that its function is to give politicians a say in interest and exchange rates.

The UK (although in principle favourable) and Denmark have so far opted out of the single currency, while Sweden has announced that it will not participate initially. Greece has been informed that its application will be rejected for the time being. All the other EU states have agreed to adopt the euro and have been accepted, albeit sometimes controversially, as passing the financial qualifying tests. (For a more extensive treatment of the political and economic background to the single currency, see **EMU** and **Convergence criteria**.)

Single European Act (SEA)

The SEA of 1986, the first major revision of the 1957 Treaty of Rome, came at a time of dissatisfaction with the EC's institutional arrangements. Having absorbed the UK, Ireland, Denmark and Greece, and being in the process of absorbing Spain and Portugal, the EC had grown too unwieldy to work properly. The single market was bogged down in trivial disagreements. It was a period of radical thinking. In 1984 Altiero Spinelli had wanted to reform the EC from top to bottom, putting the European Parliament at its centre. The Stuttgart Declaration of 1983 had proposed new areas of co-operation leading, like Spinelli's proposals, to a European Union. The SEA, responding to these undercurrents and coinciding with the advent of Jacques Delors as Commission president, fell far short of the hopes of the extreme reformers, but in reality, by extending the scope of qualified majority voting (QMV), setting a deadline of 1992 for the completion of the single market and strengthening the powers of the Parliament, it gave the EC new momentum, weakening the national right of veto and so reviving the prospects for integration – developments the more surprising, in retrospect, for occurring not merely under the watchful eye of Margaret Thatcher but with her active encouragement. She for her part doubtless wished the EC to concentrate on the task of organising a transparent internal market and accepted that a degree of supranational control was indispensable to that end, little suspecting that the enhanced role of QMV would prove to be the thin end of a giant wedge. It is nonetheless noteworthy that Denmark initially rejected the Treaty as transferring too much authority to the European Parliament, while the Irish High Court ruled that it entailed an amendment to the Irish constitution, requiring a referendum.

The SEA (*Acte Unique*) was so named because it covered a wide field and its authors were determined that it should go through as one package. Its main provisions concerned the single market. To remove trade barriers, Commissioner Cockfield had identified some 300 necessary actions, most of which were blocked by the lack of unanimous agreement in the Council of Ministers. By making these actions subject to QMV the Treaty aimed to turn the common market into a reality by the end of 1992. The SEA also addressed the democratic deficit, giving the European Parliament the right to be consulted twice over certain types of legislation (the co-operation procedure) and to veto accession treaties and Association Agreements (the assent procedure). To ease the pressure on the European Court of Justice a new Court of First Instance was created, and there were a number of lesser measures. In addition, some general concepts, which were to loom larger in the Maastricht Treaty, made their first appearance, such as cohesion (that is, more money for the poorer states and regions) and foreign policy co-operation.

Single market

From the outset, a single, or common, internal European market was the primary stated purpose of the 1957 Treaty of Rome. The promise of its creation had been a virtual condition of Marshall Aid after World War II, and the six signatories of the 1951 European Coal and Steel Community Treaty turned their attention to forming a wider customs union as soon as their dream of a European army ended with the collapse of the European Defence Community in 1954. The arrangements envisaged in the Treaty of Rome were no mere free trade area. They entailed a common external tariff; the abolition of internal customs duties; the removal of distortions to competition; the harmonisation of relevant laws; the adoption of a common agricultural policy; freedom of movement for persons, goods, services and capital; and the creation of various supranational bodies to execute the Treaty's ambitious purpose.

By 1968 the customs union was complete, but during the next 15 years progress on the single market was blocked by all manner of non-tariff barriers. Up to 70 forms were needed by truck drivers crossing EC borders; public contracts were reserved for national companies; product standards and professional qualifications were neither harmonised nor given mutual recognition; service industries were largely confined to their own member state; capital movements were not liberalised; and differential rates of VAT and duty were distorting trade. By an irony of history, it was largely on British initiative that the EC was able to recapture its momentum. Margaret Thatcher supplied much of the political drive, Commissioner Cockfield produced a crucial White Paper and an Anglo-French report to the European Parliament also had a significant impact. Meanwhile, Jacques Delors was about to take up his first Commission presidency in 1985. The enlargement of the Community had made unanimity increasingly difficult to reach, and in the new mood it was agreed that Lord Cockfield's proposals to remedy the defects of the single market could only be implemented by qualified majority voting in the Council of Ministers. This was duly enacted in the 1986 Single European Act.

Delors and Cockfield threw themselves into the revived single market programme to great effect, producing 282 Directives and Regulations, of which over 90% had been passed by the Council of Ministers and nearly 80% were being implemented in member states by the target date of December 31st 1992. Delors perceived market integration in the context of economic and political integration, characteristically pushing any measure which conduced to his larger vision; as a consequence, the single market concept soon expanded to embrace such ideas as the removal of passport controls, the introduction of a single currency, police co-operation and tax harmonisation, ideas which were to take more concrete shape in the Treaties of Maastricht and Amsterdam. Others, including Thatcher, regarded the single market as a finite end in itself, irritated at the excessively detailed regulation which accompanied it and resistant to the open-ended amplifications which were being attached to it and which raised fundamental issues of national sovereignty.

The specific single market measures (most of which also apply in the European Economic Area) are too numerous to itemise. Many of them go into detail beyond what is needed for the setting of acceptable standards, engendering a sense that the EU is out of touch, especially among consumers and small businesses. Other measures give rise to concern for the opposite reason, that of being too sweeping. The 1997 Amsterdam summit used the single market as a pretext to aim at corporate tax, capital gains tax and social policy, as well as such more appropriate targets as service-sector barriers, late payment and government-originated distortions to trade. Thus the single market, like so much else in the EU, reflects the unfinished debate about the rival merits of an integrated federal Europe or a Europe of independent, if closely linked, member states.

The Six

Belgium, France, Italy, Luxembourg, the Netherlands and West Germany – the six original signatories of the 1951 Treaty of Paris and the 1957 Treaty of Rome, which created the European Coal and Steel Community and the European Economic Community respectively. The Six was a term used to distinguish the Community from the seven founder members of EFTA. Subsequent changes made both numbers obsolete.

Slovakia

For much of its history part of Hungary, Slovakia was amalgamated into Czechoslovakia in 1918, became a Nazi puppet state in World War II, was returned to Czechoslovakia after the war and fell under Soviet domination until the collapse of communism in Eastern Europe in 1989. Freedom brought with it a revival of nationalist sentiment and Slovakia became a separate state in 1993. An ambivalent attitude to reform, continued use of secret police and other human rights failings have led the Commission to conclude that Slovakia is not yet ready for membership of the EU. In a reciprocal spirit of rejection, an unabashed Slovakia has withdrawn its application.

Slovenia

The most northerly of the former Yugoslav republics, Slovenia has been the object of repeated annexation, division and invasion since the collapse of the Austro-Hungarian Empire in World War I. Fears of Serbian domination led to a declaration of independence in 1991 as Yugoslavia broke up. Relatively prosperous by East European standards, Slovenia has a GNP per head not far short of that of the poorest EU member states and has been accepted as a candidate for early admission to the Community, which now accounts for two-thirds of its external trade.

Small countries

Europe's mini-states are for the most part protectorates of, or otherwise closely linked to, larger European countries. These special relationships determine their arrangements with the EU. Applications for EU membership by small but independent states are complicated by their lack of sufficient resources to play a full part in the Community's governance and by the incongruity of their having equal veto rights with the major nations.

⇒ **Andorra**, a republican tax haven, over which until 1993 Spain (in the name of a bishop) and France (in the name of its president) held joint sovereignty, has been part of the Community's customs union since 1991, but has not applied for EU membership.

⇒ **The Channel Islands** of Jersey and Guernsey are self-governing crown dependencies and together constitute the leading British-linked tax haven. Although not part of the EU they enjoy free movement of goods under the UK's Treaty of Accession. The **Isle of Man** has a similar status.

⇒ **Cyprus**, a former British protectorate which became a republic in 1960, has been partitioned since its invasion by Turkey in 1974. The EU does not recognise the Turkish Republic of Northern Cyprus, and although Cyprus has had an Association Agreement since 1973 and has been recommended by the Commission for full membership of the Union, its constitutional impasse remains an impediment.

- ⇒ **Gibraltar** falls within the ambit of the Treaty of Rome as a British dependency (ceded by Spain in 1713). A partially self-governing democracy, it is disputed territory between the UK and Spain, a problem exacerbated by its being a peninsula, with its airport on reclaimed land.
- ⇒ **Liechtenstein**, a principality and a tax haven linked to Switzerland, is a member both of EFTA and (unlike Switzerland) of the EEA. It has not applied for EU membership.
- ⇒ **Malta**, a former British dependency and a republic since 1974, has had an Association Agreement since 1970. Its application for full membership in 1990 received only a cautious welcome from the Commission, which was troubled by the country's economic backwardness, its protectionism and the hostility to the EU of its powerful pro-communist Labour opposition party.
- ⇒ **Monaco**, a principality, a tax haven and a protectorate of France, is in customs union with France but has no formal agreement with the EU.

Other very small European states include the **Republic of San Marino**, an Italian protectorate in customs union with the EU; and the **Vatican City**, which is independent.

The Snake

In its first effort at creating a zone of currency stability, the EC attempted in 1971 to fix European parities closer to each other than to the dollar, but with some flexibility (the Snake). The Snake rapidly died with the collapse of the dollar-based Bretton Woods system on which the post-war monetary order had been founded, but was reborn in 1972 as the Snake in the tunnel, a system whereby European currencies could fluctuate within a narrow band either side of the dollar. This creature did not last long either, killed off by the currency turmoil that accompanied the 1973 oil crisis. (See also **EMU** and **Werner Report**.)

Soames affair

By 1969 President Charles de Gaulle had been fighting European integration for a decade. In 1962 Walter Hallstein had foiled the French Fouchet Plan for a new model Europe based on co-operation between nation states. De Gaulle vetoed the UK's application to join the Community in 1963 and again in 1967, having in the meantime embarked on a boycott of European institutions and threatened to pull France out of the Community. It was therefore not entirely surprising that de Gaulle now privately discussed with Sir Christopher Soames, the British ambassador, the possibility of France allying with the UK to create a free trade area, incorporating the Six as well as the Seven. The idea (in the rather unlikely event that it could have succeeded) was all that the UK should have hoped for, but, anxious not to offend its prospective partners, it leaked de Gaulle's proposals to the USA, West Germany and other countries, provoking loud cries of treachery by the French. Within months de Gaulle had resigned, and the UK was on its way into the Common Market.

Social Chapter

The Social Chapter, formally known as the Protocol on Social Policy, is a litany of well-meaning 1970s corporatist nostrums about employment conditions. Anxious, however, to demonstrate its free-market credentials, it does not neglect to mention 'the need to maintain the competitiveness of the Community economy'. The Chapter was based on the 1989 Social Charter and was originally to be incorporated in the 1992 Maastricht Treaty as an expanded version of the social provisions contained in the Treaty of Rome. In the event, however, John Major's British government rejected it, whereupon it was extracted from the main body of the text and signed by the other 11 member states as a binding Protocol. This Protocol, which also constitutes the British opt-out, permits the signatories to use the legal instruments and the institutions of the Community, including the European Court of Justice, in pursuing the objectives of the Chapter and enforcing them at law. On coming to power in 1997 the Labour government carried out its manifesto pledge to cancel the British opt-out, clearing the way for the incorporation of the Chapter into the main body of the 1997 Treaty of Amsterdam. At the same time Prime Minister Tony Blair promised that the Chapter would not be allowed to undermine the UK's competitiveness – a promise on which it might be hard to deliver, given that most EU social legislation is determined by qualified majority voting.

I cannot think of a single more effective way to create poverty and unemployment in southern Europe.

Antonio Martino, former Italian foreign secretary, on the Social Chapter, March 1997

On the Continent the Chapter has generally been regarded as little more than a restatement of social market principles already embodied in national employment law, with the difference that global competitive pressures are leading to labour market reforms in individual member states, whereas the Chapter, being part of the *acquis communautaire*, is irreversible. British industry has long viewed it with suspicion, seeing it as a licence to undo some of the reforms instituted by Margaret Thatcher. Apologists for the Chapter reply that the British opt-out was largely ineffective, since labour market legislation could be brought in under other articles of the Treaty of Rome; they also argue less convincingly that the wording of the Chapter is too unspecific to create a threat to employment flexibility, missing the point that framework principles are a standard Community prelude to detailed regulation.

Social Charter

Easily confused with the Social Chapter of the Maastricht Treaty or the impotent European Social Charter agreed by the Council of Europe in 1961, the Social Charter (or Charter on the Fundamental Social Rights of Workers) was signed in 1989 by all the EU member states except the UK. The Charter was an initiative of Jacques Delors, who argued that European business would become more humane and more successful if the EU standardised employment rights, a view opposed by Margaret Thatcher on the grounds that over-regulating the labour market would discourage employers from creating new jobs and that employment legislation should be a national affair. There followed a Social Action Programme comprising 47 legislative proposals, most of which have in fact been implemented in the UK. The Commission planned to incorporate the Social Charter into the Maastricht Treaty. Further British opposition prevented this, and in the event it was annexed to the Treaty in the form of a Protocol on Social Policy, informally always known as the Social Chapter.

Social dumping

An expression to describe the superior competitiveness of another country arising from lower labour costs, less job protection or less regulation. The accusation has sometimes been made, especially in Paris and Brussels, against the UK, on the grounds of its former opt-out from the Social Chapter and its Thatcherite labour market conditions. The implication that competitive labour costs are discreditable might have some force if these were a product of, for example, disregard of safety standards at work. But when the advantage is a result of employment flexibility and low non-wage costs, the charge of social dumping betrays little more than antipathy to the Anglo-American model of free markets.

In the wider context of competition from Asia, Latin America and Eastern Europe, where low wages not infrequently coincide with abusive practices and environmental neglect, social dumping raises fundamental, and not easily answered, questions about the merits of unregulated free trade.

Social market economy

A somewhat vague term, originally associated with the free marketeer Ludwig

Erhard, to denote a market economy which is nevertheless concerned with social issues. Subsequently the expression came to describe a mixed economy in which the free play of market forces is constrained by social security features.

Social partners

Eurospeak for what the British used to call the two sides of industry.

SOCRATES

The European Community's programme for trans-European co-operation in education, targeted at schools and universities. (See also **ERASMUS**.)

Solidarity tax

The unpopular tax surcharge introduced after German reunification and earmarked for reconstruction costs in Eastern Germany.

Il sorpasso

The moment in the 1980s when Italy, boosted by its black economy, allegedly overtook the UK to become the world's fifth largest economy (after the USA, Japan, Germany and France). Margaret Thatcher's characteristic response was that in that case Italy's contribution to the EC's budget should be higher. By 1998 it seemed that the UK had resumed fifth position and was challenging France for fourth.

Sovereignty

Not to be confused with power, sovereignty is to a nation what free will is to an individual, namely the right to take independent action, however constrained by external circumstances.

When signing a Treaty of Accession, a member state, in addition to agreeing to co-operate with other members in various policy areas, also grants supremacy to Community law and delegates certain authorities indefinitely to EU institutions. The delegation of authority, however, even if notionally in perpetuity, does not affect sovereignty as long as it is reversible without breaking the law.

It is generally acknowledged that the member states of the EU still (if only barely) retain their sovereignty, since they could in the last resort secede from the EU. For example, in the case of the UK the primacy of Community law derives from Parliament's European Communities Act, which Parliament itself has the power to repeal. Such a repeal would entail abrogating the UK's Treaty of Accession, but this would be a diplomatic obstacle rather than a constitutional one.

Sceptics and federalists are in agreement that membership of EMU has constitutional implications, since participants will lose control over their currency and their monetary policy, which are among the defining characteristics of an autonomous state. EMU is likely also to lead eventually to the ceding to the EU of powers of taxation and spending. The originators of the Maastricht Treaty and its successor, the Treaty of Amsterdam, repeatedly stated that the purpose of EMU, as of the Treaty provisions on justice, border controls and foreign affairs, was to advance the creation of a unified European state.

Those who consider NATO obligations tantamount to sharing sovereignty are mistaken. Countries can (and do) withdraw from NATO if they choose to do so. Indeed, the capacity to enter into or to annul such treaties is part of the definition of sovereignty in international law. More relevant in the military context is the fact that member states' ability to defend their interests, in the last resort by arms, will be impaired by joining EMU, since their gold and foreign exchange reserves will be transferred into supranational ownership and the Maastricht Treaty deprives governments of the right to finance exceptional expenditure through borrowing from their central banks.

The notion that the force of global markets makes sovereignty a fiction is another fallacy. The essence of sovereignty is not that it confers omnipotence but that it allows a country to choose its response to events. Canada's independence from the USA, Switzerland's from the EU, and Japan's and Singapore's from the rest of the world prove that neither size nor geography are relevant to sovereignty. A city state and an economic giant may be similarly affected by shocks in financial markets, yet each can determine freely whether to react by, for example, floating or refixing its currency, tightening or relaxing foreign investment rules, protecting or deregulating its financial sector. Such decisions represent the practical exercise of sovereignty.

The encroachment of Community law and the wide scope of the powers granted to European supranational institutions have combined to make sovereignty an explosive issue of principle to those who set store by national independence. It is no reply to suggest that a small share in EU decision-making provides the same 'effective sovereignty' as autonomy; such a line of reasoning is tantamount to equating a province to a self-governing nation. As for 'pooled sovereignty' – a phrase in vogue among diplomats and directors of multinational companies – this has no more meaning than pooled personal identity.

Whether sovereignty resides in the people or the institutions of constitutional government is a matter for debate. In the European context the blurring of the concept is part of the wider process of disparaging the nation state in favour of an as yet amorphous federation, itself intended by its creators to evolve ultimately into a new country, with all the attributes of sovereignty which they rebuke as obsolete or chauvinist in individual nations. (See also **Federalism**.)

Spain

Spain joined the Community at the same time as Portugal in 1986, a previous application in the 1960s having been rejected on the grounds of General Franco's dictatorship. The EU's fifth largest state, Spain has two commissioners (like Germany, France, Italy and the UK) and 64 MEPs, which places it between the 87 MEPs of France, Italy and the UK and the 31 of the next largest state, the Netherlands. Spain joined NATO in 1982, but its commitment has been half-hearted and in 1986 it withdrew from the integrated military structure.

The country's regions play a strong role in its affairs, making it a natural supporter of the Committee of the Regions and one of the largest beneficiaries of the Union's structural funds. Overall, the country is a substantial net cash recipient from the Community. With its history of political extremism and its corruption scandals, Spain sees the EU as a safeguard of freedom and prosperity as well as a welcome escape from the stagnant legacy of protectionism and corporatism inherited from its years of authoritarian rule.

Spain's relationship with the UK has been coloured by disputes over Gibraltar and the Common Fisheries Policy. Many Britons, especially in fishing communities, suspect Spanish officialdom of condoning a cynical attitude towards compliance with Community rules and regulations, although it has to be said that accusations abound on both sides and that the Spanish position on fish quotas has been upheld in the English law courts. Moreover, Spain's overall record of implementing Directives is above the average for EU member states.

Although the peseta devalued during the 1992 ERM crisis, Spain was accepted in 1998 as a first-wave participant in the single currency, having achieved a considerable degree of fiscal discipline. This feat, together with the successful hosting of the Olympic Games in 1992, symbolised the country's progress in shaking off the consequences of 40 troubled years, starting with the Civil War in the 1930s and continuing with a prolonged period of international isolation until Franco's death in 1975.

Spinelli, Altiero (1907–86)

An Italian journalist, a romantic communist and an opponent of Mussolini's fascism, Altiero Spinelli spent ten pre-war years in prison and his World War II years in internment, exiled to an island, where he wrote a federalist manifesto. Anti-Church, anti-American, anti-British, anti-nationalist, anti-capitalist, he saw the war as creating the revolutionary conditions through which popular socialism could flow like 'molten lava'. Spinelli joined the Commission in 1970. In 1979 he became one of the first directly elected MEPs as part of the communist group. His major work as an MEP was the 1984 Draft Treaty establishing the European Union, which reflected his view of the European

Parliament as a potential constitution-making body (or constituent assembly), able to enact a new constitutional Treaty if ratified by a majority of the large member states. Since this role was reserved under the Treaty of Rome for unanimous agreement among the member states, Spinelli's Treaty eventually fizzled out, although it paved the way for the Single European Act of 1986 and in some ways anticipated the Maastricht Treaty of 1992. (See also **Crocodile Club**.)

Sport (1)

In the late 1990s Competition Commissioner Karel Van Miert began to target sport, starting with Formula One motor racing and Association Football. At issue were fundamental questions. Is sport a business, subject to Community laws on restraint of trade, or a voluntary activity like a club? And if professional sport is a business, does that interpretation extend to its regulation and to those many areas where the dividing line between amateurs and professionals is blurred?

In 1995 Van Miert had won an important legal victory, assuring professional footballers of freedom to play without restriction for clubs throughout the EU. In 1998 he signalled his intention to challenge as an abuse of dominant position the monopoly enjoyed by the FIA, the Formula One ruling body – a monopoly which enabled it to decide track venues for races and to command vast television fees. At the same time, Van Miert offered a not dissimilar challenge to football's governing authority, UEFA. Against him, it was argued that sports without firm central direction easily decline into lax standards. With large sums at stake, the stage was set for complex legal battles before the European Court of Justice.

Sport (2)

Recognising the hold of sport on popular affections, the Commission seeks to identify the EU with sporting events. A vintage year was 1992, in which the Community sponsored the Tour de France and took advantage of the coincidence that both the Winter and the Summer Olympics were taking place in Europe. A naive attempt to have member states' athletes compete in a unified EU team at Barcelona was vetoed by the European Olympic Committee, but the Community, despite the Olympic Charter's ban on political propaganda, spent over $15 million on advertising during the opening ceremonies. The result was a spectacular show in which the darkened stadium was transformed into the 12-star European flag by spectators waving blue and yellow torches. Other sports which the Community sponsors include yachting (the 'Treaty of Rome' has twice participated in round-the-world races), tennis (the European Community Championship for indoor tennis has been supported financially by the Commission since 1986) and swimming. In 1991 the European Sports Forum was set up, a body which brings together government and EU officials, together with various national sports federations, to advise the newly created sports sector of DG X – doubtless a welcome development to those who believe in the image-building opportunities of state-sponsored sport.

Stability Council

See **Stability Pact** and **Euro-X**.

Stability Pact

The Stability Pact, or Stability and Growth Pact, adopted by the European Council in 1997, is designed to prevent any national relapses into fiscal indiscipline after the introduction of EMU. Countries chosen for entry into the single currency will be required, on pain of penalties, to continue indefinitely to meet the convergence criteria. However, in deference to French wishes for a less rigorously monetarist regime, a council of finance ministers (known variously as Euro-X, the Stability Council and the Stability and Growth Council) is planned as a counterweight to the European Central Bank. This informal body would co-ordinate the economic policies of participating countries. Since the Maastricht Treaty places control of monetary policy in the hands of the Central Bank, stipulating independence from political interference, it is far from clear how clashes between the Central Bank and Euro-X would be resolved. Those countries which do not participate in the single currency are bound by similar constraints under the excessive deficit procedure of the Maastricht Treaty. (For a fuller analysis, see **EMU**.)

Stage

The EU's work experience scheme offering graduates the opportunity of an internship in the Commission. Poorly paid, *stagiaires* console themselves with the knowledge that the *stage* is an unrivalled means of making contacts and often leads to a permanent job in one of the Community's institutions.

Strauss-Kahn, Dominique (1949–)

As minister for economics, finance and industry in Lionel Jospin's government, Dominique Strauss-Kahn steered France through the 1998 EMU negotiations, supporting wide membership of the euro but controversially favouring the politicisation of the European Central Bank.

Structural funds

The collective name given to four (or perhaps more properly five) funds set up to assist underdeveloped, declining or economically stagnant regions of the EU.

The European Regional Development Fund (ERDF), created in 1975 and accounting for about half the EU's structural budget, targets underdeveloped regions and areas suffering from industrial decline. The ERDF meets part of the costs of each programme, the balance being provided by the relevant member state, and gives priority to schemes which contribute to Union policy aims. Over the years, the main beneficiaries have been Spain, Portugal, Greece, Ireland and Italy. The UK, which was largely responsible for initiating the ERDF as a counterweight to the bias inherent in the Common Agricultural Policy (CAP), has proved to be a relatively unsuccessful applicant. Ireland, by contrast, despite its sharp rise up the EU's league table of comparative wealth, has remained a magnet for funds.

The European Social Fund (ESF), created under the original Treaty of Rome, is designed to combat long-term and youth unemployment through vocational training and retraining, again complementing subsidies made by member states. The ESF accounts for about a quarter of the structural budget and overlaps to a considerable extent with the ERDF, in that around half its appropriations are aimed at the same objectives.

The European Agricultural Guidance and Guarantee Fund (FEOGA) is confusingly split into two parts. The (larger) Guarantee section is a central feature of the CAP and is deployed on price support. The Guidance section counts as a structural fund and is designed to assist rural restructuring and non-farm development, as well as subsidising depressed areas and those with special problems, including mountainous and Arctic regions. Like the ESF, it overlaps with the ERDF, spending about half its allocation on similar programmes. The fourth structural fund, the Fisheries Guidance Instrument, is much smaller and focuses on assistance to the fishing industry.

The Cohesion Fund was created by the 1992 Maastricht Treaty with the aim of accelerating economic convergence in the run-up to EMU. At the time the Commission wanted to double the amount of aid spent on the four least prosperous states, Spain, Portugal, Ireland and Greece. The Cohesion Fund targets infrastructure, with particular reference to the environment and to transport, energy and telecommunications, and is included in the EU budget under the same rubric as the four older funds.

From small beginnings, the structural funds had grown by 1998 to some 35% of the EU budget, with between a half and two-thirds of their disbursements going to underdeveloped regions. The variance in ingenuity and determination shown by the member states in applying for grants meant that there was no close correlation between subsidy and need – not, at least, as measured by national wealth. From a broader perspective, despite a remarkable percentage increase in the amount of the funds, they remained insignificant for all but a few of the recipients. In total they accounted for about 0.4% of EU-wide GDP, enough to weigh heavily with Ireland and to permit extensive fraud, but not enough to achieve the overall redistributive effect advocated by the 1977 MacDougall Report.

The forthcoming enlargement of the EU raises the question of the future distribution of the available funds. The favoured candidates for membership are markedly more impoverished than the poorest current member states and equally populous (Poland has about the same population as Spain, while the Czech Republic and Hungary have about the same as Greece and Portugal). In 1985 Greece had threatened to veto the accession of Spain and Portugal at the last minute unless it received additional subsidies. This resulted in the Integrated Mediterranean Programmes (IMPs), of which the beneficiaries were Greece and the most backward regions of southern France and Italy (the IMPs were discontinued in 1992 and effectively replaced by the Cohesion Fund). The next round of enlargement is likely to give rise to even more complex and acrimonious brinkmanship. The Commission's plan to reduce from 50% to 35–40% the proportion of the EU's population classed as living in areas which qualify for assistance is already contentious enough. Germany, the UK and the Netherlands will not wish to increase their contributions; Spain, Ireland, Portugal and Greece will be equally determined not to suffer a reduction in their receipts. Despite much talk about the necessity of reform, the impasse will not be easily resolved.

Differences over the allocation and financing of the structural funds may also lead to more fundamental questions. Support for declining industries, although it can help to mitigate social disruption, legitimises protectionism and is ultimately anti-competitive. As long as the EU's structural funds are confined to easing transition, this problem is containable. But longer-term payments from one set of countries to another will need greater political consensus than presently exists. Modern economies are helped to adjust flexibly to change through automatic counter-cyclical fiscal stabilisers, as prospering sectors pay more tax while struggling regions receive more benefits. The rigid EU system represents an entirely different concept. The advent of EMU in 1999 may well cause dislocation, the more serious because of Europe's low labour mobility. In that case the need for a review of the nature and scale of EU transfer payments will become irresistible if the Union is to escape a dependency culture in depressed regions combined with a politically contentious misdirection of taxpayers' money from the wealthiest countries.

Stuttgart Declaration

Now almost forgotten, like the Genscher-Colombo Plan which preceded and prompted it, the Stuttgart Declaration of 1983 was made by the European Council and presaged the transformation of the Community into the European Union. It began the process of negating the national right of veto, increasing the powers of the European Parliament and advancing the single market, as well as urging greater co-operation in the political, economic, industrial and security fields. More than a decade after President Charles de Gaulle's retirement it signalled France's conversion to the cause of federalism. Intent on her budget negotiations over the British rebate, Margaret Thatcher accepted the Declaration, properly known as the Solemn Declaration on European Union, perhaps underestimating the encroachment on national sovereignty that it threatened. The Declaration led to the Dooge Committee on institutional reform and the Adonnino Committee on a People's Europe, both of which made proposals which were to find expression in the Single European Act of 1986 and the Maastricht Treaty of 1992.

Subsidiarity

A Eurospeak term, conveying the impression of a principle that decisions should always be taken at the national level close to the citizen, unless they have to be taken at the EU level; and as such relied upon by the then Conservative government to reconcile the British electorate to the 1992 Maastricht Treaty, where the term makes its first Treaty appearance. Subsidiarity has two flaws: it is too vague a principle to be relied upon in law; and its meaning is not what it purports to be, for the concept presupposes that authority resides at the higher level unless it is delegated downwards to member states.

The Maastricht Treaty specifies that subsidiarity applies only to areas outside the Community's exclusive competence, thereby preventing its use to restore powers to member countries. The Treaty also allows the Community to take action if a given objective cannot be 'sufficiently' achieved at national level or can be 'better' achieved by the Community. This formulation was designed to reassure those who feared a centralising superstate. But it is the Commission which determines whether to delegate a decision to the member states, and it is the Court of Justice which interprets the Treaty according to the doctine of ever-closer union. Thus the power of the nation state to invoke subsidiarity against federalising legislation is slim indeed. The 1997 Treaty of Amsterdam further clarifies the subordination of the principle of subsidiarity to Community law and the *acquis communautaire*.

Sweden

Sweden was a founder member of the Council of Europe, EFTA and the Nordic Council, but its policies of non-alignment and neutrality, which had kept it out of both world wars, were long an impediment to joining the EC. In 1991, as the collapse of Soviet communism ended the Cold War and the single market gained momentum, Sweden applied for membership and was admitted in 1995 to what had by now become the European Union. Disillusionment, however, soon set in and the 52% referendum vote in favour of ratification in 1994 would probably have been reversed by 1997 if the vote had been retaken in the light of experience.

Once very prosperous, based on its rich natural resources, Sweden was governed by Social Democrats for all but seven years from 1932 to 1991, developing the so-called Swedish model of society, with a strong emphasis on welfare and the maintenance of a high moral tone. Heavy taxes, sluggish growth and an eventually unsustainable level of public debt led, however, to an urgent need for the reforms carried out by the centre-right administration elected in 1991, which embarked on a programme of liberalisation and deficit reduction. Today Sweden's prosperity is around the EU average, although the return to power of the Social Democrats in 1994 heralded a reversion to the statist policies of the past.

Sweden retains its traditional concerns for education, open government and the environment, as well as for typically modern social causes. Indeed, it was disappointment over the Union's ineffectiveness in such areas, rather than resentment of excessive Commission interventionism, that led to Sweden electing no less than half of its 22 MEPs from anti-European parties in the 1995 European elections. The country is not a member of the ERM and has decided not to participate in the first wave of EMU.

Switzerland

Switzerland has its own ways of doing things. Known for its banking secrecy, its neutrality, its attachment to government by referendum and its reluctance to join supranational bodies (it is still not a member of the UN and only joined the Council of Europe in 1963 and the World Bank and the IMF in 1992), Switzerland has long stood aloof from the EC. It was, however, a founder member of EFTA and in 1992, as the single market gained momentum and Austria, Sweden, Finland and Norway opened negotiations to join the EU (as the EC was now becoming), Switzerland also applied, simultaneously signing the EEA treaty which would link EFTA to the Union.

At this point, the old Swiss sense of separate identity reasserted itself and at the end of 1992 the electorate rejected the EEA by referendum, thereby effectively shelving Switzerland's application for membership of the EU. The country has a host of bilateral economic arrangements with the EU, but its determination to protect its own interests was evidenced in 1994 when it voted to ban foreign lorries from using Alpine roads with effect from 2004, by which time two new road-rail tunnels will have been built.

Switzerland's antipathy to centralised power is reflected in its constitution, which recognises four official languages and vests considerable authority in its communes and cantons, making the country a genuine confederation. Its economy is wealthy and the Swiss franc has for many years been the strongest currency in Europe – too strong at times for the comfort of Swiss industry. Switzerland shares with Norway, the other notable non-member of the EU, the distinction of being the most prosperous major country on the Continent.

T

Tax

Historically, the Commission has directed its attention only to the harmonisation of indirect tax, chiefly VAT, from which source it also collects much of its own budgetary funding. Late in 1997, however, it began to develop theories to justify intrusion into direct tax. These theories included the concept of protecting the revenue base of high-tax countries by eliminating loopholes and obliging other member states to raise their tax levels. As an interim step, the Commission has proposed a code of conduct to curb the special tax incentive regimes which exist in Dublin, Belgium, the Netherlands and various offshore islands, as well as in Luxembourg. The Commission has also canvassed a Directive on savings tax, which would have a devastating effect on the City-based international bond market. Any broad intervention in national corporate or income taxation would have to take into account that taxes as a percentage of GDP vary from around 35% in the UK and Spain to over 40% in Germany and over 50% in Sweden, and that top corporate rates range from 57% in Germany to 31% in the UK. (See also **Fiscal dumping**.)

Thatcher, Margaret (1925–)

Margaret Thatcher and Charles de Gaulle share the distinction of being the two most redoubtable supporters of the sovereign state and most adamant opponents of supranationalism in the EC's brief history. Having defeated Edward Heath to lead the Conservative Party in 1975, Thatcher became prime minister in 1979 and promptly engaged the Community in battle over the size of the British contribution to the budget. Her demand 'Give us our money back' reflected her sense of injustice that the UK was the second biggest net contributor after Germany, while being far from the second richest member state. To Europeans brought up to view the Community's own resources as sacrosanct, her combative language struck a jarring note. For nearly five years they accused her of a commercial attitude unworthy of the Community's high purpose, but in 1984 President François Mitterrand finally settled the issue at Fontainebleau with the British rebate.

A slayer of dragons (including her militant union opponents in the UK and the Argentinian junta of General Galtieri in the 1982 Falklands War), Thatcher had no patience with the bureaucratic procedures and compromise deals with which coalition European politicians were at ease. Yet vigorously though she swung her handbag, she made little progress in resisting European integration. She had a formidable opponent in the Commission President Jacques Delors, as de Gaulle had had in Walter Hallstein. Unlike de Gaulle, however, she had no significant European political allies, for her language was abrasive and Helmut Kohl and Mitterrand were as determined as Delors to press on with federation.

Despite her reservations about the direction Europe was taking, Thatcher initiated one of the EU's main positive achievements – the single market programme, designed by a British commissioner, Lord Cockfield. The Single European Act of 1986, which gave force to the single market, greatly increased the scope of qualified majority voting. It was not easy to foresee that the volume of intrusive legislation which would follow, in the name of harmonisation of standards, would go far beyond the minimum necessary for the creation of the internal market. Still less was it predictable that a broader precedent was being set for replacing unanimity (that is, the sovereign right of veto) by majority voting – an outcome which Thatcher deplored.

Over the years she made some inroads on the costly Common Agricultural Policy, without obtaining the radical reform she sought. As for EMU, after holding out initially against British participation in the ERM, she agreed in 1989, under the threat of cabinet resignations, to enter 'when the conditions were right'. The following year she was forced by colleagues against her better judgement to enter at what proved to be an unsustainable exchange rate. Her refusal to sign the Social Charter was less controversial, but in 1990 she fell from power, ousted through divisions in her own party caused in large part by dissent over her handling of European issues.

Thatcher was resented by Europhiles from the outset. Her attachment to British parliamentary democracy they saw as 'Little Englanderism'. Her labour market reforms and her assessment that NATO and the American alliance were the bedrock of security struck them as clinging to Anglo-Saxon, as opposed to European, attitudes. When her Bruges speech of 1988 laid out her vision of voluntary co-operation between sovereign nations rather than direction by supranational European institutions, her opponents replied by disparaging the very idea of sovereignty. A robust defender of the free market, her suspicion of Delors was enhanced by his rapturous reception at the British Trades Union Congress of 1988.

To a Europe attuned to welfare and the social market economy her doctrines sounded unfeeling. Nevertheless, even her detractors accept that the CAP needs comprehensive reform; that the EU suffers from a democratic deficit; that EMU is fraught with difficulties; and that the UK's restored economic strength is in large measure due to her influence. She can doubtless be faulted for her antipathy to German reunification and her choice of a tone which would win her few Continental friends, but she remains a memorable witness to uncomfortable truths in the annals of the EU.

Third way

A phrase perhaps coined by the National Front, but now appropriated by Tony Blair's New Labour, the third way used to mean an alternative to capitalism and communism, or, more mildly, left and right. In Europe it means a compromise between Anglo-Saxon laissez-faire economics and the Continental social market, designed to avoid the alleged brutality of the one and uncompetitiveness of the other. The Dutch economy is sometimes quoted as a model.

Tietmeyer, Hans (1931–)

An economist, civil servant and, since 1990, an orthodox central banker, Hans Tietmeyer became president of the Bundesbank in 1993, from where he has dispensed a stream of enlightened scepticism about EMU in measured language which never trespasses into fields reserved for politicians. His evidence to the German government and the Council of Ministers concerning the selection of candidates for the single currency warned that few countries genuinely qualified under the Maastricht convergence criteria.

Tobacco

An EU draft directive agreed in 1997 will lead to a phased ban, starting from 2002, on virtually all cigarette company advertising and sponsorship of sporting events. Formula One motor racing will be the last sport to lose its tobacco sponsorship, having gained an exemption until 2006. The moral high ground thus seized by the Commission was, however, undermined by the fact that the Community continued to subsidise some 200,000 inefficient European tobacco growers, chiefly in Greece and Italy, to the extent of about £750 million per year, much of which was spent fraudulently.

Trade Unions

Despite the EU's left-of-centre corporatism, trade unions play little part in its policy formation. This lack of influence is not primarily due to the movement's traditional antipathy to the Common Market as a rich man's club, an attitude which largely evaporated in the 1980s. Nor is it due to a belief that the Community is insensitive to social needs – on the contrary, member states have gone a long way in the other direction, lavishing protection on the workforce to the point where in France and Germany the cost of employing people is almost prohibitive. The reason for the trade unions' impotence is that their focus is national and they remain wedded to collective bargaining and old-fashioned thinking at a time when globalisation and the pressures of EMU call for a new approach. The prospect of an independent European Central Bank with a strong anti-inflationary stance is a sobering reminder of the waning voice of unions on European issues of genuine economic importance.

Trans–European networks (TENs)

The Maastricht Treaty envisaged integrated Europe-wide transport, telecommunications and energy networks, financed nationally but aided by Commission feasibility studies and by the resources of the Cohesion Fund and the European Investment Bank. The priorities reflected traditional structural funds themes – cross-border technical compatibility ('interoperability' in Eurospeak), assistance to outlying areas, aid to poorer regions and the enhancement of the infrastructure of the single market.

Transparency

The EU's Treaties display ostensible devotion to the principle of transparency. Nevertheless, secrecy dogs the deliberations of the Commission and the Council of Ministers. The Court of Justice does not record dissenting opinions, nor will the Central Bank publish minutes of its interest rate discussions. The obscure language of the Maastricht and Amsterdam Treaties is more charitably ascribed to bureaucratic drafting than to a desire for concealment or calculated indifference to public understanding, but the end result is the same. The European Parliament's proceedings, by contrast, are open. The problem there is that few in the outside world are much interested in them.

As the EU's decision-making powers have expanded, the need for transparency has become sufficiently apparent to have prompted some steps in the right direction. Legislative votes of the Council are now occasionally published; national parliaments are to be allowed (at least in theory) more time for scrutiny of draft legislation; and the Community's institutions are providing more information to the European Parliament. Nevertheless, the habits of concealment and unaccountability die hard and the EU's southern member states are notably less concerned about openness than the northern ones.

Treaty of Amsterdam

The Treaty of Amsterdam, agreed in 1997 and due for ratification in 1998, was intended as a sequel to the Maastricht Treaty, with the emphasis on institutional reform to facilitate enlargement and address the EU's democratic deficit. The concept was that a Community designed originally for six rich nations needed a new structure to accommodate up to 25 countries, some of them relatively poor. Much of the Treaty takes the form of amendments to and renumbering of earlier

Treaties, making it hard to follow and interpret. The Europhile verdict is that it achieved little, partly because of Germany's unwontedly negative attitude, apparently arising from Chancellor Helmut Kohl's desire to avoid any action that might derail EMU. By contrast, others see the Treaty as significantly shifting responsibilities from the member states to the Community.

The Treaty's principal purpose is to create 'an area of freedom, security and justice' and to give the EU a say in 'fundamental rights'. The Schengen Agreement is to be incorporated into the *acquis communautaire* through abolishing internal frontier controls, with the EU assuming responsibility for immigration, external borders, visas and asylum (the UK and Ireland have certain opt-outs of limited effectiveness). New anti-discrimination rights are introduced and the Social Chapter, a protocol of the Maastricht Treaty, is transferred into the main body of the text. The Maastricht Treaty is to be amended to permit Community-level action against organised crime and EU fraud. To that end the role of Europol is to be strengthened, perhaps foreshadowing its emergence as a European FBI, and there is wording suggestive of an incipient harmonisation of criminal law, a matter of concern to the UK with its unique common law safeguards. As a result of these changes, the Justice and Home Affairs pillar of the Maastricht Treaty is renamed Police and Judicial Co-operation in Criminal Matters.

The Treaty deals somewhat disjointedly with defence and foreign affairs, declaring the WEU to be an 'integral part' of the 'common foreign and security policy' while stating that NATO obligations are to be 'respected'. Majority voting in the Council of Ministers is to be extended in the field of foreign policy, but not defence. Glossing over the member states' divergent views on neutrality, NATO membership and the US military presence in Europe (not to mention specific issues such as the Balkan and Iraqi conflicts), the Treaty stipulates that policy questions are to be resolved by the six-monthly presidency of the Union. The Commission is to be 'fully associated' with any 'common measures' in this area.

In the field of institutional reform, the Treaty attempts little. It does, however, confirm the role of subsidiarity as essentially strengthening the superiority of Community law over domestic law, probably including even national constitutions. The principle of respecting the national identities of member states slips down the list of priorities and the right of veto is reduced by the introduction of qualified majority voting into 16 new areas. The Treaty removes from national governments, after an interim period, their right of initiative to make proposals to the Council, which thereafter will accept proposals only from the Commission. The main beneficiary of the Treaty is the European Parliament, which gains extensive further powers of co-decision.

By permitting the flexible use of Community institutions, or 'closer co-operation', on the part of individual groups of states wishing to accelerate their own mutual integration, the Treaty for the first time condones a two-speed Europe, albeit as a last resort. Nevertheless, there is no concession to the idea of a 'Europe of Nations'. Indeed, one remarkable clause would permit the European Council to suspend the voting rights of a member state considered to be guilty of contravention of the Treaty's 'fundamental principles'. Briefings indicate that this is intended as an emergency measure in the event of, for example, a *coup d'état*, but however impeccable the intention the clause appears to challenge the essence of national sovereignty.

Treaty of the Elysée

The 1963 Treaty of the Elysée, signed by Charles de Gaulle and Konrad Adenauer, marked a new chapter in Franco-German co-operation. The fundamental basis of the understanding was that Germany would gain national rehabilitation and open markets for German industrial goods in exchange for political influence for France and high prices for French farmers. The pact was strengthened by the instinctive personal friendship of the two leaders. Nevertheless, in its early years, the Treaty barely survived profound differences of opinion over the shape of the Community, de Gaulle favouring a Europe of Nations, while Adenauer and Walter Hallstein favoured supranationalism. In subsequent years, the alliance has overcome sharp differences over NATO, German reunification, interest rate policy, nuclear testing and Bosnia; and in 1997 and 1998 it faced a new test over EMU as France disagreed with Germany about the direction of the future European Central Bank.

The reasons why Franco-German co-operation has remained such a powerful force are both institutional and political. Regular summit and ministerial meetings, exchanges between students and children and the creation of joint military and economic bodies give a formal structure to what is essentially a marriage of convenience. By pre-agreeing a position on all Community questions of importance, France has been able to lever its influence off Germany's economic weight, while Germany has been able to shelter behind French diplomacy to avoid the charge of attempted hegemony. Both nations routinely refer to their partnership as the driving force behind European integration.

Ambitious for the UK to occupy a place at the heart of Europe, John Major sometimes gave the impression of being barely aware of the significance of the Elysée Treaty. Tony Blair is more fortunate in his timing, although (quite apart from Italian sensitivities) his prospects for forming a genuine troika will have 35 years of history to surmount.

Treaty on European Union

The 1992 Maastricht Treaty was formally entitled the Treaty on European Union. From the constitutional standpoint it came in two parts:

⇒ amendments to the Treaty of Rome and the Single European Act, principally to institute EMU
⇒ the creation of the European Union, principally through the addition of the intergovernmental 'pillars' on foreign, home and judicial affairs.

The 1997 Treaty of Amsterdam amended the Treaty on European Union and further amended the previous Treaties. It also added a new title on closer co-operation, or flexibility, which was constitutionally important because it cut across the previously clear distinction between Community activities and government-to-government relations. As a broad guide to this complex structure, the much revised Treaty of Rome, now known officially as the Treaty establishing the European Community, constitutes the supranational institutional part of the EU governing EMU and the single market, while the revised Treaty on European Union covers the provisions governing co-operation between member states. Thus the Union today is essentially constituted by those two Treaties together with the various Accession Treaties and the comparatively unimportant European Coal and Steel Community and Euratom Treaties. Given the furore which the Maastricht Treaty caused in 1992 and the extent of the subsequent alterations and additions made at Amsterdam, it is convenient to refer to the original Treaty as Maastricht, leaving the title Treaty (or Treaties) on European Union to denote the consolidated and amended version.

Treaty of Maastricht

See **Maastricht Treaty** and **Treaty on European Union**.

Treaty of Paris

The first of Europe's three founding Treaties, concluded in 1951 and establishing the European Coal and Steel Community. It is due to expire in July 2002.

Treaty of Rome

Europe's central Treaty, signed in 1957 and second of the three founding Treaties to be concluded (the first was the 1951 Treaty of Paris; the third, also signed in 1957, was the Euratom Treaty). The Treaty of Rome established the European Economic Community (later shortened to the European Community). It was succeeded by various amending Treaties, three of which, the

Single European Act of 1986, the Maastricht Treaty of 1992 and the Amsterdam Treaty of 1997, significantly expanded its scope. The text of the Treaty of Rome is not, therefore, canonical, but is constantly changed to reflect new Treaties. These alterations make it difficult to follow, since out-of-date documents often refer to Articles which no longer bear the same numbers. (See also **Treaty on European Union**.)

Trichet, Jean–Claude (1942–)

One of the main architects of the *franc fort*, the policy of sustaining the French franc at a constant rate against the D–Mark, Jean–Claude Trichet became governor of the Banque de France in 1993 after serving in the Treasury. His anti–inflationary stance, regarded by some as a contributory factor in the high level of French unemployment, brought him into intermittent conflict with President Jacques Chirac. Nevertheless, in November 1997 France astonished the other EU member states by unsuccessfully proposing him as a last-minute alternative candidate to Wim Duisenberg for the post of head of the future European Central Bank (ECB). This *démarche* was widely assumed to reflect the French wish for political influence over the ECB, despite the Maastricht Treaty's insistence on its independence.

Troika

The current presidency of the Council of Ministers, together with its immediate successor and predecessor. The point of this three–member group (literally a three–horse sledge) is to provide continuity to EU foreign policy. This is no easy matter, as illustrated by the 1998 Iraqi crisis, when the presidency was held by the UK, which supported the USA in threatening the use of force against the dictator Saddam Hussein, while the previous incumbent was Luxembourg, which supported compromise, and the next one would be the neutralist Austria. (See also **Common Foreign and Security Policy**.)

Turkey

Although a Muslim country, Turkey has long aspired to join the EU, with which it concluded an Association Agreement in 1963. Turkey is a key member of NATO, but vehement Greek opposition and widespread concern over the country's approach to human rights have combined to defer its EU application indefinitely. This outcome has been welcomed by Germany, which already has 2.8 million Turkish residents and fears being overwhelmed by Kurdish refugees fleeing Turkish persecution. Frustration at its continuing exclusion from the EU prompted Turkey in 1997 to threaten the withdrawal of its candidature, switch aircraft orders from Airbus to Boeing and hint ominously of integrating northern

Cyprus into Turkey. Turkish feelings had been inflamed by the fact that the country had been accepted into a customs union with the Community in 1993 and had met its obligations, whereas the Community, under Greek pressure, had not honoured its side of the bargain, which involved financial aid.

Twinning

When two towns twin with each other, the European Commission makes cash available for joint projects in return for which it urges the mayors to swear an oath in favour of European unification. The suggested form of wording is:

We, the mayors of …
Confident that we are responding to the deeply felt aspirations and real needs of our townspeople … and believing that the work of history must be carried forward in a larger world …

Give a solemn pledge
To foster exchanges … in every area of life so as to develop a living sense of European kinship …

And to join forces to help secure, to the utmost of our abilities, a successful outcome to this vital venture of peace and prosperity –

European Union

(See also **European identity** and **Propaganda**.)

Two-speed Europe

Devoted to transport metaphors, Europhiles often press the case for participating in moves towards European integration by reference to the danger of missing the train, thereby losing out to those in the fast lane (with scant regard for consistency, they may also object that those who lag behind obtain an unfair economic advantage). The UK's and Denmark's Maastricht Treaty opt-outs, the UK's opt-out from parts of the Treaty of Amsterdam and the fact that not all the member states will join the first wave of EMU have already created a *de facto* two-speed Europe. The admission to the EU of the neutral states of Austria, Finland, Ireland and Sweden is another, though less frequently remarked upon, instance of accommodating incompatible policies. Given the prospect of the EU growing less homogeneous with the accession of former Eastern bloc countries, such divergence seems inevitable.

Proponents of a two-speed Europe fall into two camps: on the one hand, integrationists, impatient to accelerate the process of unification and unwilling to be held up by the slowest ship in the convoy; and on the other hand countries that wish to slow or halt the federal momentum but are prepared to forswear the use of the veto provided that they can be left out of policies they consider fundamentally unsuited to their national interests. Opponents of flexibility are similarly divided between those who fear that it is an excuse for creating a privileged inner club within the EU and those who fear that it will lead to the ultimate break-up of the Community. The debate centres on the question whether the EU's institutions should be allowed to become involved in policies where there is no unanimity among the member states. The 1997 Treaty of Amsterdam, endorsing the principle of closer co-operation, comes down on the side of encouraging the selective use of EU mechanisms by groups of states bent on integration.

Those interested in fine distinctions claim to detect a five-speed Europe: the first wave of participants in the single currency; the remaining member states; the approved early candidates to join the EU; those whose application has been deferred; and Turkey. There is more than a little force to such reasoning, which serves as a reminder that the EU's institutional arrangements were designed for six, not 21 or more members; and that the accession of relatively impoverished new countries can be financed only by taking more from the present contributors or handing out less to the present beneficiaries.

U

The UK and Europe

From the outset, the UK's attitude to the emerging institutions of the European Community has been ambivalent. Winston Churchill considered that the UK was 'with' but not 'of' Europe, 'associated, but not absorbed'. The country took no part in the discussions that preceded the Treaty of Paris in 1951 and sent only an emissary to the Messina Conference in 1955 which culminated two years later in the Treaty of Rome and the establishment of the EEC. By contrast, the UK was a founder member of the Council of Europe in 1949 and of the European Free Trade Association (EFTA) in 1960.

Retreat from Empire and the 1956 Suez fiasco (where the UK was humiliatingly forced by the USA to abandon an Anglo-French incursion to secure the canal from Egyptian expropriation) inaugurated a low point in British confidence. Twice in the 1960s, first under the Conservative Harold Macmillan in 1963 and next under the socialist Harold Wilson in 1967, the government's application to join the Community (which would have meant abandoning EFTA) was vetoed by President Charles de Gaulle. In an epoch of high tariffs the Commonwealth was too far-flung to provide a viable alternative and in the dispirited mood of the times successive prime ministers could offer no better prospect than the hope that Europe's vigorous economic revival, led by Germany, would somehow brush off on the UK.

Unless you are prepared to moor yourself off the coast of Europe, you are not really fit and ready to become a member of our European Community.
General de Gaulle, explaining why France could not accept the UK's application to join the Common Market, 1963

De Gaulle's retirement gave Edward Heath the opportunity to succeed in 1971 where his predecessors had failed. By dint of assurances that the UK would not turn its back on the Commonwealth, that its fishing industry would be protected from the Common Fisheries Policy and that its sovereignty was not in jeopardy, Heath got the European Communities Act of 1972 through Parliament, assisted by the rebellion of Roy Jenkins against the Labour Party's new-found hostility to Europe. Perhaps the Bill would have passed anyway, but its merits were exaggerated, its defects glossed over and a legacy of mistrust was left which dogs the European question to the present day.

Returned to government in 1974, Wilson headed a Labour Party whose collective opinion had shifted. His first act in Europe was to embark on a token renegotiation of the Tory terms of accession, to be followed by a nationwide referendum, in which the all-party pro-European campaign led by Heath and Jenkins repeated the earlier assurances, laying particular stress on the promise of economic growth and the safeguard to national interests provided by the veto. The pro-Europeans outspent the opposing independence campaign by more than ten to one and the final vote showed a majority of just over two-thirds in favour of the UK retaining its membership of the Common Market.

De Gaulle's objection to British membership had been based not only on fear of admitting a rival to French leadership but also on his cool assessment of the UK as insular, maritime, pro-American, tied to the Commonwealth and naturally inclined to free trade. To this list could justly have been added the UK's outspoken press, its common law, its adversarial style of democracy – and also its lack of commitment to the Community. Indeed, by 1983, four years after Margaret Thatcher obtained power in the 1979 election, Labour had yet again switched sides and was formally in favour of withdrawal.

Thatcher's early years were largely taken up by argument over the UK's excessive contribution to the European budget, a dispute not settled until 1984, when the UK was granted its abatement, or rebate. More positively, the UK was an enthusiastic proponent of the single market and of the Community's enlargement by incorporating the former East European communist countries, which were starting to embrace democracy and open markets. These enthusiasms reflected the UK's concept of Europe as a free trading area bound together more by voluntary co-operation than by the compulsion implicit in supranational institutions. Yet paradoxically the Single European Act of 1986 did more to extend majority voting than any other of Europe's key Treaties. Thatcher's later term of office coincided with the growing influence of her political contemporary, Helmut Kohl, and with Jacques Delors' first presidency of the Commission; in clashes reminiscent of those between de Gaulle and Walter Hallstein Thatcher strenuously resisted a new onslaught of federalism, which Delors no less resolutely pursued.

In 1990 Thatcher resigned, brought down largely by the defection of cabinet colleagues and former colleagues, led by the Europhiles Geoffrey Howe and Michael Heseltine. Her successor, John Major, promised a fresh policy at the heart of Europe. He was soon disillusioned. The collapse of the ERM, into which he had, as chancellor, brought the pound, led to recriminations with Germany; the Maastricht Treaty was passed in the House of Commons by only three votes, despite the opt-outs which Major had won from the final stage of EMU and from the Social Chapter; the Commission found backdoor ways to introduce social legislation; and the question of whether or not to join the single currency turned into an internecine Conservative battleground. Germany and France increasingly disregarded the British voice in Community affairs, a situation exacerbated by disagreement over the Bosnian crisis and bitter disputes over fish and beef.

By 1997 the wheel had turned full cycle again – now it was Major who was isolated in Europe and Labour which had made another U-turn to proclaim itself as the pro-European party (while nevertheless promising to defend national interests against creeping federalism). In that year's elections victory went to Tony Blair, whose hopes of a co-leadership position in a Europe shaped in some measure by British interests were similar to Major's own unfulfilled expectations in 1990.

Europe without the UK is a mere torso.
Chancellor Helmut Kohl, Bad Homburg, April 1997

Few in high office have cared to explain to the British people that sovereign independence within the framework of the EU is largely a contradiction in terms. There have been rare occasions when the federal tide might conceivably have been stemmed – for example, at the time of the Soames affair and when Denmark refused to ratify the Maastricht Treaty in 1992. But even if such opportunities really existed, they were fleeting and easy to miss and any vacuum has always been filled by the consistent will of the Commission and of Germany, bent alike on the goal of a unified Europe.

It is facile to speculate that the Community might have evolved differently if the UK had participated fully in its formation from the outset. The fact is that the UK perceived itself as being equally linked to Europe and to the Anglo-Saxon world, comprising the USA, the Commonwealth and the English-speaking countries of Asia; and this perception was no nostalgic fantasy, but was grounded in shared history and culture as well as in patterns of trade and investment. Thus the European question seems destined to rumble on indefinitely unless a new institutional relationship is forged which recognises the UK's differences with Europe as candidly as its common interests.

UKREP

See **Permanent representatives**.

Uniform electoral procedure

The 1957 Treaty of Rome stipulated that elections to the European Parliament should be held under a uniform procedure. Interpreted strictly, this would mean the same form of proportional representation, the same voting age, the same national or regional list system, the same electoral thresholds, and so forth. The subsequent 40 years have led to numerous proposals, but no solution has been found which could win the necessary unanimity in the Council, absolute majority in the Parliament and ratification by member states. In 1997 Tony Blair's Labour government presented a Bill to amend the British method of electing MEPs by abolishing constituencies and first past the post elections in favour of a new regional system based on the Continental d'Hondt formula for allocating seats. This amended procedure would resemble several systems commonly used elsewhere in Europe and would, perhaps incidentally, strengthen the leadership's control of candidates and policy.

United Nations (UN)

The UK and France are permanent members of the UN Security Council, together with China, Russia (succeeding the Soviet Union) and the USA. There are also ten non-permanent members, each elected for a two-year term. Disunity among the great powers has frequently prevented the Security Council from carrying out the peacekeeping role envisaged for it when the UN Charter was signed in 1945. Under the EU's Common Foreign and Security Policy the European member states confer with each other regularly and vote together whenever possible. Integrationists have even canvassed the idea that the British and French seats on the Security Council should be merged into a single EU seat. Policy differences on substantive issues, however, have often reduced European co-operation to little more than friendly exchanges of information.

United States of Europe

A resonant expression, associating Europe's aspirations for power and prosperity with the federal political model of the USA. In 1946, in the immediate aftermath of World War II, Winston Churchill famously used the phrase in a speech in Zurich to describe his vision of a Europe made peaceful by Franco-German *rapprochement*. The origins of the phrase, however, are at least 150 years old. Victor Hugo used it after the revolutions of 1848 to express his own dream of a peaceful and united Continent. Indeed, the contrast of America's freshness and simple purpose with Europe's convoluted politics has inspired European idealists since the American Declaration of Independence in 1776. 'United States of Europe', then, is not so much a working blueprint for European integration as an evocation of the New World, designed to lend grandeur to the horse-trading and grinding detail of EU negotiations and to cloak the ambitions of European federalists in the aura of manifest destiny.

The USA and Europe

In the history of post-war US-European relations, three main themes stand out. First, US determination to contain Soviet communism. It was this that led to the Berlin Airlift, the formation of NATO and the commitment to station US troops and missiles in Europe. Second, enlightened economic self-interest. It was this that led to the Marshall Plan and the reconstruction of Europe as a market for American goods. Third, unremitting support for European integration.

Isolationism is a recurrent temptation to Americans – the attraction of a retreat from foreign entanglements into the security of their own rich and self-sufficient democratic society. But NATO and Marshall Aid established the USA for 50 years after World War II as a European power, a development that often wounded French pride but was warmly welcomed by the UK, America's traditional ally, and by Germany, whose eastern borders faced the Warsaw Pact armies. It is scarcely too much to say that the American presence saved Europe from succumbing, whether politically or militarily, to the Soviet Union.

Throughout this period, the USA strongly favoured European federation. It saw Europe's fragmentation as the cause of protectionism, narrow markets and wars in which American servicemen had died. A united Europe would be a stronger buffer against communism, a richer outlet for American exports, an assurance against another European war. Mistrustful of the British Empire and its successor, the Commonwealth, the USA pressured the UK to abandon Commonwealth preference and be fully absorbed into the Common Market. There was an element of over-simplification in Washington's approach, typified by Henry Kissinger's query: 'Who do I call when I want to speak to Europe?' The assumption was that if a United States of America was the ideal political system on one side of the Atlantic, then a United States of Europe must be the ideal counterparty on the other side. The complexities of European history were a challenge to the USA's patience.

The collapse of the Soviet Empire around 1990 and the growing assertiveness of the EU after the 1992 Maastricht Treaty belatedly cast some doubts into US thinking. The Community no longer needed the American nuclear shield and in matters of trade it regarded itself as a rival more than a partner – the GATT negotiations in 1994 were especially painful. As for foreign affairs, an amalgam of discordant policies within the EU produced a lowest common denominator strategy, rendering the Atlantic alliance indecisive, as was cruelly clear in the Bosnian and Gulf crises. Even the single currency was tinged with chauvinism; the euro was presented by Brussels and Paris as a future competitor to the dollar. In 1997 and 1998 an array of eminent American economists, who had previously dismissed EMU as a foolish idea waiting to be discarded, came out in alarm to denounce it as a recipe for dislocation which, far from cementing the Union, might lead to a fatal weakening. For the first time, some thoughtful Americans wondered aloud whether the USA's interests had been best served by supporting European attempts to build a monolithic technocracy in preference to a 'Europe of Nations'. But by now the USA's ability to influence events had waned and the Continent had travelled a long way down the federal path.

V

Van Miert, Karel (1942–)

From unlikely beginnings as a Belgian socialist protester against NATO's deployment of Pershing missiles in Europe, Karel Van Miert has become the Community's competition commissioner, charged with resisting state monopolies, government bail-outs and private sector anti-competitive behaviour. Appointed in 1995 as successor to Leon Brittan, Van Miert has from time to time fallen foul of the German, French and British governments and has been accused both of interfering too much and of giving way too easily. Nevertheless, despite a tendency to stray from his brief, his affable determination has won him friends in one of the Commission's most difficult jobs.

Variable geometry

A flexible EU, in which members states may choose in which activities to participate. (See also **Two-speed Europe** and **Closer co-operation**.)

VAT

The Cockfield Report of 1985, which preceded the introduction of the 1986 Single European Act, advocated greater standardisation of indirect taxes in order to further the completion of the single market. This process of harmonisation is popular in the Commission for its relative ease of administration (a share in national VAT revenues also forms part of the financing of the EU budget). Harmonisation is, however, made problematic by political, cultural and economic factors. For example, there are wide national differences in the degree of reliance on indirect, as opposed to direct, taxation, ranging from Greece, where indirect tax is low, to Denmark, where it is high; certain countries attach particular importance to low VAT on basic necessities or on items such as books; the Protestant countries tend to levy special duties on spirits; and taxes on petrol and cigarettes are affected by health and environmental policies.

VAT harmonisation may also have unintended effects on competitiveness. Thus the London art market, already damaged in 1995 by the imposition of 2.5% VAT on imports, will be largely driven to New York, Geneva and Hong Kong if the rate rises as planned to 5% in 1999, when the Commission hopes in addition to impose an artists' royalty on sales of modern pictures. These measures, designed to make London conform with the inactive markets of the rest of the EU, take no account of the fact that art is mobile and its market global.

Veto

The veto power of member states (known more emolliently as the unanimity requirement) is central to the structure of the EU. From the earliest days of the Common Market, integrationists such as Jean Monnet and Walter Hallstein argued that ever closer union implied the erosion of the right of individual nations to veto legislation; otherwise progress could always be blocked in the Council of Ministers by one recalcitrant state, however small. President Charles de Gaulle countered that the loss of the veto meant the transfer of power to technocrats and would expose France to being overruled by foreigners; to that extent, he considered the Treaty of Rome flawed. This dispute led to France refusing all co-operation with the Community in 1965, a crisis only resolved by the Luxembourg Compromise, under which it was conceded that decisions affecting a vital national interest would have to be unanimous, even if the Treaty specified majority voting.

By the early 1980s the Luxembourg Compromise had been virtually shelved and the Single European Act of 1986 brought a vast increase in qualified majority voting (QMV). The unanimity principle still exists for accession treaties (Greece relies on it to keep Turkey out of the EU), Treaty amendments, appointments to the Commission, changes to the Community's revenue-raising power and the resolution of certain disputes with the European Parliament. Voluntary co-operation in home affairs and foreign policy (the two inter-governmental pillars of the Maastricht Treaty) is also by definition subject to unanimity. But single market measures, the budget, EMU, the Common Agricultural Policy and implementation of agreed foreign policy, together with a growing number of other areas, are now determined by QMV, the scope of which was most recently enlarged by the 1997 Treaty of Amsterdam.

The concept of variable geometry allows countries to opt out of unwanted policies rather than being obliged to choose between vetoing them or accepting a majority verdict. Whether this flexibility weakens or strengthens the power of the nation state *vis-à-vis* the EU's federalising institutions is an important and much debated question. (See also **Two-speed Europe** and **Closer co-operation**.)

Visegrad states

The Czech Republic, Slovakia (together Czechoslovakia until 1993), Hungary and Poland, formerly satellites of the Soviet Union and members of the Warsaw Pact, which met at Visegrad in 1991 and agreed to co-operate in seeking membership of NATO and the EU as a route to total integration into Western Europe. All four countries are members of the Council of Europe and have Association Agreements.

W

Waigel, Theo (1939–)

As German finance minister since 1989 and head of the CSU, the Bavarian-based junior partner of the CDU-dominated ruling coalition, Theo Waigel was discomforted in 1997 by his party's disenchantment with EMU and by the criticism he had encountered from being identified with Chancellor Helmut Kohl's unpopular economic policies. He survived to pilot Germany through the difficult negotiations in 1998 over the selection of the president of the European Central Bank and the admission of countries to the single currency.

Warsaw Pact

The mutual defence treaty, lasting from 1955 to 1991, which gave the Soviet Union the pretext to station troops throughout the Iron Curtain countries, so ensuring its domination until the sudden collapse of East European communism. (See also **Brezhnev Doctrine**.)

Werner Report

The Werner Report prefigured in 1970 many of the features which marked later efforts to achieve monetary union. It was a period of intense currency instability, with a strong D-Mark and a weak French Franc both parting company from the dollar, itself suffering from a US balance of payments crisis. In 1971 the post-war monetary order based on the dollar, known as Bretton Woods, collapsed; and in 1973 the Yom Kippur War in the Middle East led to a quadrupling of oil prices, accompanied by global stagnation and inflation. A less propitious period for introducing monetary union could scarcely be imagined, and the project soon disintegrated, after two attempts at fixing European parities (the Snake and the Snake in the tunnel) had fallen apart. The episode was a humiliating failure, but it taught the Commission that Treaty law and a supranational central bank were essential ingredients for success if the plan were ever to be relaunched.

WEU (Western European Union)

More or less defunct for some 45 years, the WEU was designated in the 1992 Maastricht Treaty as the future defence component of the EU. It originated in 1948 as the Brussels Treaty Organisation, changing its name in 1954 with the addition of West Germany and Italy to its existing membership of the UK, France and the Benelux countries. The stimulus for change was the collapse of the European Defence Community, Jean Monnet's dream of a European army, but the WEU's military function was made irrelevant by NATO, and any broader role was overshadowed by the emergence of the Common Market. With the ending of the Cold War, however, the EU (and especially France) has become more assertive, doubtless calculating that it now has less need of NATO's nuclear deterrent. Hence a revived interest in developing a more independent European military capability, albeit partly under the NATO umbrella, building on the newly formed 50,000-strong Eurocorps and the institutional framework of the WEU.

Portugal and Spain joined the WEU in 1988, and Greece in 1995. In 1992 Iceland, Norway and Turkey became associate members and Ireland, Denmark, Austria, Finland and Sweden (all except Denmark neutrals) became observer members. In 1994 the Baltic states, Poland, the Czech Republic, Slovakia, Hungary, Romania and Bulgaria were made associate partners. But in real terms this amounted to little more than bureaucratic fodder for the meetings of the WEU's Council of Ministers, Permanent Council and Assembly of member state parliamentarians. For despite aspirations of a more cohesive European defence identity, the 1991 Gulf War and the 1992–95 Bosnian crisis showed that in an emergency only NATO and individual nations (chiefly the USA, but also France and the UK) could muster the resolve and fire power to take resolute action. In the Gulf War, French airborne capabilities were hampered by not being networked into NATO's high-tech enemy-recognition system; in Bosnia, the EU was at sixes and sevens over all aspects of its policy; and despite the Petersberg declaration of 1992, in which the WEU agreed to contribute forces to peacekeeping in Europe, it sent only 35 policemen to help Albania in 1997.

Europe can only speak with one voice when it has nothing to say.
Jean-Pierre Chevènement, French interior minister

The relationship of the WEU to NATO is ambivalent. NATO's success in deterring Soviet aggression for half a century stands in contrast to the WEU's inactivity. Nor could European forces mount any sustained action without the help of US surveillance and logistics, a dependence recognised in the Luxembourg Declaration of 1993, in which the WEU defined itself as the European pillar of NATO. Yet Europe longs to prove that it is a genuine world power, with a Common Foreign and Security Policy to match its economic weight and a military arm in support. British attachment to NATO and scepticism over the WEU is thus a microcosm of the long-running debate about whether the EU is to become a federal state or to remain a confederation of independent democracies. If history is a guide, Europe's political will towards integration is such that the most likely outcome is a somewhat reluctant Germany co-operating with France to produce the embryonic army which failed to come into existence after World War II, with the UK acting as an ally and the neutral member states watching from the sidelines.

White Wednesday

On September 16th 1992 a crescendo of currency speculation culminated in the withdrawal of the pound and the lira from the ERM and the devaluation of the peseta. Since this spelled the ruin of Prime Minister John Major's policy of tying sterling to the D-Mark zone, it was initially called Black Wednesday, the more so as millions had been spent on foreign exchange markets trying to prop up the pound. Later, as the new-found freedom assisted the UK's recovery from recession and the predicted inflation failed to occur, the day came to be reassessed and is now equally often known as White Wednesday.

Widening

Enlarging the membership of the EU. Often contrasted with (and sometimes considered incompatible with) deepening, or further integration of the existing members' activities. (See also *Acquis communautaire* and **Two-speed Europe**.)

Wilson, Harold (1916–95)

As Labour prime minister, Harold Wilson applied to join the EC in 1967. President Charles de Gaulle vetoed the UK's entry, as he had previously vetoed Harold Macmillan's application. Wilson's motives, like Macmillan's, were defensive; he believed the UK to be in irreversible decline and hoped that Europe's economic success might somehow come to the rescue. Having lost the 1970 election to Edward Heath, Wilson won back power in 1974. By now the UK was in the EC, but the Labour Party had become more sceptical. After a token renegotiation of the Tory terms of accession, Wilson held a referendum in 1975, which endorsed continued British membership. The referendum campaign repeated the exaggerated promises and downplaying of risks which had marked Heath's entry negotiations.

Wirtschaftswunder

West Germany's post-war economic miracle, engineered by Ludwig Erhard, Chancellor Konrad Adenauer's free-marketeering minister of economics from 1949 to 1963.

Women's rights

See **Discrimination**.

Working Time Directive

Adopted by qualified majority voting in 1993, with member states having three years to incorporate it into domestic law, the Working Time Directive was a Commission social measure masquerading as a health and safety measure – the difference being that health and safety rules fall under the Treaty of Rome and are of universal EU application, whereas social rules are governed by the Social Chapter of the Maastricht Treaty, from which the UK had at the time an opt-out. The UK's appeal against the circumvention of its Maastricht exemption was overruled by the European Court in 1996, although the British submission that no genuine medical issues were at stake was not seriously challenged.

The Directive imposes a maximum 48-hour working week together with minimum periods of daily and weekly rest, holidays and breaks. It applies only to certain sectors of activity, although the Commission has plans to extend it across a broader field. Some UK businessmen suspected the Directive of an unspoken agenda – that of preventing British companies from retaining a competitive edge through flexible employment practices. (See also **Social dumping.**)

World Trade Organisation (WTO)

The Geneva-based successor to the GATT, set up in 1995 after the conclusion of the Uruguay Round of GATT negotiations. The WTO's agenda for 1999 is a resumed attempt to reduce agricultural subsidies – a project likely to encounter resistance not only in France but also elsewhere in Europe as well as in the USA.

Z

Zollverein

The best known 19th century customs union, under which most German states progressively adopted the external Prussian tariff in exchange for the elimination of internal trade barriers. In this way (and through Bismarck's military defeat of Bavaria and Austria in 1866) Prussia came to dominate what was to become Germany, replacing Austria as the main centre of power in the German-speaking world. Under Bismarck, Germany became a united country, with a nationwide law, a single currency and a common banking system. Parallels with Chancellor Helmut Kohl's ambitions for the EU do not appear entirely fanciful.

APPENDICES

1 Chronology of the EU

	European Community	The world
1945	End of World War II	
	UN Charter signed	
1946	Churchill's Zurich speech calls for United States of Europe	Iron Curtain descends on Eastern Europe
1947	Marshall Aid begins	India and Pakistan gain independence
1948	Berlin blockade	State of Israel founded
1949	Council of Europe founded	Mao establishes People's Republic of China
		North Atlantic Treaty signed
		Comecon formed
1950	Schuman Plan	Korean War starts
1951	Treaty of Paris creates ECSC	
1952	EDC Treaty signed	
1953		Korean War ends
		Stalin dies
1954	EDC collapses	Vietnam War begins
		Algerian revolt starts
1955	West Germany joins NATO	Warsaw Pact signed
	Messina Conference	
1956	Anglo-French Suez Canal crisis	Hungarian uprising crushed
1957	Treaty of Rome creates EEC	Sputnik 1 (first spacecraft) launched
	Euratom Treaty signed	
1958		Mao's Great Leap Forward (1958–61)
1959		Japanese GNP trebles over 8 years (1959–67)
1960	EFTA Convention signed	
1961	Berlin Wall erected	USA joins Vietnam War
1962	CAP launched	Cuban missile crisis
		De Gaulle ends Algerian War

	European Community	The world
1963	De Gaulle vetoes UK membership of EC Treaty of the Elysée	J.F. Kennedy assassinated
1964		
1965	Empty chair crisis	
1966	Luxembourg Compromise France partially withdraws from NATO	Cultural Revolution in China (1966–78)
1967	De Gaulle again vetoes UK	
1968	Internal tariffs ended	'Prague Spring' crushed Martin Luther King murdered
1969		Man lands on the moon
1970		
1971	Common Fisheries Policy Birth of the Snake	Collapse of Bretton Woods system
1972	Norway rejects EEC	Nixon and Mao reopen US–China relations
1973	Accession of Denmark, Ireland and UK Death of the Snake	Yom Kippur War precipitates oil crisis USA withdraws from Vietnam
1974		Nixon resigns
1975	British referendum endorses membership European Regional Development Fund established Lomé Convention signed	
1976		Mao Zedong dies
1977		
1978		
1979	First direct European elections EMS and ERM initiated	Egypt and Israel sign accord Ayatollah Khomeini replaces Shah in Iran Soviet troops enter Afghanistan
1980		
1981	Accession of Greece	Deployment of Pershing missiles in Europe

	European Community	The world
1982		Falklands War
1983		
1984	Spinelli's draft Treaty on European Union Thatcher negotiates British rebate	
1985		
1986	Single European Act Accession of Spain and Portugal	Gorbachev initiates *glasnost* and *perestroika*
1987		Stockmarket crash
1988		Soviet troops withdraw from Afghanistan
1989	Berlin Wall falls	Collapse of communism in Eastern Europe Tiananmen Square massacre
1990	UK joins ERM German reunification	Break-up of Yugoslavia
1991		Soviet Union disintegrates War with Iraq over Kuwait
1992	Single market programme completed UK leaves ERM Maastricht Treaty; Danes reject it Switzerland rejects EEA	
1993	Danes accept Maastricht at second attempt ERM collapses	
1994	EEA comes into force Norway again rejects membership	Mandela becomes president of South Africa
1995	Accession of Austria, Finland and Sweden	Dayton Peace Accord in Yugoslavia
1996	Beef crisis EMU Stability Pact agreed	

	European Community	The world
1997	UK government adopts Social Chapter	Hong Kong returned to China
	Treaty of Amsterdam	Asian economic crisis
1998	Selection of single currency countries	Russian financial collapse
1999	*Launch of single currency*	
2002	*Euro to become legal tender*	

2 Lomé Convention signatories

Africa
Angola
Benin
Botswana
Burkina Faso
Burundi
Cameroon
Cape Verde
Central African Republic
Chad
Comoros
Congo
Côte d'Ivoire
Djibouti
Equatorial Guinea
Eritrea
Ethiopia
Gabon
The Gambia
Ghana
Guinea
Guinea-Bissau
Kenya
Lesotho
Liberia
Madagascar
Malawi
Mali
Mauritania
Mauritius
Mozambique
Namibia
Niger
Rwanda
São Tomé & Principe
Senegal

Seychelles
Sierra Leone
Somalia
Sudan
Swaziland
Tanzania
Togo
Zaire
Zambia
Zimbabwe

Caribbean
Antigua & Barbuda
Bahamas
Belize
Dominica
Dominican Republic
Grenada
Guyana
Haiti
Jamaica
St Christopher & Nevis
St Lucia
St Vincent & The Grenadines
Surinam
Trinidad & Tobago

Pacific
Fiji
Kiribati
Papua New Guinea
Solomon Islands
Tonga
Tuvalu
Western Samoa
Vanuatu

3 Composition of the European Parliament, January 1998

	PES	EPP	UFE	ELDR	EUL/NGL	Greens	ERA	IEN	IND	Tot.
Belgium	6	7	—	6	—	2	1	—	3	25
Denmark	4	3	—	5	—	—	—	4	—	16
Germany	40	47	—	—	—	12	—	—	—	99
Greece	10	9	2	—	4	—	—	—	—	25
Spain	21	30	—	2	9	—	2	—	—	64
France	16	11	18	1	7	—	12	11	11	87
Ireland	1	4	7	1	—	2	—	—	—	15
Italy	18	15	24	4	5	4	2	—	15	87
Luxembourg	2	2	—	1	—	—	1	—	—	6
Netherlands	7	9	2	10	—	1	—	2	—	31
Austria	6	7	—	1	—	1	—	—	6	21
Portugal	10	9	3	—	3	—	—	—	—	25
Finland	4	4	—	5	2	1	—	—	—	16
Sweden	7	5	—	3	3	4	—	—	—	22
UK	61	18	—	2	1	1	2	1	1	87
Total	**213**	**180**	**56**	**41**	**34**	**28**	**20**	**18**	**36**	**626**

PES – Party of European Socialists   Left-of-centre MEPs from all EU states
EPP – European People's Party   Right-of-centre MEPS from all EU states (mainly Christian Democrats, British Conservatives, Spanish Popular Party and French UDF)
UFE – Union for Europe   Mainly Forza Italia and French Gaullists
ELDR – European Liberal, Democratic and Reformist Group   Centre and Liberal parties
EUL/NGL   Miscellaneous green, left and neo-communist parties
Greens   Ecologist parties
ERA – European Radical Alliance   French Radicals and miscellaneous regionalists
IEN – Independent Europe of the Nations Group   Eurosceptics
IND – Independents   Including French National Front

4 Qualified majority voting

Country	Council votes	Population (million)	Population per vote (million)	EU population (%)	Votes (%)
Germany	10	81.4	8.1	22.0	11.50
UK	10	58.1	5.8	15.7	11.50
France	10	57.7	5.8	15.6	11.50
Italy	10	57.2	5.7	15.4	11.50
Spain	8	39.1	4.9	10.6	9.20
Netherlands	5	15.4	3.1	4.2	5.75
Greece	5	10.4	2.2	2.8	5.75
Belgium	5	10.1	2.0	2.7	5.75
Portugal	5	9.8	2.0	2.6	5.75
Sweden	4	8.8	2.2	2.4	4.60
Austria	4	8.0	2.0	2.2	4.60
Denmark	3	5.2	1.7	1.4	3.40
Finland	3	5.1	1.7	1.4	3.40
Ireland	3	3.6	1.2	1.0	3.40
Luxembourg	2	0.4	0.2	0.1	2.30
	87	370.4	4.3	100.0	100.00

5 European Currency Unit

Composition of the ECU basket and weights of the component currencies in the ECU, September 1st 1998

1 ECU =	Currency	Country	Weight (%)
0.6242	D–Mark	Germany	31.6
1.332	Franc	France	20.1
0.2198	Guilder	Netherlands	9.9
3.431	Franc	Belgium/Luxembourg	8.4
151.8	Lira	Italy	7.7
0.1976	Krone	Denmark	2.6
0.00855	Punt	Ireland	1.1
0.08784	Pound	UK	13.1
1.44	Drachma	Greece	0.4
6.885	Peseta	Spain	4.1
1.393	Escudo	Portugal	0.7

Notes
1. The composition of the basket was fixed in 1993. It does not include the currencies of the new EU member states (Austria, Finland and Sweden), but it does include the pound, the Danish krone and the Greek drachma, which will not participate immediately in the euro.
2. The euro will be exchangeable on a 1-for-1 basis with the ECU.
3. At September 1st 1998 the ECU was worth DM1.97, $1.11 and £0.67 (ie £1 = 1.50 ECUs).

6 Directorates-General

DG I	External Relations
	– North America, Australia, Far East
	– Europe, Russian Federation
	– South Mediterranean, Middle East, Latin America, South-East Asia
DG II	Economic and Financial Affairs
DG III	Industry
DG IV	Competition
DG V	Employment, Industrial Relations, Social Affairs
DG VI	Agriculture
DG VII	Transport
DG VIII	Development
DG IX	Personnel, Administration
DG X	Audiovisual Media, Information, Communications
DG XI	Environment, Nuclear Safety
DG XII	Research and Development
DG XIII	Telecommunications and IT
DG XIV	Fisheries
DG XV	Internal Market, Financial Services
DG XVI	Regional Policies and Cohesion
DG XVII	Energy
DG XVIII	Financial Services (now part of DG II)
DG XIX	Budgets
DG XX	Financial Control
DG XXI	Customs and Indirect Taxation
DG XXII	Education, Training and Youth
DG XXIII	Enterprise Policy, Distributive Trades, Tourism and Co-operatives
DG XXIV	Consumer Policy

7 Selected statistics

Country	GDP[a] (Ecu billion)	GDP per head[a] (Ecu '000s)	Relative GDP per head[b]	Deficit/ 1997 GDP[c] (%)	Debt/ 1997 GDP[d] (%)
Belgium	222	22.0	111	2.6	124
Denmark	150	28.8	116	−1.3	67
Germany	1,916	23.5	109	3.0	62
Greece	104	10.0	67	4.2	109
Spain	490	12.5	77	2.9	68
France	1,283	22.2	105	3.0	57
Ireland	70	19.4	103	−0.6	66
Italy	1,042	18.2	103	3.0	123
Luxembourg	15	37.5	164	−1.6	7
Netherlands	335	21.8	108	2.1	73
Austria	189	23.6	108	2.8	66
Portugal	89	9.1	69	2.7	62
Finland	110	21.6	98	1.4	59
Sweden	201	22.8	98	1.9	77
UK	1,225	21.1	98	1.9	52
EU 15	7,467	20.2	100	2.6	72
USA	7,360	28.3			
Japan	3,223	25.8			

a   Projected nominal 1998 GDP translated at September 1998 exchange rates.
b   Purchasing power parity relative to EU average at March 1998.
c   Maastricht Treaty convergence criterion 3%.
d   Maastricht Treaty convergence criterion 60%.

Figures based on Eurostat estimates

8 Selected information

Country	Date of accession	Institution joined	Population (million)	Seats in European Parliament	Council votes
Belgium	1958	EEC	10.1	25	5
Denmark	1973	EC	5.2	16	3
Germany	1958	EEC	81.4	99	10
Greece	1981	EC	10.4	25	5
Spain	1986	EC	39.1	64	8
France	1958	EEC	57.8	87	10
Ireland	1973	EC	3.6	15	3
Italy	1958	EEC	57.2	87	10
Luxembourg	1958	EEC	0.4	6	2
Netherlands	1958	EEC	15.4	31	5
Austria	1995	EU	8.0	21	4
Portugal	1986	EC	9.8	25	5
Finland	1995	EU	5.1	16	3
Sweden	1995	EU	8.8	22	4
UK	1973	EC	58.1	87	10
EU 15			370.4	626	87